# Story Circle

# Story Circle

Digital Storytelling Around the World

Edited by

*John Hartley and Kelly McWilliam*

WILEY-BLACKWELL

A John Wiley & Sons, Ltd., Publication

This edition first published 2009

© 2009 by Blackwell Publishing except for editorial material and organization © 2009 John Hartley and Kelly McWilliam

Blackwell's publishing program has been merged with Wiley's global Scientific, Technical, and Medical business to form Wiley-Blackwell.

*Registered Office*
John Wiley & Sons Ltd, The Atrium, Southern Gate, Chichester, West Sussex, PO19 8SQ, United Kingdom

*Editorial Offices*
350 Main Street, Malden, MA 02148-5020, USA
9600 Garsington Road, Oxford, OX4 2DQ, UK
The Atrium, Southern Gate, Chichester, West Sussex, PO19 8SQ, UK

For details of our global editorial offices, for customer services, and for information about how to apply for permission to reuse the copyright material in this book please see our website at www.wiley.com/wiley-blackwell.

The right of John Hartley and Kelly McWilliam to be identified as the authors of the editorial material in this work has been asserted in accordance with the Copyright, Designs and Patents Act 1988.

*Library of Congress Cataloging-in-Publication Data*

Story circle : digital storytelling around the world / edited by John Hartley & Kelly McWilliam.
   p.   cm.
Includes bibliographical references and index.
ISBN 978-1-4051-8059-7 (hardcover : alk. paper) – ISBN 978-1-4051-8058-0 (pbk. : alk. paper)
1. Interactive multimedia. 2. Digital storytelling. 3. Storytelling–Data processing. I. Hartley, John, 1948– II. McWilliam, Kelly.
  QA76.76.I59S785 2009
  006.7–dc22

                     2008045563

A catalogue record for this book is available from the British Library.

Set in 10.5/13pt Minion by SPi Publisher Services, Pondicherry, India
Printed and bound in Singapore by Fabulous Printers Pte Ltd

001   2009

# Contents

# List of Figures

# List of Tables

# Acknowledgments

*Story Circle* surveys new work done around the world, but it arose from a very particular context: the Creative Industries Faculty at Queensland University of Technology (QUT). Over a period of years many people have lent their help and goodwill to the enterprise, and we would like to thank them. They include quite a few of the authors; special thanks go to Jean Burgess, Helen Klaebe, Angelina Russo, Jo Tacchi, and Jerry Watkins. From QUT we would also like to thank all those who participated in our workshops; and Justin Brow, Brad Haseman, Greg Hearn, Paul Makeham, Lucy Montgomery, Tanya Notley, and Christina Spurgeon. Brad provided valuable institutional support from the Faculty Research Office. We have also been ably supported to an extent we do not deserve by Claire Carlin, Rebekah Denning, Tina Horton, Nicki Hunt, and Eli Koger. Eli has been invaluable on the technical and presentational side – she makes things work beautifully and look beautiful.

Beyond our own patch we have enjoyed working with pioneers Joe Lambert and Daniel Meadows. Joe has been especially helpful with the book; and Daniel helped us to kick off digital storytelling at QUT in the first place. Glynda Hull and Knut Lundby encouraged our work, particularly in the pre-conference on digital storytelling that they organized at the International Communication Association conference in San Francisco in 2007. Helen Simondson and her colleagues at the Australian Centre for the Moving Image (ACMI) in Melbourne have been crucial to the development of digital storytelling in Australia; we thank them for holding the "First Person" conference on digital storytelling at ACMI in February 2006 (see www.acmi.net.au/first_person_transcripts.htm).

We gratefully acknowledge the support of the Australian Research Council for our research projects: John Hartley for an ARC Federation Fellowship, and Kelly McWilliam for an ARC Postdoctoral Fellowship (Industry). We acknowledge the support of the ARC for the "New Literacy, New Audiences" Linkage project, which was held within the ARC Centre of Excellence for Creative Industries and Innovation. At different times it has supported the digital storytelling research of Hartley, McWilliam, Russo, Watkins, and also Ellie Rennie, whose work does not feature in this collection but who was creatively and intellectually involved in the early stages of that project.

There would be no book without the support and encouragement of our publisher, Jayne Fargnoli. We are grateful to her – once again – for taking on a topic that is not yet fully embedded in educational courseware. Naturally, we hope to repay her trust by accelerating that process with this book.

We thank Sage Publications Ltd for granting permission to reproduce some sections of Wu Qiongli's chapter from her paper "Commercialization of digital storytelling: An integrated approach for cultural tourism, the Beijing Olympics and wireless VAS," published in the *International Journal of Cultural Studies* 9(3), 2006: 383–94.

# Notes on Contributors

**Jean Burgess** is a Postdoctoral Research Fellow in the ARC Centre of Excellence for Creative Industries and Innovation, Queensland University of Technology (QUT). She works on cultural participation and user-led innovation in new media contexts, focusing particularly on digital photography, online video, and applications of digital storytelling. With Joshua Green, she is the author of *YouTube: Online Video and Participatory Culture* (2008).

**Nico Carpentier** is a media sociologist working in the Communication Studies Departments of the Free University of Brussels (VUB) and the Catholic University of Brussels (KUB). He is co-director of the VUB research center CEMESO and a board member of the European Communication Research and Education Association (ECREA – formerly ECCR). Among other works, he has coedited *The Ungraspable Audience* (2004), *Towards a Sustainable Information Society* (2006), and *Reclaiming the Media: Communication Rights and Democratic Media Roles* (2007).

**Maria Chatzichristodoulou**, a.k.a. Maria X, is a curator, producer, and PhD researcher in digital performance at Goldsmiths, University of London. Previously Co-director of the Fournos Centre and co-founder/Co-director of the Medi@terra Festival (Athens, Greece, 1996–2002), Maria lectures at Birkbeck and Goldsmiths, University of London. In 2007 she initiated and co-directed the three-day event, INTIMACY. She is co-ordinator of the Thursday Club (Goldsmiths) and coeditor of the forthcoming *Interfaces of Performance* (see www.cybertheater.org, www.intimate performance.org).

**Margaret Anne Clarke** graduated from the University of Liverpool with a PhD in twentieth-century Brazilian literature. Her research interests include contemporary Brazilian digital cultures and writing and the use of computer and multimedia applications for language learning. She has published articles in all these areas. She is Senior Lecturer in Portuguese at the University of Portsmouth.

**Marie Crook** has produced several high-profile radio-storytelling projects for BBC local radio. She continues to consult on storytelling projects and works as a freelance facilitator and consultant.

**Lisa Dush** is a lecturer in the Writing across the Curriculum program at the Massachusetts Institute of Technology (MIT) and the director of Storybuilders, a business that helps individuals and organizations tell stories with digital media. She is writing a doctoral dissertation for the University of Massachusetts Amherst on the organizational implementation of digital storytelling.

**John Hartley** is Distinguished Professor and ARC Federation Fellow at Queensland University of Technology (QUT) and Research Director of the ARC Centre of Excellence for Creative Industries and Innovation. He is among the pioneers of media and cultural studies and has published 20 books, translated into 13 languages, including *The Politics of Pictures* (1993), *Popular Reality* (1996), *Uses of Television* (1999), *A Short History of Cultural Studies* (2003), and *Television Truths* (2008). He is Editor of the *International Journal of Cultural Studies*.

**Sissy Helff** is an assistant professor in British and Postcolonial Literature and Culture at the University of Frankfurt, Germany. Her publications include *Unreliable Truths: Indian Homeworlds in Transcultural Women's Literature* (2008) and the two coedited volumes *Transcultural English Studies: Theories, Fictions, Realities* and *Transcultural Modernities: Narrating Africa in Europe* (both 2008). She is a Visiting Researcher at the University of Leeds, where she is currently working on the book *"Out of Place?" The Location of African Migration in Culture and the Arts*.

**Jenny Kidd** is a Research Associate of the University of Manchester, working in the Centre for Applied Theatre Research. In 2005 she completed a PhD at Cardiff University on the subject of Digital Storytelling, with the

"Capture Wales" project as a primary focus. Her research interests include cultural consumption, alternative media, and various forms of digital storytelling.

**Helen Klaebe** is a senior research fellow in the Creative Industries Faculty at Queensland University of Technology (QUT). Her PhD examined new approaches to participatory public history using multi-artform storytelling strategies. She is the author of *Onward Bound: The First 50 Years of Outward Bound Australia* (2005) and *Sharing Stories: A Social History of Kelvin Grove* (2006). Helen also consults as a public historian, focusing on engaging communities in urban renewal projects; and regularly designs and manages co-creative media workshops for commercial and public-sector organizations.

**Joe Lambert** is the co-founder and Executive Director of the Center for Digital Storytelling (CDS) in Berkeley, California. Along with Dana Atchley and Nina Mullen, he developed the Digital Storytelling Workshop. Joe has written *Digital Storytelling: Capturing Lives, Creating Community* (2002) and the *Digital Storytelling Cookbook* (forthcoming). Prior to his work in new media, Joe was Executive and Artistic Director of the theater company Life on the Water, and a community organizer with numerous organizations in California and Texas.

**Patrick Lowenthal** is an Assistant Professor of Instructional Technology at Regis University, Denver, Colorado, USA. He has a background in adult education, training, and development, and instructional design and technology. His research interests are related to online learning and computer-mediated communication, issues related to post-secondary teaching and learning, problems of practice, and new literacy and media studies.

**Knut Lundby** is professor of Media Studies in the Department of Media and Communication, University of Oslo, Norway. He was founding director of InterMedia, University of Oslo, researching design, communication, and learning in digital environments. Knut is the Director of the international Mediatized Stories project, focusing on "Mediation Perspectives on Digital Storytelling among Youth." He is the editor of *Digital Storytelling, Mediatized Stories: Self-representations in New Media* (2007).

**Kelly McWilliam** is an ARC Postdoctoral Research Fellow (Industry) in the Creative Industries Faculty of Queensland University of Technology (QUT), where she researches romance in digital media. She has ongoing interests in the social impact of media participation, including digital storytelling, and in popular culture, particularly around genre, gender, and sexuality. She is the author of *When Carrie Met Sally: Lesbian Romantic Comedies* (2008) and the co-author, with Jane Stadler, of *Screen Media: Analysing Film and Television* (2009).

**Daniel Meadows** has been described by the American commentator J. D. Lasica as "one of the icons of the Digital Storytelling movement." As a photographer he is recognized as a prime mover in the new documentary movement of 1970s Britain. He lectures in Photography and Participatory Media in the School of Journalism, Media and Cultural Studies at Cardiff University. He has written five books and was Creative Director of the BBC's Digital Storytelling project "Capture Wales" from 2001 to 2006.

**Angelina Russo** is an Associate Professor in the Faculty of Design, Swinburne University of Technology, Melbourne, and a Research Fellow of the ARC Centre of Excellence for Creative Industries and Innovation. She researches the connections among museum communication processes, multimedia design, and digital content creation. She is Chief Investigator on the research project "Engaging with Social Media in Museums," which brings together three Australian museums and the Smithsonian Institution in the USA to explore the impact of social media on museum learning and communication.

**Helen Simondson** is the Manager of Events at the Australian Centre for the Moving Image (ACMI), in charge of ACMI's digital storytelling project. She holds undergraduate qualifications from Deakin University and postgraduate qualifications from the Victorian College of the Arts. She has worked as a choreographer and movement director for a range of companies and projects including the Australian Opera, Victoria State Opera, Dance North, Sydney Dance Company, and Playbox Theatre.

**Jo Tacchi** is an Associate Professor in the Creative Industries Faculty, Queensland University of Technology (QUT) and Centre Fellow of the ARC Centre of Excellence in Creative Industries and Innovation. She is a media anthropologist specializing in ethnographic research on old and new media technologies. She holds a PhD in social anthropology from University College London, and works on a range of media research and development projects in Australia and the Asia and Pacific region.

**Lora Taub-Pervizpour** is an Associate Professor and Chair in the Media and Communication Department at Muhlenberg College, Pennsylvania, USA. She has contributed chapters to the *Encyclopedia of Television* (ed. H. Newcomb, 1997), *Continental Order? Integrating North America for Cybercapitalism* (ed. V. Mosco and D. Schiller, 2001), and *Television Studies* (ed. T. Miller, 2002).

**Nancy Thumim** is an LSE Fellow in the Department of Media and Communications at the London School of Economics and Political Science. She completed her PhD on mediated self-representations in 2007.

**Jerry Watkins** is a Senior Lecturer in the Faculty of Design, Swinburne University of Technology, Melbourne, and Research Fellow with the ARC Centre of Excellence for Creative Industries and Innovation. He has a 20-year track record in communication design and multimedia production. He has provided creative and strategic consultancy to some of the world's leading organizations, and has delivered digital content workshops for UNESCO and UNDP. His interdisciplinary research examines communication, participatory content creation, and social media.

**Julie Woletz** holds an MA in German Language and Literature and is completing a PhD at Goethe University, Frankfurt, Germany. Her thesis, "Contexts of Interaction within Computer Interfaces," analyzes prototypes and cultural requirements for an interface theory as a convergence of information sciences and media studies. She lectures at the universities of Frankfurt and Cologne, and is an IT consultant. Her research interests include digital media, new media cultures and practices, and human computer communication and interaction.

**Wu Qiongli** (Leila Wu) holds an MA from Queensland University of Technology (QUT), Australia, where she was involved in the Kelvin Grove Urban Village "Sharing Stories" project. Her interests lie in the practice and commercialization of digital storytelling in China. She is creative director and overseas board director at Beijing Blue Moon Culture (BMC), a computer graphics and 3-D animation company.

# Part I

# What Is Digital Storytelling?

# 1

# Computational Power Meets Human Contact

## *John Hartley and Kelly McWilliam*

Everyone loves a story. Not everyone loves a computer. "Digital storytelling" is a workshop-based practice in which people are taught to use digital media to create short audio-video stories, usually about their own lives. The idea is that this puts the universal human delight in narrative and self-expression into the hands of everyone. It brings a timeless form into the digital age, to give a voice to the myriad tales of everyday life as experienced by ordinary people in their own terms. Despite its use of the latest technologies, its purpose is simple and human.

The late Dana Atchley developed "digital storytelling" in California in the early to mid-1990s, with his partner Denise Aungst (later Atchley), with Joe Lambert and his partner Nina Mullen, and with programmer Patrick Milligan (Lambert 2006: 8–10). Although digital videos existed before that time in various forms, they were overwhelmingly the productions of experts – digital artists and filmmakers, for the most part. Atchley's innovation was to develop an exportable workshop-based approach to teach "ordinary" people – from school students to the elderly, with or (usually) without knowledge of computers or media production – how to produce their own personal videos. But despite the term "digital" in digital storytelling, the emphasis is on the *story* and the *telling*. Workshops typically commence with narrative and expressive "limbering-up" exercises, designed to loosen up everyone's storytelling capabilities. This feature is called the *story circle* – hence the title of this book. It may include verbal games, making lists (loves and hates), and writing make-believe scenarios, as well as scripting what will become each person's own story. The idea is not only to tap into people's implicit narrative skills, but also to focus on the telling, by prompting participants to share their ideas, and to do so spontaneously, quickly, and in relation to all sorts of nonsense as well as to the matter at hand. Thus, although individual stories can often be confessional, moving, and express troubles as well as triumphs, the process of making them can be noisy, fun, and convivial.

While the practice developed as a response to the exclusion of "ordinary" people's stories in broadcast media, it was facilitated by the increasing accessibility of digital media to home users, with digital cameras, scanners, and personal computers all becoming increasingly accessible to the domestic market in the 1990s. Digital storytelling also emerged as part of broader cultural shifts, including a profound change in models of media communication. As contemporary societies move from manufacturing industry to knowledge-based service economies, the entire array of large-scale and society-wide communication is undergoing a kind of paradigm shift, across the range of entertainment, business, and citizenship. Changing technologies and consumer demographics are transforming the production and consumption of media content of all kinds. The one-way broadcasting model of traditional media industries is evolving into peer-to-peer communication networks. These changes have been most pronounced in the explosion of user-created content in digital media, from games to online social networks. Similar changes are also being recognized in academic agendas, with interest shifting beyond analyses of the political economy of large-scale practices, or the ideology of industrially produced texts, and toward consumer-generated content production, distribution, and consumption.

Digital storytelling is now practiced around the world in increasingly diverse contexts, from cultural institutions and community development programs to screen innovation and commercial applications. It represents something of a social movement. It also occupies a unique place in consumer-generated media. The phenomenal success of YouTube shows that the Internet is now fully mature as an audiovisual medium, and the success of social networks like MySpace shows the broad hunger for human contact in the digital age. To these powerful social networking tools the digital storytelling technique adds individual imaginative vision, a "poetics" of expression, and the necessary technical competence, offering people a repertoire of creative skills to enable them to tell their own unique stories in a way that captures the imagination of others – whether close family members or the whole world.

At this moment in media history, digital storytelling represents an important fulcrum around which these larger trends pivot. It is at once an emergent form, a new media practice, an activist/community movement and a textual system:

- As a *form*, it combines the direct, emotional charge of confessional disclosure, the authenticity of the documentary, and the simple elegance of the format – it is a digital sonnet, or haiku.
- As a *practice*, digital storytelling combines tuition of the individual with new narrative devices for multiplatform digital publishing across hybrid sites.
- As a *movement*, it represents one of the first genuine amalgamations of expert and consumer/user-led creativity.
- And as an elaborated *textual system* created for the new media ecology, digital storytelling challenges the traditional distinction between professional and amateur production, reworking the producer/consumer relationship. It is a contribution to (and test of) contemporary thinking about "digital literacy" and participation, storytelling formats, and content distribution.

Accordingly, *Story Circle* provides a comprehensive international study of the digital storytelling movement, locating it in current debates on user-led media, citizen consumers, media literacy, and new media participation. Since first emerging in the 1990s, digital storytelling has grown exponentially. It is practiced in the UK, the USA, Australia, Japan, India, Nepal, and Belgium, among other countries, both developed and developing. It is used by schools, universities, libraries, museums, community organizations from health to arts activism, and broadcasters, including notably the BBC. It has the potential for commercial applications. Yet little has been written on digital storytelling, outside of occasional "how-to" guides by practitioners, and both business and educational textbooks that – rightly – extol the virtues of storytelling for learning (see Pink 2005, McDury and Alterio 2002). Beyond such practical tips for busy professionals, there has been little of substance to analyze and situate digital storytelling in the context of new media studies (but see Lundby 2008). *Story Circle* fills the gap.

## Foundations: Development of the Movement

The digital storytelling "movement" has been around for a long time. The movement itself was launched by Atchley (www.nextexit.com/) at the American Film Institute in 1993, where the first workshop was held. A year later, workshops were incorporated as the main activity and product of

**Table 1.1**  Opening years of major digital storytelling programs, by continent

| Year began | 1994 | 2001 | 2002 | 2003 | 2005 | 2006 |
|---|---|---|---|---|---|---|
| Name | Center for Digital Storytelling | "Capture Wales," BBC | Australian Centre for the Moving Image | Kids for Kids | Men as Partners, EnGender Health | Million-Youth-Life-Stories, Museu da Pessoa and Aracati |
| Country | USA | Wales | Australia | Israel | South Africa | Brazil |
| Continent | North America | Europe | Australasia | Asia | Africa | South America |

what would become the Center for Digital Storytelling (CDS) in Berkeley, California, directed by Joe Lambert (www.storycenter.org), the primary organization associated with this new media practice (Nissley 2007: 91). In association with the BBC, and with the crucial support of Menna Richards, Controller of BBC Cymru-Wales, Daniel Meadows accomplished an innovative reworking of the Californian model, adapting it to the "media ecology" of UK public broadcasting. "Capture Wales" (www.bbc.co.uk/wales/captures) was launched in 2001. That program has been so successful that besides the hundreds of stories in its own online archive, digital stories have aired regularly on BBC television and radio, and a number of BBC regions in England have produced their own versions.

Thousands of people have participated in a digital storytelling workshop in recent years at different international locations. Hundreds of workshops have been held, with at least one on every continent except Antarctica (Lambert 2006: 1; and see Table 1.1). This diffusion of a community media practice in a global mediasphere has been facilitated by increasingly diverse modes of uptake, and the development of an increasingly sophisticated (albeit largely informal) infrastructure (Howley 2005, Hartley 1996). In terms of the latter, for example, digital storytelling is facilitated by growing numbers of organizations, festivals, conferences, and competitions that are dedicated to or substantially focused on the practice, from the Nabi Digital Storytelling Competition in Korea to the Island Movie Contest in Hawaii. There are commercial products targeting digital storytelling practitioners, such as MemoryMiner digital storytelling software. Adobe markets

Photoshop Elements and Premiere Elements as "effective digital storytelling tools in your classroom."[1] There are networks of trainers and organizations providing an extended online community around digital storytelling; for instance, "Stories for Change" is a community website funded by MassIMPACT in the USA; and the "Digital Storytelling Network" in Australia.[2] Some education providers have begun to list "becoming a Digital Storytelling Facilitator" as a possible career path for their graduates, as in Australia's Swinburne University of Technology's Bachelor of Design (Multimedia Design).[3] Joe Lambert (2000) once commented, "I always thought of our work in Digital Storytelling as what we used to call 'movement building.'" The current level of activity around the world is proof positive that the movement is not "building"; it is "built."

## Diffusion: Uneven Development

However, digital storytelling has not been taken up evenly "around the world." Digital divides, among other differences in the accessibility, valuation, and uses of digital storytelling, persist (Bucy and Newhagen 2003). For example, while digital storytelling is widely used across North America, Europe, and Australasia, it is less developed in Asia, Africa, and South America. Most of the workshops held on those continents have been run or led by Western organizations or Western workshop facilitators and, by and large, have not resulted in ongoing local programs (although, as Table 1.1 demonstrates, there are exceptions). A case in point: Jennifer Nowicki of USA-based Creative Narrations led a digital storytelling workshop in Southern China for Shantou University's English Language Program in 2007 but, since Nowicki returned to the USA, the university has no plans to facilitate its own digital storytelling workshops. Indeed, digital storytelling is still most popular in "digitally saturated areas," in Knut Lundby's words, which is unsurprising, given the West's first-player advantage in the development of a consumer market for digital technologies (Lundby, this volume; Xiudian 2007).

One impediment to the diffusion of the movement is that parts of Asia, particularly Japan and South Korea, draw on different conceptions of "digital storytelling," which has likely affected the reach of the CDS/BBC models. For instance, the Entertainment Lab at the University of Tsukuba in Japan is typical in its use of "digital storytelling" to denote computer technologies, drawing on a "generic" conception of *digital* storytelling, rather than the "specific" conception that characterizes CDS-based digital *storytelling* (for more on "generic" vs. "specific" digital storytelling, see McWilliam 2008).[4]

Nevertheless, in most places where digital storytelling is located, the practice can usually be directly linked to the CDS. For example, at least three of the five programs (besides the CDS) listed in Table 1.1 were set up by the CDS. Daniel Meadows attended a CDS workshop before returning to the UK and playing a key role in setting up the "Capture Wales" program with the BBC; CDS co-founder Joe Lambert visited Australia to help set up the Australian Centre for the Moving Image's programs; and Amy Hill of the CDS delivered the first "Men as Partners" workshops in South Africa (for extended discussion of the latter, see Hill 2006). Lambert also visited Brazil, where his dissemination of the CDS's practices were incorporated into the Million Life Stories program (see Clarke, this volume); the Museu da Pessoa (Museum of the Person), one of the organizations behind the Million Life Stories program, also co-hosted the "International Day for Sharing Life Stories" with the CDS on May 16, 2008. However, the Israeli Kids for Kids programs – located in Asia, where digital storytelling is significantly less popular – is only indirectly linked to the CDS, which nevertheless remains the central organization associated with both the community media practice itself and its globally networked distribution.

On May 16, 2008 the first "Listen! – International Day for Sharing Life Stories" was held, co-organized by the CDS and the Museu da Pessoa in Brazil. It was announced as follows:

> We are part of an international movement of practitioners who view listening, collecting and sharing life stories as a critical process in democratizing culture and promoting social change. We want this day to be especially dedicated to celebrating and promoting Life Story projects that have made a difference within neighborhoods, communities, and societies as a whole …
>
> We will encourage participation in the day through many possible events, including:
>
> - Story Circles in people's homes, at workplaces, schools, community centers, virtual environments
> - Public open-microphone performances of stories
> - Exhibitions of Stories in public venues, as image, text, and audiovisual materials
> - Celebratory events to honor local storytellers, practitioners, and organizations

- Open houses for organizations with a life story-sharing component
- Online simultaneous gatherings, postings, and story exchanges
- Print, Radio and Television broadcast programming on life stories, and documentaries that feature oral histories and story exchanges.[5]

The event was supported by groups from all over the world, whose reports can be found online (see n.5).

## *Story Circle*: Around the Book

### *Part I: What Is Digital Storytelling?*

In Part I, introductory chapters by the editors provide a conceptual framework for and an international survey of digital storytelling.

### *Part II: Foundational Practices*

Part II of the book contains important reflections by two digital storytelling pioneers, Joe Lambert and Daniel Meadows, as well as a contribution from Helen Simondson of the Australian Centre for the Moving Image (ACMI), whose programs have led the way in that country, and one from Marie Crook of the BBC on the use of the technique for radio broadcasting.

In a way that is now characteristic of the movement, Joe Lambert combines his curiosity about the details of the practice – how to tell a good story using digital affordances – with "big-picture" issues including global tensions between cosmopolitanism and fundamentalism, problems of access and participation in a digital environment, and the value of progressive arts and educational activism that seeks to emancipate individual freedom ("tell stories") while building a sense of community ("listen deeply").

One innovation in this section is Daniel Meadows's dialogic presentation with Jenny Kidd, who conducted a doctoral research project on "Capture Wales" and whose findings are interspersed with Meadows's own narrative. In this way, human story and conceptual analysis are kept in touch with each other.

In her review of digital storytelling at ACMI, Helen Simondson raises the general problem of how cultural institutions with statutory collecting, archival, and exhibitive missions can come to terms with consumer-generated content, and the DIY culture of participatory media. The problems are not only institutional, they are also ideological. Curators and artists are not used to sharing their spaces with what they see as unsophisticated or sentimental work made by amateurs. And "ordinary people" don't usually see themselves as bearers of national aesthetic values. As Simondson shows, ACMI's Memory Grid is making both sides think afresh about their role as performers of public culture.

As the form disperses to new platforms, Marie Crook shows how the movement's commitment to the expertise and autonomy of the participant remains crucial, even in a context where the target demographic includes those who may seem least expert, for instance people seeking to gain literacy skills in reading and writing (never mind "digital" literacy). Nevertheless, argues Crook, they are "experts in their own story," and this is what needs to be brought out, without the instrumental purposes of the broadcaster or learning provider getting in the way. Thus despite the difference between broadcast radio and digital storytelling, the "story circle" remains the crucial element.

## Part III: Digital Storytelling around the World

The middle part of the book pursues digital storytelling around the world, although it does turn out that "the world" is never quite where you may think it is. Thus Part III opens with an account of African life as it is lived not in Africa but in Wales, and to make the cosmopolitan point the authors Sissy Helff and Julie Woletz are located in Frankfurt. Naturally such a context raises issues not of ethnic belonging but of the performance of the self in conditions of cross-cultural flows that include histories of racial conflict and colonialism. However, the stories analyzed by Helff and Woletz are "affirmative" of the self rather than critical of the context. They find this an appropriate although sometimes irritating "narrative means for generating modern transcultural Britishness."

Next comes Brazilian storytelling analyzed from Portsmouth. Margaret Anne Clarke traces the "One Million Life Stories of Youth" project in Brazil. She considers how the digital storytelling form, including workshop practice and the mode of subsequent dissemination, may adapt to the Brazilian context. She concludes that with flexible implementation to suit local conditions, digital storytelling can contribute to the "construction of fully democratic frameworks" by fostering collective and individual memories and voices.

In Australia, rapid urban development overlies sites of historic significance to the settler community. The history of such sites is also the memory of people living in and around the area. Here digital storytelling is integrated into oral history, and the very act of recording their memories prompted participants into further animated bursts of sharing. Thus the "Sharing Stories" project described by Jean Burgess and Helen Klaebe was just that; a means for people to share their stories with their families, with each other, with cultural institutions, and with the new generation of developers and users of the places where the stories were set. Along the way, everyone learnt about difference, they shared responsibility for the authority of their own history with formal institutions, and the project as a whole mapped a micro-public linked by narrative.

Media anthropologist Jo Tacchi reports on a large-scale research project in South and Southeast Asia (India, Nepal, Sri Lanka, and Indonesia). The project as a whole belongs to the field of "development communication," working with international agencies to promote information technologies and self-expression among excluded populations. Tacchi herself is interested in the promotion of *voice* in a development context, and found digital storytelling an ideal way to combine Information and Communication Technologies (ICTs) with "finding a voice" for the empowerment of marginalized people, such that they may achieve creative agency in the processes of social change that affect them.

Knut Lundby contextualizes the digital storytelling movement in the light of developments in Norway, Denmark, and Sweden, but more particularly in relation to sociological theory. He discusses the shift from "media" to "mediations" as the participatory turn and consumer productivity diffuse through both time and space, to reconfigure the relationship between agency and structure. Similarly, Nico Carpentier describes two digital storytelling projects in Belgium in terms of anarchist theory and Foucauldian notions of power. Nancy Thumim brings us full circle to the UK, with an analysis of aspects of "Capture Wales" and "London's Voices," which she analyzes in terms of the tensions between the activism of digital mediators and the positioning of members of the public, who she sees as being put in their place by initiatives such as these, which undermine the very notion of the "ordinary person" while seeking to represent it. She finds similar tensions in relation to issues of community and quality.

*Part IV: Emergent Practices*

The final part of the book presents various emergent practices, some of which go very much against the grain of what has gone before. They show how digital storytelling is evolving – or how it may need to evolve – to adapt to different contexts and for new purposes. The idea of Part IV is to present a number of possible directions not necessarily predicted in the digital storytelling "movement," which may take forward some of its energies into hitherto uncharted territory. Thus it is not intended to be comprehensive – after all, the possible interpretations of the phrase "digital storytelling" are almost infinite. Instead, the chapters in Part IV offer instances of emergent practices rather than a comprehensive map.

One direction not taken in the digital storytelling movement as we have explored it in this book is towards role-play games and MMOGs (massively multiplayer online games) that foster peer-to-peer relations in multiplayer environments, of which perhaps the best known is "Second Life." Here, we offer a rather different take on the role-play scenario, where the digital narrative involves exploring an "endless forest" as a deer. Naturally there are other possibilities! However, using this example, where storytelling does not involve verbal language at all, Maria Chatzichristodoulou argues that self-representation in digital narrative can be taken much further than is normal in digital storytelling. Such a context points to "digital narratives that are experiential, multiple, and relational."

Another direction not taken by most of those involved in the digital storytelling movement is toward commercialization. However, there may well be many market-based applications of the technique that are non-exploitative and fun. Wu Qiongli takes up the challenge of this idea in her chapter by developing a business plan for the extension of the practice in China. She sees opportunities in tourism services, the digital content industries, and in electronics retailing. Marketized applications of digital storytelling may seem to contradict its libertarian origins, but in fact many liberating aspects of popular culture, from music to online social networks, can thrive in a commercial environment, perhaps more readily than in the control culture of formal education or in the hierarchical specializations of art. Long term, the prospects for the wide adoption and retention of digital storytelling without some exposure to markets are extremely limited.

The next chapters return to the slightly more familiar ground of education. Lora Taub-Pervizpour raises some awkward questions in her discussion of digital storytelling as a tool for engaging marginalized youth. She finds this process fraught with "profoundly contradictory and conflicted situations," as she raises questions about the mutual responsibilities of story producers and storytellers, and their different investments in popular culture. Her chapter offers one way to get beyond the tensions noted by Thumim. Self-reflexive effort is needed by facilitators and activists, who may have more to learn from the process of "empowering" marginalized groups than the people involved. Patrick Lowenthal extends the theme of how digital story-telling may fare in the educational context with his analysis of issues related to its institutionalization as a school-based activity. The theme of institu-tionalization is important because organizations are "agents" in their own right, with purposes that may differ from those of either participants or facilitators. These institutional realities and how practitioners navigate them may determine the success or otherwise of digital storytelling initiatives. A question always to be faced is how emancipationist intentions can be pursued using the agency of large-scale institutions which also have their own control imperatives. One way to address such issues is to confront organizational culture directly, as Lisa Dush does. She explores the difficulties, from training to distribution, faced by organizations in general when they try to adopt digital storytelling. She develops a "syntax" based on genre theory to assist in illuminating implementation difficulties in organizations.

Finally, Jerry Watkins and Angelina Russo argue that the original model of digital storytelling from the CDS and BBC Wales results in an individual-ist but prescriptive mode of expression, in a genre that is more reactive than interactive. Against this, they argue for a "strategic team-based approach to participatory content creation." Working with cultural institutions like museums, libraries, and galleries, they stress the importance of collabora-tive and team-based "microdocumentary" production, bringing organiza-tions together with communities of interest in "co-creative systems," which focus not so much on self-expression as on interactivity and the potential for distribution afforded by Web 2.0 platforms.

All of the chapters in Part IV tend toward a view of the future of digital storytelling that conforms more explicitly to the collaborative, iterative, experiential, dialogic, and socially networked characteristics of Web 2.0 (and its successors). As digital literacy improves, there is also increasing discom-fort with a model of propagation that assumes a radical asymmetry between expert facilitators (teachers or artists) and participants ("ordinary" people), whose capabilities are assumed to be close to zero. Digital storytelling can learn from other domains, for instance MMOGs and Web 2.0 interactivity, and from other contexts, commercial and institutional. Digital storytelling was invented before most of the affordances of Web 2.0 were available, but there is no need to dismiss it as a transitional stage that has been overtaken by new developments (each of which throws up its own problems). Instead, digital storytelling can learn from new applications and existing contexts while retaining its own purposes and hard-won achievements in emergent practices that suit the times.

## The Future: Computing Human Contact

Digital storytelling has certainly traveled the world, and it remains a powerful tool for both emancipationist and instrumentalist agendas. However, it must adapt in order to survive, and among the challenges it faces are those raised in the course of this book. Although it developed in the context of Californian festival culture and European public broadcasting, it has matured in the age of YouTube. Is it possible to retain the celebratory, affirmative, confessional, and therapeutic "romanticism" of digital storytelling within a global structure of socially networked entrepreneurial consumerism? Is it possible for teachers to be facilitators, or will their best efforts go toward reproducing organizational inequalities, further disempowering the very disenfranchised voices they were trying to hear?

The only way to resolve such questions is in practice. Digital storytelling is organized around workshop practices and teaching programs that bring big organizations and expert professionals into skin-to-skin contact with "ordinary citizens." Instead of leaving things as it finds them it is an interfering attempt to propagate the means for digital expression, communication, interaction, and social networking to the whole population. The hope is that all sides get something valuable from the experience and perhaps a more permanent added value to take away and keep. None of this is easy to do without creating further problems. Thus diversity, experimentation, flexibility, and openness to change are more likely to produce valuable outcomes than fixed rules or – worse still – critical disengagement. However, it is clear from this book that critical observers entertain various misgivings about digital storytelling, including:

- as a *form*, it is too sentimental, individualistic, and naively unselfconscious;

- as a *practice*, the means of delivery are too teacher-centric, too caught up in institutional powers and structures;
- as a *movement*, its propagation and dissemination strategies are hopeless – most digital stories persist only as unused archive; and it has a very low profile on the Net, making little use of interactivity and social networking;
- as a *textual system*, the potential for "serious" work is underdeveloped – there is too much attention to self-expression; not enough to the growth of knowledge.

These misgivings need to be seen as a spur to action rather than cause for withdrawal. Digital storytelling is an experiment, so it is capable of iterative self-correction and improvement, as long as enough people stick around long enough to push it forward. *Story Circle* shows how the experiment is going so far. To deal with the problems it is important for everyone involved to maintain a reflexive and critical attitude within a supportive and human purpose. Digital storytelling is a good way to explore how individuals can help each other to navigate complex social networks and organizational systems, which themselves rely on the active agency of everyone in the system to contribute to the growth of knowledge. Digital storytelling uses computational power to attempt human contact. It would be a surprise if we got that right first time; but a pity if we stopped trying.

## Notes

1   MemoryMiner digital storytelling software (www.memoryminer.com/) and Adobe Digital Storytelling (www.adobe.com/education/digkids/storytelling/index.html).
2   "Stories for Change" (storiesforchange.net) and "Digital Storytelling Network" (www.groups.edna.edu.au/course/view.php?id=107).
3   See www.swin.edu.au/corporate/careers/Design-MultimediaDesign.pdf
4   The Entertainment Lab at the University of Tsukuba (www.graphic.esys.ts ukuba.ac.jp/research.html); Department of Digital Storytelling, ZGDV Computer Graphics Centre (www.zgdv.de/zgdv/zgdv-en/r-d-departments/digital-story telling); Digital Storytelling Effects Lab (disel-project.org/).
5   See www.ausculti.org/about.html; www.storycircles.org and storiesforchange. net, and digitalstorytelling.ci.qut.edu.au/

# 2

# TV Stories
## From Representation to Productivity

## *John Hartley*

### To Have Great Poets …

Alfred Harbage, pioneering historian of Shakespeare's audience, followed the dictum of the great American poet of democracy Walt Whitman (1995 [1883]: 324), who wrote: "to have great poets, there must be great audiences too." Harbage (1947) says: "Shakespeare and his audience found each other, in a measure they created each other. He was a quality writer for a quality audience … The great Shakespearian discovery was that quality extended vertically through the social scale, not horizontally at the upper genteel, economic and academic levels."

I've always been interested in the "great Shakespearean discovery," which has motivated my research and writing about television ever since *Reading Television* (Fiske and Hartley 2003 [1978]). In that book, I coined the term "bardic function" to describe the active relationship between TV and viewers, where, we argued, TV programming and mode of address use the shared resources of narrative and language to deal with social change and conflict, bringing together the worlds of decision makers (news), central meaning systems (entertainment), and audiences ("vertically through the social scale") to make sense of the experience of modernity.

This chapter revisits the notion of the "bardic function." It is an attempt to locate self-made and personally published media, including both community-based initiatives like digital storytelling and commercial enterprises like YouTube, within a much longer historical context of popular narration (see also Hartley 2008a for further discussion of the bardic function in relation to the "consumer productivity" of sites like YouTube). The challenge inherent in such an attempt is to understand whether, and if so how, the *cultural function* of the television medium has been affected by recent technologically enabled change. Most important in this respect is the social (and global) dispersal of production. Can TV still serve a "bardic function" after it has evolved from *broadcast* to *broadband* (and into a further, *mobile* phase)? Broadcast TV has been a household-based "read-only" medium, with a strong demarcation between highly capitalized expert-professional producers and untutored amateur domestic consumers. Broadband (and mobile) "TV" is a customized "read-write" medium, where self-made audio-visual "content" can be exchanged among all agents in a social network, which may contain any number of nodes ranging in scale from individual, to family and friends, to global markets. What continues, and what changes, under such conditions, and what new possibilities are enabled?

## Talk about Full Circle!

Blaming the popular media for immoral, tasteless, sycophantic, sexist, senseless, and disreputable behavior is nothing new. Tut-tutting at the off-duty antics of media personalities also has a long history. Both were present – and already formulaic – at the earliest foundation of European storytelling, in this case sometime before the fourteenth century; perhaps as far back as the sixth. This was the period when Taliesin ("Radiant Brow"), the Chief Bard of Britain, flourished, or at least when the verses attributed to him were written down. Taliesin "himself" was both myth and history: a sixth-century historical bard at the court of King Urien of Rheged in North Britain (who was also both historical and a figure in Arthurian myth); and a legendary Taliesin who starred in Welsh poems associated with his name in the *Book of Taliesin* (Guest 1849, Ford 1992).

On the occasion when he first revealed his magical poetic powers, this fictional Taliesin delivered a series of poems denouncing the king's existing corps of four and twenty bards. Part of the trick of getting himself noticed, evidently, was to rubbish the opposition:

| | |
|---|---|
| *Cler o gam arfer a ymarferant* | **Strolling minstrels** are addicted to evil habits. |
| *Cathlau aneddfol fydd eu moliant* | **Immoral songs** are their delight. |
| *Clod orwas ddiflas a ddatcanant* | In a **tasteless manner** they rehearse the **praise of heroes**. |

| | |
|---|---|
| *Celwydd bob amser a ymarferant* | **Falsehood** at all times they use … |
| *Morwynion gwinion mair a lygrant* | The **fair virgins** of Mary they **corrupt** |
| *A goelio iddynt a gwilyddiant* | Those who put **trust** in them they bring to **shame,** |
| *A gwyrion ddynion a ddyfalant* | And **true men** they **laugh to scorn,** |
| *A hoes ai amser yn ofer y treuliant* | And **times and seasons** they spend in **vanities** … |
| *Pob parabl dibwyll a grybwyllant* | All kinds of **senseless stories** they relate. |
| *Pob pechod marwol a ganmolant* | All kinds of **mortal sins** they praise. |

Taliesin, *Fustl y Beirdd* ["Flail of the Bards"] (Nash 1858: 177–9)[1]

If you substitute "TV and pop culture" for "strolling minstrels," and in terms of cultural function there's every reason why you should, it is surprising how familiar and contemporary is this list of evil, immorality, tastelessness, lies, exploiting women, abusing trust, humiliating innocent citizens, time-wasting vanity, and senselessness. It's just the kind of thing that people say about the "tabloid" media, popular entertainment formats, and media celebrities (e.g., see Turner 2005). Taliesin's name, which by the time these lines were composed was itself a popular "brand" or "channel,"[2] was used to reproach the other bards, "so that not one of them dared to say a word" (Guest 1849). Clearly, a *competitive system* of knowledge-providers was already well developed in pre-modern oral culture, in which "media professionals" vied openly for both institutional patronage and popular acclaim.

Later commentators on Taliesin have supposed that the composer of this invective against strolling minstrels – who were the *distribution system* for pre-modern popular media – was likely to have been a thirteenth- or fourteenth-century monk, usurping Taliesin's name for a contemporary dispute. There was no love lost between monks and minstrels. Their mutual loathing was occasioned not only by a difference between sacred/clerical and secular/profane worldviews, but also by a medieval antecedent of the modern antagonism between public service and commercial media, education and entertainment, high and popular culture, artistry and exploitation, intellectuals and showmen. Proponents of the former persistently called for official regulation of the latter; which by the tenth century had already occurred in the legal code of Hywel Dda (King Hywel the Good), laying down the infrastructure for cultural distinctions that persist to this day.[3]

Generically, the despised but ubiquitous medieval "popular media" – the romances and narrative verse collected under the name of Taliesin and others – were comparable to the style of variety, magazine, and current affairs shows on television. The overall mix in a given performance did not follow the Aristotelian unities of place, time, and action, but included successive snippets of news, fantasy, ballad, romance, travel, discovery, and morality, all presented in an entertaining package that borrowed freely from other suppliers but made sure audiences knew which noble sponsor was behind it (by praising same to the skies) and which poetic brand – in this case the top "brand" of Taliesin – was bringing them these pleasures:

> Written down from the mouths of the wandering minstrels ... the poems ascribed to Taliesin in particular, are for the most part made up of allusions to local, sometimes historical events, references to the Mabinogion, or fairy and romance tales of the Welsh, scraps of geography and philosophy, phrases of monkish Latin, moral and religious sentiments, proverbs and adages, mixed together in wonderful confusion, sometimes all in the compass of one short ballad. (Nash 1858: 34–5)

Welcome to television, Taliesin-style.

## Bardic Television: "From the Hall of the Baron to the Cabin of the Boor"

When we coined the term "bardic function," John Fiske and I wanted to identify the cultural rather than individual aspect of television. We did not share the then predominant approaches to audiences, derived as they were from psychology (media effects on individual behavior), sociology (the "uses and gratifications" of television), and political economy (consumers as effects of corporate strategies). Such approaches looked for a linear chain from TV (cause) to audiences (effect); as in "TV causes violence." We approached TV audiences from a cultural perspective and a literary training, which meant:

1. seeing television and its audiences as part of an overall *sense-making system*, like language and its elaborated or "literary" forms and genres, both verbal and visual;
2. seeing culture not just as a domain of aesthetics, but also, and primarily, one of identity formation, power, and struggle; *the performance of the self in the context of power.*

Within this envelope of meaningfulness a "whole way of life" is established, made sense of, lived, and changed, rendering media consumption as an *anthropological* sense-making activity (e.g., Richard Hoggart, Raymond Williams, Claude Lévi-Strauss, Marshall Sahlins, Edmund Leach; see Hawkes 1977). Combining the cultural approach with a mode of analysis derived from *semiotics*, which is interested in how the overall sense-making system works to generate new meanings at various levels of symbolism (e.g., Ferdinand de Saussure, Roland Barthes, Umberto Eco, Yuri Lotman), we argued that TV brought together in symbolic unity, by means of special-ized textual forms from cop shows to quiz shows, the worlds of a society's leadership (top) and its general population (bottom), just as had the Tudor propagandist William Shakespeare. As John Milton put it in 1667, in his rationale for a narrative poetry that sought to explain the human condition, the ideological purpose of the performance was to "justify the ways of God to men" (*Paradise Lost* 1.26). For "God" we may now read "power"; and instead of poetry we have realism, but the *function* remains: justifying the ways of power to audiences.

In deference to the literary, historical, and anthropological antecedents of our work, and to television's own oral-musical modes of address, not to mention the contextual fact that at the time Fiske and I worked in Wales, we called that justification process the "bardic function." The antecedents of popular entertainment with political import go as far back at least as the medieval bards, heralds, minstrels, and troubadours whose job it was to "broadcast" the exploits, ferocity, largesse, and (mis)adventures of the high and mighty. In other words, the "bardic function" retains some ancient aspects, not only those relating to universal human creative talent, but also in organizational form and purpose:

> That bards or persons gifted with some poetic and musical genius existed in Britain, as in every other country in the world at every age, may be conceded, and that among the Celtic tribes, perhaps in an especial manner, the capacity for recording in verse the deeds of warriors and the ancestry of chieftains, was held in high esteem, and the practice an honorable occupation. (Nash 1858: 24)

Why is such an occupation honored; of what use is it to the polity? For those he served directly, the bard was of high importance as the broker of knowledge for the family (which stood in place of the state at the time). Bardic song brought in new information and ideas to the court, while simultaneously broadcasting to the world the employer's claims to fame. The bard was:

> the genealogist, the herald, and to some extent the historian of the family to which he was attached, kept alive the warlike spirit of the clan or tribe, the remembrance of the old feuds or alliances, and whiled away those tedious hours of an illiterate age … To some extent a man of letters, he probably fulfilled the office of instructor in the family of his patron or chief. (Nash 1858: 27)

For the remainder of society, a "mass medium" was needed to broadcast the adventures and to advertise the merits of the winners in the medieval "economy of attention" (Lanham 2006). Such a medium existed in the minstrelsy, although, as we have seen, it had its clerical detractors:

> Besides these regularly acknowledged family or domestic Bards, there was in Wales, in the eleventh and twelfth centuries, and from thence downwards, a very numerous class of itinerant minstrels, who, like the Troubadours, Jongleurs, or Gleemen, wandered from place to place, seeking reward for the entertainment they afforded by their musical acquirements, and their recital of songs and tales for the amusement of all classes, from the hall of the baron to the cabin of the boor. (Nash 1858: 27; for the regulation of gifts and "vagabond" minstrels see pp. 33, 179)

Fiske and Hartley (2003 [1978]: 64–6) list seven qualities in common between bards and television. Both are:

1. *mediators* of language;
2. expressions of *cultural* needs (rather than formal purity or authorial intention);
3. *socio-central*;
4. *oral* (not literate);
5. *positive and dynamic* (their storytelling mode is to "claw back" anomalous or exogenous events such that nothing in the external environment remains unintelligible or outside of the frame of bardic textualization; and everything they publish is intelligible to the general audience);
6. *myth-making*;
7. sources and repositories of *common sense* and *conventions* of seeing and knowing.

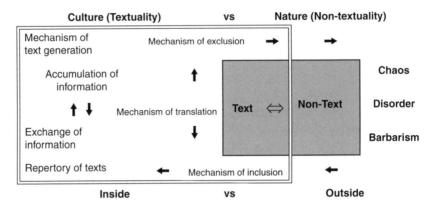

**Figure 2.1**   The "Tartu school" semiotic model of culture (Sonesson 1997; 2002)

In short, the "bardic function" is to textualize the world meaningfully for a given language community: this has been expressed diagrammatically by Göran Sonesson (see Figure 2.1).

Fiske and Hartley (2003 [1978]: 66–7) also enumerate the functions performed by TV in its bardic role:

1. to *articulate* cultural consensus;
2. to *implicate* individuals in the cultural value-system;
3. to *celebrate* the doings of cultural representatives;
4. to *affirm* the practical utility of myths and ideologies in the context of conflict (both real and symbolic);
5. to *expose*, conversely, perceived inadequacies in the cultural sense of self;
6. to *convince* audiences that their status and identity as individuals is guaranteed;
7. to *transmit* a sense of cultural membership.

By this analogy – although I am trying to show that it was more than an analogy; it was more like an evolutionary buildup of cultural and organizational resources – the "bardic function" of popular television works to "sing the praises" of its dominant culture in the same way that Celtic bards and minstrels lauded, lamented, and sometimes laughed at their overlords in an oral culture. Both connect political power and textual pleasure in a specialized form of expression that is accessible to everyone in a given language community, and which serves the function of ordering the social, natural, and supernatural worlds. Although bardic tales were *about* knights and princesses, they were *for* everyone (as they remain, in fantasy genres).[4] Like Taliesin in Celtic Britain, television uses high-level narrative conventions and its own oral/aural (rather than literate) relationship with audiences to spin topical but timeless stories out of the doings of contemporary characters, many of these the latter-day equivalent of the kings, beasts, and heroes of the Middle Ages, albeit in the convincing guise of detectives, prostitutes, journalists, celebrities, neighbors, and foreigners.

## Narrative and Polity – "Representation of the People"

Be it noted that the order of bards and popular television alike are specialized institutionalized agencies for this broader cultural function. They take it on and professionalize it within evolving historical, regulatory, and economic contexts, and of course in so doing they tend to narrow its potential, to exclude outsiders (the general public) from productive or creative participation, not least to maintain the price of their skills, and to restrict the infinite potential of semiosis to definite forms with which their own institutionalized "mechanism of translation" (see Figure 2.1) can comfortably cope. These institutional agencies can optimize storytelling's scale (a story can be reproduced many times) and its diffusion (a story can be heard by many people); but they also increase both formal and bureaucratic rigidity in narrative production and thus reduce adaptability to change.

Such a view of the "bardic function" must retain a "top-down" approach to storytelling, because it focuses on a centralized, "institutional" form of production, rather than storytelling at the "anthropological" level of everyday life. Bardic tales were about the elite who commissioned the bards to tell them. They were made by specialist professionals close to the centers of power. They were intended for the enjoyment of one and all, and designed to be diffused throughout the social strata and across the land or indeed the world, as in the global career of Arthurian stories. Broadcast television certainly cast the semiotic net more widely, telling tales of ordinary life using characters from across the social spectrum (a vernacular innovation pioneered in Chaucer's *Canterbury Tales*). However, in neither the bardic nor the broadcast context did "ordinary" people play much of a direct role in the production of these tales. During the heyday of television, the domestic TV audience could participate only by gathering round and enjoying official versions performed by professional bards and minstrels. They were not encouraged to take up the metaphorical harp for themselves and have a go too, using the shared forms and conventions of the style.

The concept of the "bardic function" was developed specifically to account for the storytelling mode of a mass medium, in which few storytellers "sang" universally accessible narratives about socially favored characters to many auditors, and thereby gave shape, and sometimes purpose, to the polity as a whole. A limitation of this top-down perspective, as Wyn Griffith pointed out in relation to the period of the medieval princes immortalized in bardic song, is that "we do not know what the common man [much less woman or child] thought of it all" (1950: 80): neither their own words nor stories of their lives are preserved in text, which at this stretch of time is the only archive remaining to tell us something about the culture. The same might be said of mass media, which tend to tell stories of ordinary life *to* "the common man" and woman and child, in the form of comedy, soap opera, and reality television, but nevertheless, simply for reasons of scale, cannot accommodate more than samples of expression *by* them.

But now, everyone with access to a computer can not only "sing" for themselves, they can also personally publish the results to everyone else. The shift from the broadcast to the interactive era, from analogue to digital technologies, and from expert/professional production to DIY or "consumer-generated" content – from "read-only" to "read-and-write" media, for consumers as well as professionals – has opened up the idea of the "bardic function" to new interpretation, and to a new challenge.

A new *interpretation* must include this widely distributed capability, with myriad storytellers, not just top bards. How far into "ordinary" life might the production and performance of stories go? In terms of oral cultures like those of pre-modern Europe, such an interpretation would require attention not just to "court" bards but also to "folk" songs and stories, from art to anthropology, from the productivity of a social institution to that of language. A new interpretation of the "bardic function" would need to take a much stronger interest in what has come to be called "amateur," DIY, or consumer-created content. The *challenge* is to understand how such a diffused system might work to propagate coherent sense across social boundaries, among different demographics, and throughout social hierarchies. In other words, how does a fully distributed narrative system retain overall systemic unity? If everyone is speaking for themselves, then who speaks for everybody?

This is a similar question to one of the central problems of democracy itself, which is always beset by secessionist tendencies (see Collier and Hoeffler 2002), and only seems to work at any scale once it has abandoned direct decision-making in favor of some form of representative delegation, so that the demos is included symbolically rather than literally in the decision-making process of the polity. As with democracy, so with musical or dramatic storytelling – the challenge is to find a way to think about, to explain, and to promote mass participation without encouraging splits, divisions, migrations, and anarchy on the one hand, or an incomprehensible cacophonous plurality of competing voices on the other, or an authoritarian/elitist alternative to both. The challenge is also a negative one – how *not* to associate "more" with "worse"; mass participation with loss of quality?

Can one imagine a "bardic function" that pervades the polity, that keeps open the possibility of communication and meaningfulness across demographic boundaries and social hierarchies, providing leadership as to what "we" know and imagine, while simultaneously permitting myriad unique experiences to be connected to (and differentiated from) common knowledge and popular entertainment? And can one imagine stories told by *just anyone* as simultaneously democratic in expression yet retaining the admired qualities of professionally crafted work?

Such an extended function is like *language* itself rather than being the direct product or purpose of a state or other institutional "provider." A language unites the unpredictable unique utterances produced by all speakers with the systematic coherence required for them to be heard, understood, and responded to by any hearer within the given language community. Nevertheless, language too has been subjected to institutional organization, official regulation, and historical evolution; and it has developed complexity in both form and content.

In medieval courts, language was institutionally differentiated from action; bards from knights, *prating* from *prowess*. Each function was separately organized into its own "order" with its own regulations, rituals, and specialist schools. Bards were servants of the king (or state), from which position – like media barons – the successful ones achieved influence, status, and wealth. However, in one sense, and in the long run, they were even more powerful than kings. For they were the creators of a kind of cultural wealth that was and remains in short supply and great demand – immortality through fame. Kings and knights were not known until praised. So of course they all did whatever it took, in a competitive system, to make sure that their actions were noted and remembered (including paying for that service). The "age of chivalry" was a product of those who recorded it, not directly of the knights whose actions were celebrated. In the long run you were only as brave or successful as Taliesin et al. said you were; the memory of your very existence depended upon story. This was the origin of both literature and heraldry. Bards, minstrels, and heralds performed the same job; that of noting exactly who was whom, what they did to deserve their honor, and which family or court should get the credit (College of Arms n.d.).

Kings and knights were not known until they were praised; the common people were not known at all. A full-scale "economy of attention" (Lanham 2006) was in place, comprising a competitive social network market in which everyone's value was determined by what everyone else in the system knew and said about them (Potts et al. 2008). This was a "virtualization" or "textualization" of what had since very ancient times been a literal and material practice. The Achaeans, for instance, measured honor directly, in booty won in battle. It was called *geras*. After a battle the "spoils of war" (captured arms, people, towns, etc.) were literally divided up among the winning warriors by the victorious general or king; and the bigger your pile the more you were honored. Conversely, a small pile was an insult, so further conflict or defection was likely over the "distributive fairness" of the division of spoils (Balot 2001: 87–8).[5] But of course we only know all this because a poet – in this case Homer – duly noted it down, recording both the system of *geras* and the amount apportioned to Achilles, Ajax, Hector, etc.; by which "honors" the immortality of these heroes is still measured today.

## "Olympic Games of the Mind"

For humans, storytelling itself is a form of schooling in the capabilities of language. It teaches us how to think (plot), what to think about (narrative), the moral universe of choice (character), and the calculation of risk (action), motivated by desire for immortality (fear of death). If learning via storytelling is so important, you might expect to find it institutionalized, brought out from the realm of tacit or informal knowledge into the scientific realm of explicit expertise. For even if it is the case that storytelling is, as it were, an evolutionary adaptation, it does not follow that natural talent will thrive naturally. As well as any natural propensity among individuals, its propagation requires social coordination to extend it throughout the population via progressive stages of tutelage to attain higher levels of complexity, and "the oxygen of publicity" to make it all seem worth attempting. Thus, even though everyone can tell a story, storytelling needs infrastructural investment if it is to answer the needs of an increasingly adept population in a growth economy. If stories are teachers, how can storytelling be taught? Are there social institutions devoted to propagating the skill among the many, rather than restricting its benefits to the few?

Historically, part at least of the answer to that question was bardic. Bardic schools were instituted in medieval times in Wales and Ireland to systematize the order of bards and to teach subjects we might now recognize as law, history, geography, genealogy, language, literature, music, science (e.g., natural history, magic), and religion, as well as – indeed through – the strict regulations appertaining to bardic poetry in terms of form and meter (cynghanedd, englynion, etc.).[6] Such schools were far from informal, but they were oral and vernacular in mode, unlike ecclesiastical schools (from which modern schooling is descended), which were literate and Latinate. Bardic schools precipitated into the general population people who were skilled in the craft aspects of storytelling as well as knowledgeable in the topical issues, powers, and celebrities of the day.

One of the earliest social mechanisms used to improve bardic quality was the *eisteddfod* (literally, "sitting"). The first eisteddfod was held (it is said) in the court of Rhys ap Gruffudd, prince of Deheubarth in South Wales, in 1176.[7] This "grand festival" was an open, international competition, announced a year in advance, to find the best bard and the best minstrel. Competitors congregated at Lord Rhys's residence, Cardigan Castle, and each was given hospitality while the two winners received "vast gifts." These professional eisteddfodau continued periodically until the decline of the bardic order by the seventeenth century. They were revived by Iolo Morgannwg (Edward Williams), "a stonemason of ill-controlled genius" (Griffith 1950: 143), on Primrose Hill in London in 1791, as a vehicle for the expression of passionate amateurism and (largely fabricated) antiquarianism.

From 1860 the National Eisteddfod was held each summer. It continues today as one of the main cultural events of Wales, held entirely in Welsh, to determine and showcase the winners of bardic, musical, and literary competitions (among others – there are sections for science and media as well). It is also a popular annual holiday event, attracting an average of over 150,000 visitors each year, from a population of three million of whom about a fifth are Welsh speakers (Stevens and Associates 2003: 11–16). A cross between folk festival (e.g., Glastonbury in England; Woodford in

**Figure 2.2**    A Prince of Wales visits Cardigan Castle, more than 800 years after the first eisteddfod was held there by a previous Prince of Wales. *Picture courtesy of the* Tivyside Advertiser *and Cadwgan/Cardigan Castle*

Australia), scholarly convention,[8] and *Pop Idol*, the National Eisteddfod has remained a national but amateur institution of language and learning for many decades.

Writing of this "one-nation Olympic games of the mind," Wyn Griffith asked: "Where else can you find a people eager to devote a week to crowding into a peripatetic festival devoted to the arts, ordinary people, working people, men and women of all ranks, rich and poor?" (Griffith 1950: 152). Despite his conviction that "there is nothing quite like it anywhere else in the world" (136), there are in fact quite a few things like it. Carnivalesque singing and poetry competitions abound, in folk, urban, and school settings. Some of them are modeled on and retain the title of the eisteddfod, including well-established networks in Australia and South Africa.[9] Some don't use the Welsh word, but eisteddfodau they are; for example:

> several hundred people ascended to the Waswantu Plateau in the southern Peruvian Andes to celebrate and compete in an annual song contest that marks the height of carnival festivities in the region … Competing groups

regaled the assembled crowd and judges throughout the day with newly composed songs that ranged, in usual carnival fashion, from the bawdy to the biting, the raunchy to the reflective. (Ritter 2007: 177)

These events maintain a strongly local and self-made character. They are not swamped by global media and power; rather they are an exercise in rereading it. The Andean event described above attracted the attention of ethnomusicologist Jonathan Ritter because, "late in the day … the 'Falcons of Mt. Wamaqo' entered the ring of rocks marking the performance area and offered its final round entry, a song entitled 'Osama bin Laden'." As Emma Baulch has commented, writing about the punk music scene in Bali: "due to the global dissemination of mass mediation, people now collectively imagine existences that differ from the social realities in which they live. Thus the electronic media's impact on the imagination serves not just as an escape but as a staging ground for action" (Baulch 2007: 110–11). Globally dispersed competitive performance carnivals like eisteddfodau (under whatever local name) are among the training camps for that staging ground. They have appropriated contemporary media, as well as using oral traditions and professional skills going back a thousand years and more. They are used for the present purposes of non-elite populations, brought together in a "great feast of amateurs of the arts" (Griffith 1950: 147); one in which a people self-organizes to propagate and improve its own use of its own language.

A connection between amateur eisteddfod and expert media remains, because the competitions held in schools and community centers and mountainsides are used by performers, parents, and professional associations alike as an apprenticeship training ground; a "beauty-pageant circuit," as it were, for voices, words, and music. Out of it can certainly come world-class talent, as demonstrated in the life and career of opera star Bryn Terfel, who was raised on eisteddfodau and now produces and sponsors them.[10] And of course mainstream or traditional media have developed their own highly coded versions of the eisteddfod, in the guise of the *Idol* format – which, it transpires, goes back to the *Bardic Idol* contest of Prince Rhys ap Gruffudd in the 1170s.

The rock eisteddfod is a hybrid form that has had success in Australia, and thence in Japan, New Zealand, South Africa, Germany, Dubai, and the UK. It is a national competitive event for schools, designed to "motivate young Australians to make positive and healthy lifestyle choices."[11] The idea is to combine music, performance, and health messages. Originally promoted by a radio station, the finals are now televised, and successful school teams may tour overseas. The "challenge" targets youth at risk of "abuse, discrimination, crime or drugs, neglect or destructive behavior." In 2008 the rock eisteddfod "Global Challenge" was held in Japan, where performances were to be staged using a contemporary remix of traditional Japanese tales.[12] Advice to contestants on the website included a presentation on "Creating a Theme," which gave examples of how to find, research, and remix a story. The similarity between these Japanese stories and those to be found under Taliesin's name in the *Mabinogion* is striking – and highly appropriate to a global eisteddfod.

## "Bamboo Shoots after the Rain" – Proliferating Global Eisteddfodau

Here are some extracts from the Japan Rock Challenge's "Creating a Theme".

### *Japanese folklore themes*

- *mukashibanashi* – tales of long ago
- *ongaeshibanashi* – stories of repaying kindness
- *tonchibanashi* – witty stories
- *waraibanashi* – funny stories
- *yokubaribanashi* – stories of greed
- *namidabanashi* – sad stories
- *obakebanashi* – ghost stories

### *Examples of stories*

- *Kintaro*, the superhuman Golden Boy
- the vengeful *Kiyohime*, who became a dragon
- *Momotaro*, the oni-slaying Peach Boy
- *Bancho Sarayashiki*, the ghost story of Okiku and the Nine Plate
- *Urashima Taro*, who rescued a turtle and visited the bottom of the sea
- *Yotsuya Kaidan*, the ghost story of Oiwa

- *Issun-Boshi*, the One-inch Boy
- *Kachi Kachi Yama*, a villainous raccoon-dog and heroic rabbit
- *Bunbuku Chagama*, a teakettle which is actually a shape-changing tanuki
- *Hanasaka Jiisan*, the old man that made the flowers bloom
- *Tamamo no Mae*, the wicked fox-woman
- *Shira-kiri Suzume*, the tongue-cut sparrow

*The chosen story*

*Taketori Monogatari (The Tale of the Bamboo Cutter)*, written in the tenth century, is the oldest surviving Japanese work of fiction. It is often referred to as the "ancestor of all romances." Theories as to the background of the story have never been proven, e.g., the names of five suitors are those of members of the Japanese court in the eighth century that the story is directed at, etc. Today it is known as a children's story, *Kaguya-hime* (Princess Kaguya), and shares similarities with *Sailor Moon*, *Cinderella*, *Thumbelina*, *Snow White*, and even *Rocket Girls* anime.

Students were advised that in remixing such a story, the purpose was to "carry a message":

The Japanese proverb – *"Ugo no takenoko"* – translates as *"bamboo shoots after the rain"*. This expression suggests that as in life, many things happen one-after-another, just as bamboo shoots bursting to the surface after the rain. And it is how we react and respond to difficult or seemingly impossible situations that defines who we are. This becomes the performance "challenge" … to explain in music, drama and dance this "message" to the audience: that life is … MISSION: POSSIBLE.[13]

# Digital Literacy – from Self-made Media to Self-made Networks

This is where digital storytelling comes in. The unusual thing about digital storytelling compared with other digital products is that it is taught. It has about it more of the eisteddfod than the software application. It prioritizes the "storytelling" over the "digital" – indeed, it is pretty hard to find on

the Web. Instead, digital storytelling thrives among the very same community centers, voluntary organizations, and arts activists who devote their
time to improving the creative and performative talents of the otherwise
untutored multitude, encouraging those with tradable talent to move into
professional levels of the system (cultural or economic), while enabling
those who would otherwise only get to stand and stare to tell their own
stories. In short, the propagation of digital storytelling is more like the
teaching of music than the marketing of media. Digital storytelling is a
"practice" rather than a "form"; a *story circle* that links tellers with other
agents across the network. On the model of other institutions of vernacular
teaching like the eisteddfod, it shows how entire institutional *networks* as
well as individual *stories* can be "self-made."

This is how the eisteddfod reconfigures the "bardic function." The oral
bardic function of storytelling *for* a culture is an evolutionary antecedent to
a networked bardic function of storytelling *by* a culture. As a result, "self-
actualization" can now be an individual activity rather than a representative
story; something we do, not something we watch. However, even individual
talent needs development, and various vernacular institutions, including
eisteddfodau, have arisen to service that need. People are not encountered
as single selves even when they are telling their own story. Instead, through
informal institutions that help the system as a whole to coordinate and rep-
licate its capabilities, individuals are encountered as connected and networked interlocutors, able to speak for themselves, but only because they
are in a context where conversation is possible with others and others are
present to add their own voices.

This being the case, a question remains about the role of professional
"bards." The original bards were the highest exponents of the literacy of the
time: they expressed the possibilities afforded by the textual system of oral
poetry; they were the innovators, the sources of growth, in short, they were
the semiotic wealth-creators of their day and they were royally rewarded for
it. From that perspective, handing over the baton to the amateur audience
may seem like a backward step, a lowering of standards, and a threat to
income (for discussion of the problem of expertise in digital storytelling,
see Hartley 2008b). The idea that each individual should tell his or her own
stories may even encourage self-regarding "look-at-me" egotism among the
"reading public." Now, it seems, we don't have to earn attention, esteem, or
honor or have it bestowed by a specialist, as in the days of heralds and bards,
because we can just say whatever we like about ourselves on Bebo. Each
citizen becomes their own Homer, their own Taliesin, blowing their own

heraldic trumpet, "harping on" in bardic style, singing their own praises. Some "experts" regard such a prospect not as democratized expression or consumer productivity, but as a nightmare scenario (Keen 2007).

However, things are clearly not as simple as this. To tell their own stories people must be able not only to record something that happened and how they feel about it, but also how it might sound to an interlocutor, what there is about it that might attract an audience's attention, and what it might tell people that they don't already know. In other words, people must learn not only the basic skills of *self-expression* but also those of effective *communication*; not only to tell stories but also to attend to their hearers' demands for information, education, and entertainment (as the Reithian mantra had it). In an open system they will also learn how to connect what they want to say with what others in the network are saying and want to hear. The standard of individual utterance and of the entire social network is cumulatively raised.

Thence the most interesting question is what digital media might be used *for*. We should wait and see, not fall for the temptation of hurling abuse at the latest upstart medium that poses some sort of competition to the entrenched professionals of the day, just as the mythical Taliesin did in his own diatribe against strolling minstrels. It's an unedifying sight, serving only to mask the real potential of the contemporary "bardic function." Instead, it would be preferable to show how the massive scaling up of storytelling expands rather than supersedes the opportunities for professional storytellers and "ordinary" people alike – consumer productivity and trained expertise are both required if the energies of all agents in the system are to be harnessed.

In such a context, professional storytellers have options.

1. *The Taliesin function* ("I'm a bard and you're not"). They can carry on doing what they do so well, and thumbing their noses at the "amateurs," for as long as the "top-down" business plan allows it.
2. *The Gandalf function* ("I'm a bard and this is how it's done"). Or, they can shift, as educators have learnt to do, from the position of "sage on the stage" to that of "guide on the side" or even "meddler in the middle" (McWilliam 2007). In other words, they can use their skills to assist the productivity of the storytelling system rather than seeking to dominate it, helping to make the intuitive skills of others explicit and goal-directed, rather than usurping them.
3. *The eisteddfod function* ("We're all bards: let's rock!"). This third option beckons. It takes up the baton of the eisteddfod, proposing amateur and

professional as options within the same system, not as opposed paradigms; thereby leading to the possibility of co-creative collaboration that massively extends the capability of the system.

Digital storytelling hovers intriguingly between functions 2 and 3; it is facilitated by professionals, sometimes incorporating professionals as co-creators. But as time elapses, things evolve. Based on the lesson of previous step changes in the growth of knowledge, it is clear that evolution is blind, and the opportunities afforded by adaptations cannot be known in advance, whether it is the opposable thumb or the digital network.

Certainly, when writing and printing were invented, no one could have predicted their eventual uses from the purposes of the inventors. The printing press in Gutenberg's day was based on agricultural machinery and used largely for religious clients. Its eventual success was not at all certain. Like many innovative startups, Gutenberg's own firm went bust. How could anyone in the 1450s have foreseen the importance of printing and publishing for the growth of the great realist textual systems of modernity – science, journalism, and the novel – since none of them existed until printing made possible the development of a modern reading public? Similarly, who today can predict the cultural function of internet affordances; the outcome of the democratization of publishing; and the population-wide extension of semiotic productivity? Here is where creative professionals might focus their attention; by seeing the bardic function as socially distributed and evolutionary, while seeking to maximize its current potential for self-expression, social networking, and knowledge creation. What can the system make possible now that it has been invented?

We don't yet know the answer to that question. It's an emergent system. In the meantime, it is sufficient perhaps to focus on what individuals have to say, especially by adding to the social conversation as many as possible of the voices belonging to the "common man and woman" who have historically left so little trace on explicit knowledge or elaborated language. This is what digital storytelling allows for. It shows how literacy belongs to the system, not to individuals, that the system requires both individual agents and organizing institutions, and that professionalism, innovation, novelty, creativity, and knowledge are, in principle, universally distributed among agents who can navigate their own way to their own objectives, creating knowledge as they go; and "performing the self," not only in the context of power but also of possibility. It remains true now as it was in Walt Whitman's day, that "to have great poets, there must be great audiences too." Digital storytelling is one way to get more of both. How that works in practice – and it's a work in progress – is the subject of succeeding chapters of *Story Circle*.

## Notes

1 David William Nash was an early debunker of the mystic (druidic and shaman- istic) claims of Celtic revivalism, such as those associated with Iolo Morgannwg, which are, however, still popular in new-age circles (Matthews 2002). Instead, Nash argued for historical and contextual analysis, and for accurate translation (Nash 1858). His work founds the argument I am seeking to advance here, that bards were a regulated part of medieval society, with an institutionalized cul- tural function that – allowing for technological change – persists. See also Ford (1992) and Guest (1849).

2 "Taliesin" remains a viable brand name to this day. It is the name of – among other things – a prominent Welsh journal, an arts centre in Swansea, and vari- ous private companies, not to mention its second life in architecture as the name of Frank Lloyd Wright's former home. In the way of these things, "bardic function" is also becoming a brand, emancipated from its origins, as for instance in a blog called "the bardic function" (eekbeat.blogspot.com/).

3 See Nash (1858: 33, 179) and Morris (1889: 12–13); also www.llgc.org.uk/ ?id=lawsofhyweldda

4 A good example being Brian Helgeland's 2001 movie *A Knight's Tale* (starring Heath Ledger), whose character "Chaucer" (Paul Bettany) imaginatively re- creates the "bardic function" with poetic verve, if not historical accuracy.

5 "In Homer, the term *geras* means a 'prize of honor, an honorific portion' … Solon's use of the term *geras* shows that he … conceives of this due recognition as a part of the distributive fairness that he tries to institute in settling Athenian strife" (Balot 2001: 87–8).

6 See cy.wikipedia.org/wiki/Categori:Barddoniaeth_Gymraeg

7 A contemporary account (accessible at llandeilo.org/rhys_ap_gruffudd.php) describes the first recorded eisteddfod, showing its characteristic elements of open competition, "public" or "state" sponsorship, and the mixture of musical and verbal arts, thus:

> 1176 – And the Lord Rhys [ap Gruffudd] held a grand festival at the castle of Aberteifi [i.e., Cardigan Castle] wherein he appointed two sorts of con- tention; one between the bards and poets, and the other between the harpers, fiddlers, pipers and various performers of instrumental music; and he assigned two chairs for the victors in the contentions; and these he

enriched with vast gifts. A young man of his own court, son of Cibon the fiddler, obtained the victory in instrumental song; and the men of Gwynedd obtained the victory in vocal song [i.e., bardic poetry]; and all the other minstrels obtained from the Lord Rhys as much as they asked for, so that there was no one excluded. And that festival was proclaimed a year before it was held, throughout Wales and England and Prydyn and Ireland and many other countries. (From the entry for 1176 in *Brut y Tywysgogion* [*The Chronicle of the Princes*], published in 1860 by the Lords Commissioners of Her Majesty's Treasury under the direction of the Master of the Rolls, reproduced in Allday 1981: Appendix IV, this quotation: 174)

8  Griffith (1950: 141) writes of pre-modern eisteddfodau: "The meetings of the bards … were not held for the purposes of entertaining an audience, nor for the production of literature: they were sessions of professionals for the study of the rules of Welsh prosody, and to let performance establish the headship of the profession and the degrees of qualifications."

9  For South Africa see www.sowetan.co.za/article.aspx?id=466044 (South African School Choral Eisteddfod). For Australia see, e.g., www.eisteddfod.org. au/aesa/history.html (Association of Eisteddfod Societies of Australia), www. queenslandeisteddfod.org.au/content/view/3/1/ (Eisteddfod Society of Queensland), and www.nationaleisteddfod.org.au/ (Australian National Eisteddfod). Among the main Welsh eisteddfodau, apart from the thousands in schools and community centres, are the National (www.eisteddfod.org.uk/ english/), Urdd Gobaith Cymru/Welsh League of Youth (www.urdd.org/ eisteddfod/?lng=en), and the International Musical Eisteddfod at Llangollen (www.international-eisteddfod.co.uk/).

10  For Bryn Terfel's biography see www.musicianguide.com/biographies/ 1608002839/Bryn-Terfel.html

11  See www.rockchallenge.com.au/modules.php?op=modload&name=PagEd& file=index&topictoview=1

12  See www.rockchallenge.jp/

13  See www.globalrockchallenge.com/jp/modules/PagEd/media/creatingatheme_eng. pdf

# 3

# The Global Diffusion of a Community Media Practice
## Digital Storytelling Online

*Kelly McWilliam*

Digital storytelling is a community media practice in a global mediasphere (Howley 2005, Hartley 1996). Referring specifically to the co-creative, workshop-based practice upon which this volume is focused, digital story-telling is widely used across North America, Europe, and Australasia, but is significantly less visible in Africa, Asia, and South America. It is most popular in the Western industrialized world, which is perhaps unsurprising given the West's dominance over key mass-market technologies, from home computing processors to platform software (Lundby, this volume, Xiudian 2007). Thus, despite its intercontinental diffusion, there are clear patterns in the global application of this form of digital storytelling.

This chapter provides an overview of those trends by charting the online presence of digital storytelling, based on a survey of 300 programs operating around the world. At the time of writing, these were the programs with a prominent online presence, whether in the form of a dedicated web page or site or simply being reported on another web page or site. Throughout the survey, digital storytelling programs are categorized, in a loosely framed quantitative analysis, according to program, host, host type (educational institution, community center, or organization, cultural institution, or "other," on which I elaborate later), location, and the year the program began (where the year was unclear, the year has been approximated and a question mark added to the record).

The larger survey from which these data are drawn includes additional details about the kind of participant targeted, the stated or implied purpose of the program, whether the program is fixed or mobile (i.e., located in a fixed position or able to travel), the sector of the program (public or private), and the source url. The survey included in this chapter was shortened for the express purpose of increased readability and is intended to provide a "bigger picture" of the overarching trends in global, organization-based digital storytelling practice. It represents the first research to offer such an evidence-based trend analysis of the practice, focusing specifically on digital storytelling programs

1.  that have a prominent online presence;
2.  which center around digital storytelling workshops; and
3.  whose online presence, whether implicitly or explicitly, suggests an ongoing, rather than a one-off organizational commitment to running those workshops.

In cases where it was unclear whether there is an ongoing commitment to digital storytelling or where including a one-off example was instructive, I have included the program in the survey that follows.

## Digital Storytelling and Co-creative Caveats

In focusing on digital storytelling programs with an online presence, this chapter is neither exhaustive nor a survey of the countless web pages of digital storytelling "resources," "how-to manuals," "teaching guides," or "useful links." As a result, by no means all digital storytelling practice attempted around the world is captured here. There are at least two reasons for this, both worth thinking about in relation to the current distribution of the form. The first reason is about absence and creative privacy and the second about digital abundance and creative publicity.

First, then, a significant proportion of digital storytelling never reaches the Internet. The Center for Digital Storytelling (CDS), to take a major example, has produced hundreds, perhaps thousands, of digital stories in over fifteen years of operation, but exhibits fewer than ten of those on its website.[1] In other words, there is a comparative absence of digital storytelling programs represented online, in terms of all the digital storytelling programs in existence (or in planning) around the world. This is not necessarily surprising. Aside from limitations on time and server space, which make exhibiting every digital story ever made a challenging task, to say the least, there are also issues of privacy. Because digital storytelling often emphasizes personal expression and story sharing, many digital stories are personal, inexpert, privately expressive, and produced for personal consumption, rather than public exhibition. In a survey of digital storytelling programs with an online presence, programs producing private stories unsuitable or unintended for online distribution will obviously not play a part; quite simply, despite being in the age of YouTube, not all self-made media are for exhibition.

Second, in focusing on specific digital storytelling programs, individual digital stories that are available on file-sharing websites like YouTube, presented outside of their programmatic context, remain an "unsurveyed" presence.[2] In conducting this survey, my interest has been in charting the development and diffusion of one particular media practice, rather than on the innumerable forms that "digital stories," however understood, may take, or on their potential sites of distribution and exhibition. Nevertheless, what the existence of sites like YouTube does point to is the enormous profusion of individual creativity publicity, for which digital storytelling is a modest, but increasingly popular, format.

## Digital Storytelling around the World: An Online Survey

Most of the 300 digital storytelling programs surveyed began operating in the early 2000s (274), or almost a decade after its emergence in California, highlighting a recent surge in popularity. Moreover, almost all occur in the public (261), rather than the private sector. The latter in particular demonstrates that despite the burgeoning popularity of digital storytelling across the public and private sectors, and a handful of influential early forays into commercial consultancies – most notably, Dana Atchley's work in the late 1990s with multinationals like Coca-Cola – it is still overwhelmingly a public practice.[3] In fact, digital storytelling programs are run in or for a comparatively small range of (mostly public) hosts, comprising educational institutions (123), community centers or organizations (71), cultural institutions (51), and "government, business and religious" hosts (55), including public broadcasters, companies and/or consultancies, health organizations, and a church. I discuss and present the survey in smaller groupings, categorized according to organizational siting, location, and popularity.

### Educational institutions

Of the 300 digital storytelling programs surveyed, more than one-third, or 123, were hosted by educational institutions and often presented by

**Table 3.1** Survey of DST online: educational institutions – K12

| Title | Host | Continent | Country | State/Region | City | Year began |
|---|---|---|---|---|---|---|
| Digital Hero Book | Khanya Schools | Africa | South Africa | | Cape Town | 2007 |
| Life 'Round Here International DST | International School of Tianjin | Asia | China | | Tianjin | 2007 |
| DST | Tomigaoka High School | Asia | Japan | | Tomigaoka | 2008? |
| Life 'Round Here International DST | Qatar Academy | Asia | Qatar | | Doha | 2007 |
| Life 'Round Here International DST | International School Bangkok | Asia | Thailand | | Bangkok | 2007 |
| Life 'Round Here International DST | Taradale Intermediate School | Australasia | New Zealand | | Hawkes Bay | 2007 |
| Life 'Round Here International DST | Te Awamutu Intermediate | Australasia | New Zealand | | Te Awamutu | 2007 |
| Portsmouth EMAS: DST | Portsmouth Ethnic Minority Achievement Service/South-East Grid for Learning | Europe | England, UK | | Portsmouth | 2006 |
| DST | Bishop Parker Combined School/ Living Archives | Europe | England, UK | | Milton Keynes | 2003 |
| Mobile Multimedia Project | Bryngwyn School | Europe | Wales, UK | | Carmarthen | 2007 |
| DST for Deaf and Hard of Hearing Pupils | First Campus and University of Wales, Newport | Europe | Wales, UK | | Pontypridd | 2007? |
| Hidden Stories | Brenda Dyck | North America | Canada | Alberta | Edmonton | 2006 |

| | | | | | | |
|---|---|---|---|---|---|---|
| DST | Surrey School Division | North America | Canada | British Columbia | Surrey | 2007? |
| Life 'Round Here International DST | The Fernie Academy | North America | Canada | British Columbia | Fernie | 2007 |
| DST | Vancouver School Board | North America | Canada | British Columbia | Vancouver | 2006 |
| Tales from Bridgeview | Bridgeview Elementary and National Film Board of Canada | North America | Canada | British Columbia | Surrey | 2006 |
| DST w/Photostory for K-8 | BYTE Conference and Rolling River School Division | North America | Canada | Manitoba | Minnedosa | 2008 |
| DST | Massassaga-Rednersville Public School | North America | Canada | Ontario | Belleville | 2006 |
| DST in Language Arts | Prairie South School Division (Prairie South E-learning) | North America | Canada | Saskatchewan | Prairie South | 2007 |
| DST | Kenai Peninsula Borough School District | North America | USA | Alaska | Kenai | 2007 |
| DST | Rancho Santa Fe School | North America | USA | California | Santa Fe | 2007? |
| DST | Poway Unifed School District | North America | USA | California | Poway | 2006 |
| DST @ Pepper Drive | Pepper Drive School | North America | USA | California | El Cajon | 2007 |
| Online Professional Learning Workshops: DST | Greenwich Public Schools Virtual Library | North America | USA | Connecticut | Greenwich | 2007 |
| Life 'Round Here International DST | Carol Morgan School | North America | USA | Dominican Republic | Santo Domingo | 2007 |
| Life 'Round Here International DST | San Jose Episcopal Day School | North America | USA | Florida | Jacksonville | 2007 |

*(cont'd)*

**Table 3.1** *(cont'd)*

| Title | Host | Continent | Country | State/Region | City | Year began |
|---|---|---|---|---|---|---|
| Voices from Africa | Tuskawilla Middle School | North America | USA | Florida | Orlando | 2006 |
| Beyond Words: DST in the Classroom | Wekiva Elementary | North America | USA | Florida | Orlando | 2006 |
| Beyond Words: DST in the Classroom | Heathrow Elementary | North America | USA | Florida | Orlando | 2006 |
| DST | Cherokee County School District | North America | USA | Georgia | Canton | 2007? |
| Life 'Round Here International DST Project | Center Elementary | North America | USA | Georgia | Waycross | 2007 |
| Senior Citizens DST Workshop | Niles Township High School – District 219 | North America | USA | Illinois | Stokie | 2007 |
| Tell Me Again | Nicholasville Elementary School | North America | USA | Kentucky | Nicholasville | 2002? |
| DST | Hendron-Lone Oake Elementary School | North America | USA | Kentucky | Paducah | 2006 |
| DST in Scott County Schools | Scott County Schools | North America | USA | Kentucky | Georgetown | 2001 |
| Life 'Round Here International DST | Marblehead Community Charter Public School | North America | USA | Massachusetts | Marblehead | 2007 |
| TEACHBoston DST Pilot Project | Boston Public Schools | North America | USA | Massachusetts | Boston | 2003 |
| DST Series | Oakland Schools | North America | USA | Michigan | Oakland | 2007 |

| Project | School / Organization | Region | Country | State | City | Year |
|---|---|---|---|---|---|---|
| DST Project | Walled Lake Consolidated Schools | North America | USA | Michigan | Walled Lake | 2005 |
| DST | Digital Storytelling Academy (TIES = Coop of 38 Minnesota School Districts) | North America | USA | Minnesota | St. Paul | 2004 |
| DST @ Dixie Attendance Center | Dixie Attendance Center, Forrest County School District | North America | USA | Mississippi | Forest County | 2005 |
| Life 'Round Here International DST | MICDS | North America | USA | Missouri | St. Louis | 2007 |
| DST | Tenafly Middle School | North America | USA | New Jersey | Tenafly | 2005 |
| Life 'Round Here International DST | St. Boniface School | North America | USA | Ohio | Cincinnati | 2007 |
| Life 'Round Here International DST | Chehalem Valley Middle School | North America | USA | Oregon | Newberg | 2007 |
| Life 'Round Here International DST | Clear Run Intermediate School | North America | USA | Pennsylvania | Tobyhanna | 2007 |
| Life 'Round Here International DST | Vincent Elementary School | North America | USA | Pennsylvania | Spring City | 2007 |
| Life 'Round Here International DST | Swiftwater Intermediate School | North America | USA | Pennsylvania | Swiftwater | 2007 |
| TechQuest: NPS Technology Training (DST) | Narragansett Pier Middle School | North America | USA | Rhode Island | Narragansett | 2006 |

(cont'd)

**Table 3.1** *(cont'd)*

| Title | Host | Continent | Country | State/Region | City | Year began |
|---|---|---|---|---|---|---|
| Life 'Round Here International DST | CrossRoads Middle School | North America | USA | South Carolina | Columbia | 2007 |
| Life 'Round Here International DST | Trenton Rosenwald Middle School | North America | USA | Tennessee | Trenton | 2007 |
| DST | Emerald Park Elementary | North America | USA | Washington | Kent | 2005 |
| Life 'Round Here International DST | San Jorge de Miraflores School | South America | Peru | | Lima | 2007 |
| DST Workshops | Scott County DST Center (Scott County Schools and Public Library) | North America | USA | Kentucky | Georgetown | 2002 |
| Relevant, Engaged, Authentic Learning | Sanford Middle School and Central Florida Zoo | North America | USA | Florida | Orlando | 2006 |

teachers or other institution-based trainers (rather than consultant facilitators), showing the form's increasing "embeddedness" in the sector. Of the total 123 digital storytelling programs based in educational institutions, 55 were located in K-12 schools, including associated after-school and/or vacation-care settings (the vast majority, 41, of which were located in North America); 42 in universities; and 26 in colleges or institutes. In all of these education-based subcategories, all of which were located in the public sector, most programs targeted student participants (63), including a handful targeting both student and teacher participants. Indeed, even in university settings, many programs were embedded in student teacher training, highlighting the immense popularity of educational applications of digital storytelling, a trend reflected in the comparative explosion of scholarly attention around educative applications (see, e.g., Banaszewski 2002, Hull 2003, Davis 2005). Similarly, many of the programs were either part of larger courses (i.e., part of media design or education courses, as in universities, colleges, and institutes) or years of study (as in schools). In other words, few digital storytelling programs were presented as standalone workshops in formal educational contexts (unlike in community contexts, where, as I discuss later, this was the norm), perhaps reflecting the familiar institutional constraints of curriculum, "limited class time and limited access to technology" in formal schooling (Bull and Kajder 2004: 49).

In schools, digital storytelling is primarily used to increase student engagement and to improve student print and media literacies, although there are necessary differences in the application of these learning goals depending on the ages and abilities of the students. In younger grades, the emphasis tends to be on personal reflection in shorter digital stories, rather than on technical skills or complicated composition. For example, at Pepper Drive School in El Cajon, California, third-graders reflect on a YMCA swimming lesson in individual digital stories comprising photographs and a 20-second voice-over, focusing on their favorite experience at the pool and overall enjoyment of the lesson.[4] In middle grades, the emphasis tends to shift to digital storytelling for improved composition and narrative construction, as well as on basic media production skills, for example, sixth-grade media studies students at Bryngwyn School in South Wales, who create digital stories not only to build media production skills, but also to try to articulate and narrate their experience at the school to assist them with as positive and seamless a transition to the seventh grade as possible.[5] In older grades, the emphasis typically shifts to more advanced print and media literacies and to wider community applications of school digital storytelling.

The Niles Township High School in Illinois in the USA, for instance, ran digital storytelling workshops not just for teachers and high school students, but also for senior citizens in their community. While students developed narrative and media production skills in class, they then shared responsibility with their teachers for running public workshops for local seniors as a means of distributing technological knowledge within the community and engaging with their community in meaningful interpersonal ways.[6]

However, even with age-appropriate differences among digital storytelling applications in K-12 schools, which might be seen to incrementally develop students' proficiencies toward teaching, there was a relatively consistent dual emphasis in middle and older grades on narrative and technology. The only exception here is with younger grades, where teachers often placed an increased emphasis on narrative over technological skill building. This is consistent with a broader trend in K-12 literacy education, where traditionally conceived core skills like reading and writing are privileged over technology-based skills (see Banaszewski 2002, Bull & Kajder 2004). At the same time, the emphasis on narrative over technology is also consistent with the origins of digital storytelling, where the practice itself developed through, but not because of, concurrent technological developments (see Lambert 2006).

In universities there was a slight but unsurprising shift in the institutional framing of digital storytelling (see Table 3.2).

While all digital storytelling programs sited in universities, colleges, and institutes are based in the public sector, there are two main trends in university-specific applications of the practice: first, digital storytelling is popular within teacher training programs in educational faculties, which is consistent with the considerable prominence of educational (and particularly K-12) applications of the practice, particularly in North America; second, digital storytelling is also prominent in media production courses, such as in multimedia and design courses, and this trend was more evenly dispersed around the world. In fact, these trends in digital storytelling in universities also held true for colleges and institutes (see Table 3.3).

Most of the colleges and institutes surveyed (18 out of 26) are vocational education providers, meaning they are providers of education which is occupation-specific and practice-led but which does not usually include a major component on general or theoretical education (see Grollmann and Rauner 2007). In those colleges and institutions, the only key difference from university applications of digital storytelling is an increased emphasis on production and expression, rather than contextual or theoretical learning, with many sited in arts and/or design courses. In Canada, Toronto

**Table 3.2** Survey of DST online: educational institutions – tertiary

| Title | Host | Continent | Country | State/Region | City | Year began |
|---|---|---|---|---|---|---|
| UWC DST | University of West Cape Town | Africa | South Africa | | Cape Town | 2005 |
| DST Training | Shantou University | Asia | China | | Guangdong | 2007 |
| Understanding Culture through DST | Keio Research Center for Foreign Language Education | Asia | Japan | | Keio | 2008 |
| DST Seminar | Osaka Gakuin University | Asia | Japan | | Osaka | 2004 |
| RMA822 Study of DST | Hanyang University | Asia | South Korea | | Seoul | 2008? |
| OD464: DST | Yonsei University | Asia | South Korea | | Seoul | 2007? |
| Digital Voices | Making Links Conference | Australasia | Australia | New South Wales | Sydney | 2007 |
| KCP403 Creative Industries Applied Research | Queensland University of Technology | Australasia | Australia | Queensland | Brisbane | 2007 |
| DST | University of South Australia | Australasia | Australia | South Australia | Adelaide | 2007 |
| DST Short Course | Victoria University | Australasia | Australia | Victoria | Melbourne | 2007 |
| DST | lab.3000/RMIT University | Australasia | Australia | Victoria | Melbourne | 2006 |
| DST Workshop | LearnScope/RMIT University | Australasia | Australia | Victoria | Melbourne | 2004 |
| DST | Technische Universität Darmstadt | Europe | Germany | | Darmstadt | 2004 |
| DST | Hogeschool Utrecht – Education | Europe | Netherlands | | Utrecht | 2004 |
| Mediatized Stories | University of Oslo | Europe | Norway | | Oslo | 2006? |
| Maestro en Educación Especial | Universidad de Cádiz | Europe | Spain | | Cádiz | 2007 |
| Created by Catalonia | Universitat Rovira i Virgili/Creative Narrations | Europe | Spain | | Catalonia | 2006 |

*(cont'd)*

**Table 3.2** (cont'd)

| Title | Host | Continent | Country | State/Region | City | Year began |
|---|---|---|---|---|---|---|
| My Digital Self-Geography | Malmö University and CDS | Europe | Sweden | | Malmö | 2003? |
| Networked DST | Malmö University | Europe | Sweden | | Malmö | 2006 |
| DST Workshop | Higher Education Academy and University of Gloucestershire | Europe | England, UK | | Gloucester | 2007 |
| DST | University of London | Europe | England, UK | | London | 2007 |
| CO32056: DST | Napier University | Europe | England, UK | | Edinburgh | 2006 |
| Mobile DST | University of Glamorgan and BBC Wales | Europe | Wales, UK | | Glamorgan | 2007 |
| DST and Incarcerated Youth | University of Alberta and unnamed youth correctional facility | North America | Canada | Alberta | Calgary | 2007 |
| Program for DST | University of Calgary and CDS | North America | Canada | Alberta | Edmonton | 2006 |
| Visual Anthropology | University of Alberta | North America | Canada | Alberta | Alberta | 2006 |
| DST Workshop | University of British Columbia | North America | Canada | British Columbia | Vancouver | 2005 |
| DST Project in Curriculum Studies | University of Ontario Institute of Technology | North America | Canada | Ontario | Oshawa | 2006 |
| Undergraduate Honors in Public History | Concordia University (Center for Oral History and DST) | North America | Canada | Québec | Montreal | 2006 |
| Computers in the Classroom | University of Regina | North America | Canada | Saskatchewan | Regina | 1999 |

| Stories of Culture and Place | University of Alaska Geography Program | North America | USA | Alaska | Fairbanks | 2005 |
|---|---|---|---|---|---|---|
| Digital Underground Storytelling for Youth/ DUSTY | University of California, Berkeley and Joseph Center for Community Enhancement | North America | USA | California | Oakland | 2001 |
| MSc and MFA in Digital Cinema | DePaul University | North America | USA | Illinois | Chicago | 2008 |
| Technology Literacy Camp | Aurora University | North America | USA | Illinois | Aurora | 2006 |
| DST Grad Class | Aurora University | North America | USA | Illinois | Aurora | 2006 |
| DST (various) | Ball State University | North America | USA | Indiana | Muncie | 2006? |
| DST and Community | New York University ITP and Xavier University | North America | USA | Louisiana | New Orleans | 2007 |
| Charlestown Digital Stories | University of Maryland, BC and Retirement Living TV | North America | USA | Maryland | Baltimore | 2006 |
| Red Cedar Writing Project | Michigan State University | North America | USA | Michigan | East Lansing | 2006 |
| DST Workshop | New Directions Technology Conference | North America | USA | North Carolina | Flat Rock | 2006 |
| Visible Knowledge | Millersville University | North America | USA | Pennsylvania | Millersville | 2002 |
| DST Workshop | University of Texas and CDS | North America | USA | Texas | Austin | 2007 |

**Table 3.3** Survey of DST online: educational institutions – colleges and institutes

| Title | Host | Continent | Country | State/Region | City | Year began |
|---|---|---|---|---|---|---|
| Intercultural Storytelling in the Virtual Reality | Studienzentrum für evangelische Jugendarbeit in Josefstal/ Arbeitsgemeinschaft der evangelische Jugend in Deutschland; Division for World Mission, Neuendettelsau; Eastern and Coastal Diocese, Evangelical Lutheran Church in Tanzania | Africa | Tanzania | | Dar es Salaam | 2003 |
| Digital Photo Albums – Storytelling | Workers Educational Association (WEA) Hunter | Australasia | Australia | New South Wales | Lake Macquarie | 2008? |
| DST | Outreach Lake Macquarie/TAFE NSW Hunter Institute | Australasia | Australia | New South Wales | Newcastle | 2006 |
| People, Place and Pastimes | Wodonga Tafe | Australasia | Australia | Victoria | Beechworth, Corryong, Mount Beauty, Tallangatta and Yackandandah | 2007? |
| CCD Creative Collaborations | Victorian College of the Arts/University of Melbourne | Australasia | Australia | Victoria | Melbourne | 2008 |
| DST | Soundhouse | Australasia | Australia | Victoria | Melbourne | 2007 |
| DST | CAE | Europe | Australia | Victoria | Melbourne | 2003 |

| | | | | | | |
|---|---|---|---|---|---|---|
| Intercultural Storytelling in the Virtual Reality | Studienzentrum für evangelische Jugendarbeit in Josefstal/Arbeitsgemeinschaft der evangelische Jugend in Deutschland; Division for World Mission, Neuendettelsau; Eastern and Coastal Diocese, Evangelical Lutheran Church in Tanzania | Europe | Germany | | Josefstal | 2005 |
| DST | Oslo University College/Jazz Assembling | Europe | Norway | | Oslo | 2006 |
| DST | Shetland College | Europe | England, UK | | Various | 2003 |
| Who Do You Think You Are? | Yale Centre for Digital Storytelling, Yale College | North America | England, UK | | Wrexham | 2006 |
| First Nations DST and ArtStudio | Emily Carr Institute of Art | North America | Canada | British Columbia | Vancouver | 2006? |
| Introduction to DST | Thames Institute of the Arts | North America | Canada | Ontario | Chatham | 2007 |
| DST | Toronto School of Art | North America | Canada | Ontario | Toronto | 2000? |
| DST | Yavapai College, Dana Atchley Center for Digital Storytelling | North America | USA | Arizona | Sedona | 2005 |
| Bringing DST to the Classroom LearnShop | Scottsdale Community College | North America | USA | Arizona | Phoenix | 2005 |

(cont'd)

**Table 3.3** *(cont'd)*

| Title | Host | Continent | Country | State/Region | City | Year began |
|---|---|---|---|---|---|---|
| DST | Phoenix College | North America | USA | Arizona | Phoenix | 2006 |
| AAE DST | Arizona Adult Education DST Institute | North America | USA | Arizona | | 2007 |
| CSC85 – DST | Mendocino College | North America | USA | California | Ukiah | 2008 |
| DST in Nature | Three Rivers Community College | Asia | USA | Missouri | Poplar Bluff | 2005 |
| DST | Korea Advanced Institute of Science and Technology | Asia | Republic of Korea | | Daejeon | 2005 |
| DST | Seoul Institute of the Arts | Australasia | South Korea | | Seoul | 2006 |
| Queensland Stories/A Picture Paints 1000 Words | ICT Learning Innovation Centre/ Education Queensland | Europe | Australia | Queensland | Brisbane | 2004 |
| DST: Summer School | Edith Russ Site for Media Art | Europe | Germany | | Oldenburg | 2003 |
| Community Net | DIMITRA in Athens: Institute for Training and Development and Digi-Tales (Europe) | Europe | Greece | | Larissa | 2006 |
| DST | Blekinge Institute of Technology | Africa | Sweden | | Karlskrona | 2005 |

School of Art's description of its "414: Digital Storytelling" course, for example, is typical: according to the School's website, it teaches students to use "photographs, video, text, music, voice-over, animation, and any other available materials" for "personal and visual storytelling." Similarly, in the USA, Phoenix College in Arizona offers "ART150: Digital Storytelling," a course designed to enable "students to find and develop their personal stories" through "the use of digital technology to create, edit, produce and archive a digital story."[7] Both emphasize practical skill-building in multimedia production and personal and/or creative expression over any larger engagement with theory and, as such, are more akin to digital storytelling applications in K-12 schooling, particularly the elementary and middle grades, than in universities.

In almost all of the education-based digital storytelling programs surveyed, there was an articulation of digital storytelling as an important pedagogical tool, a trend that, as I discuss later, has also begun to dominate digital storytelling programs in the private sector.

## Community

There were 71 community organizations – organizations that "intend to meet local needs," but do not "aim to make a profit for private or corporate gain" (Lewis 2006: 15) – surveyed with potentially ongoing digital storytelling programs, and many more holding numerous one-off workshops. That total makes community organizations, including community arts and/or media centers, the second most popular site of digital storytelling programs around the world, second only to the West's enthusiastic embrace of digital storytelling in education. This is consistent with the community theater backgrounds and motivations of the practice's founders (on which see Lambert 2006). Unlike educational hosts, however, most digital storytelling programs in community organizations are standalone programs, rather than programs embedded in larger courses.

Of the 71 community digital storytelling programs surveyed, three of the most common themes used to frame community digital storytelling are:

- *historical*: collecting public histories of community and/or place (20);
- *aspirational*: empowering storytellers, especially marginalized storytellers (42);
- *recuperative*: helping storytellers overcome adversity (4).

**Table 3.4** Survey of DST online: community centers/organizations

| Title | Host | Continent | Country | State/Region | City | Year began |
|---|---|---|---|---|---|---|
| DST | Cafesociety.org | Africa | Sierra Leone | | Freetown | 2006 |
| Bridges to Understanding | Bridges to Understanding | Africa | South Africa | | Cape Town | 2001? |
| Digital Stories | Sonke Gender Justice Network | Africa | South Africa | | Cape Town | 2007 |
| Youth Photo-reflect | PhotoVoice | Africa | South Africa | | Orange Farm | 2006 |
| Men as Partners – South Africa | Engender Health | Africa | South Africa | | Johannesburg | 2005 |
| Bridges to Understanding | Bridges to Understanding | Asia | India | | Dharamsala | 2001? |
| Finding a Voice | Akshaya Centres/QUT | Asia | India | | Akshaya | 2006 |
| Finding a Voice | Ankuram TV/QUT | Asia | India | | Ankuram | 2006 |
| Finding a Voice | Gender Resource Centre/QUT | Asia | India | | Calcutta | 2006 |
| Men as Partners – India | Engender Health | Asia | India | | Surat | 2006 |
| Finding a Voice | Hevalvaani Samudayik Radio/QUT | Asia | India | | Hevalvaani | 2006 |
| Finding a Voice | Mandaakini Ki Awaaz Samudayik Radio/QUT | Asia | India | | Bhanaj | 2006 |
| Finding a Voice | ICT4pr/QUT | Asia | Indonesia | | Various | 2006 |
| DST | Kids for Kids | Asia | Israel | | Old City Jerusalem | 2003 |
| Finding a Voice | Radio Lumbini CMC and Buddhanagar Telecentre/QUT | Asia | Nepal | | Lumbini | 2006 |
| Finding a Voice | Buddhanagar Telecentre/QUT | Asia | Nepal | | Buddhanagar | 2006 |
| Finding a Voice | CLC Madhawiliya/QUT | Asia | Nepal | | Madhawiliya | 2006 |
| Finding a Voice | Tansen CMC/QUT | Asia | Nepal | | Tansen | 2006 |

| Project | Organization | Region | Country | State/Province | City | Year |
|---|---|---|---|---|---|---|
| Finding a Voice | CMC Madanpokhara/QUT | Asia | Nepal | | Madanpokhara | 2006 |
| DST Workshop | Break the Silence Mural Project, Palestine Education Project, Middle East Children's Alliance | Asia | Palestine | | Bethlehem | 2007 |
| Finding a Voice | Kothmale Community Multimedia Centre/QUT | Asia | Sri Lanka | | Kothmale | 2006 |
| First Person: Hungarian Heritage DST Project | Tuggeranong Community Arts | Australasia | Australia | Australian Capital Territory | Tuggeranong | 2007 |
| Hi8us | Information and Cultural Exchange (ICE)/Digi-Tales (Europe) | Australasia | Australia | New South Wales | Parramatta | 2008 |
| Mobilestories: DST | Metro Screen | Australasia | Australia | New South Wales | Sydney | 2006 |
| DST | Community IT | Australasia | Australia | South Australia | Angle Park | 2008? |
| DST | Southern Westernport Learning Communities | Australasia | Australia | Victoria | Dingley Village | 2004? |
| DST | Fraynework DST | Australasia | Australia | Victoria | Carlton | 2001? |
| DST | (e)-vision Centre, TUANZ | Australasia | New Zealand | South Island | Wellington | 2006 |
| DST Workshop für MultiplikatorInnen | Reflect and Act | Europe | Austria | Vorarlberg | | 1999 |
| Verhalen van Dordrecht (Stories from Dordrecht) | Verhalen van Dordrecht (Stories from Dordrecht) | Europe | Brussels | | Dordrecht | 2006 |

(cont'd)

**Table 3.4** (cont'd)

| Title | Host | Continent | Country | State/Region | City | Year began |
|---|---|---|---|---|---|---|
| Prointegration/Digitales (Europe) | Berliner Gesellschaft für internationale Zusammenarbeit (Berlin International Cooperation Agency)/Digi-Tales (Europe) | Europe | Germany | | Berlin | 2006 |
| Dolle Zine/Digitales (Europe) | Politiek Cultureel Centrum De Balie/Digi-Tales (Europe) | Europe | Netherlands | | Amsterdam | 1999 |
| Bruxelles nous Appartient/Brussels behoort ons toe (Brussels Belongs to Us) | Bruxelles nous Appartient/Brussels behoort ons toe (Brussels belongs to Us) | Europe | Netherlands | | Brussels | 2006 |
| Kiezen Voor Je Leven – Learn for your life/Digitales (Europe) | Mira Media/Digi-Tales (Europe) | Europe | Netherlands | | Utrecht | 2007? |
| DST | Delta Garden/CDS | Europe | Sweden | | Växjö | 2002 |
| Alcohol Stories | Digitalbridge | Europe | Sweden | | Malmö | 2002 |
| Urban Echoes | Digitalbridge | Europe | Sweden | | Malmö | 2007 |
| Connexions DST | Community Service Volunteers/Media Clubhouse Islington | Europe | England, UK | | Islington | 2006 |
| Breaking Barriers DST | Breaking Barriers DST | Europe | England, UK | | Blackwood | 2004 |
| Hi8us Projects Ltd | Hi8us/Digi-Tales (Europe) | Europe | England, UK | | London | 2006 |
| Living Together | Association for Culture, Education & Communication / Digi-Tales(Europe) | Europe | Slovakia | | Bratislava | 2007 |

|  | | | | | |
|---|---|---|---|---|---|
| Bridges to Understanding Canada | Atira Women's Resource Society | North America | Canada | British Columbia | Vancouver | 2008 |
| DST Project | Atira Women's Resource Society | North America | Canada | British Columbia | Vancouver | 2006 |
| Envisioning New Meanings of Disability and Difference | Center for Independent Living in Toronto | North America | Canada | Ontario | Toronto | 2007 |
| CNH DST Project | Central Neighborhood House, Women's Program | North America | Canada | Ontario | Toronto | 2006 |
| Outta Your Backpack Media Workshop | Indigenous Action Media | North America | USA | Arizona | Flagstaff | 2007 |
| Media Justice for Indigenous Communities Workshop | Indigenous Action Media | North America | USA | Arizona | Flagstaff | 2007 |
| Indigenous Media Activism Advanced Workshop | Indigenous Action Media | North America | USA | Arizona | Flagstaff | 2007 |
| Sedona DST Workshop | Sedona DST Workshop | North America | USA | Arizona | Sedona | 2006 |
| Imagine Mars | Northpointe Neighborhood Network/NASA | North America | USA | California | Long Beach | 2002? |
| Digital Griot: Intergenerational DST | Digital Clubhouse Network – West Coast Clubhouse | North America | USA | California | San Jose | 1996? |
| Community DST Workshop | Third World Majority | North America | USA | California | Oakland | 2002 |
| Silence Speaks | Center for Digital Storytelling | North America | USA | California | Berkeley | 2000 |
| Stories of Service: Intergenerational DST | Digital Clubhouse Network – West Coast Clubhouse | North America | USA | California | San Jose | 1998 |

(cont'd)

**Table 3.4** *(cont'd)*

| Title | Host | Continent | Country | State/Region | City | Year began |
|---|---|---|---|---|---|---|
| Digital Healing: Intergenerational DST | Digital Clubhouse Network – West Coast Clubhouse | North America | USA | California | San Jose | 1997 |
| Young Brave Hearts: Intergenerational DST | Digital Clubhouse Network – West Coast Clubhouse | North America | USA | California | San Jose | 1996 |
| Digitally Abled Producers Project (DAPP) | Digital Clubhouse Network – West Coast Clubhouse | North America | USA | California | San Jose | 1995 |
| Train the Trainers | Center for Digital Storytelling | North America | USA | California | Berkeley | 1994 |
| Latino Legacy: Intergenerational DST | Digital Clubhouse Network – West Coast Clubhouse | North America | USA | California | San Jose | |
| Digital Stories Quilt | San Diego LGBT Community Center | North America | USA | California | San Diego | 2006 |
| The Color of Words | Hill Neighborhood | North America | USA | Connecticut | New Haven | 2006/7 |
| DST Workshops | Appalshop, Community Media Initiative | North America | USA | Kentucky | Whitesburg | 2005? |
| DST in the First Ward | New Media Network | North America | USA | Missouri | Columbia | 2007 |
| Our Stories | Equality Ohio and CDS | North America | USA | Ohio | Columbus | 2007 |

| Program | Organization | Continent | Country | Region | City | Year |
|---|---|---|---|---|---|---|
| DST | Portland Community Media | North America | USA | Oregon | Portland | 2007 |
| Multimedia DST | Portland Community Media | North America | USA | Oregon | Portland | 2007 |
| Youth Out Loud Summer Program | Youth Media Institute | North America | USA | Washington | Seattle | 2007 |
| Bridges to Understanding | Bridges to Understanding | North America | USA | Washington | Seattle | 2001 |
| Bridges to Understanding | Bridges to Understanding | South America | Guatemala | Tzutujil Maya | Santiago Atitlán | 2001? |
| Bridges to Understanding | Bridges to Understanding | South America | Peru | | Cuzco | 2001? |
| DST Bootcamps | Digital Storytelling Festivals | North America | USA | Various | Various | 1997 |

*Historical* digital storytelling frames the practice as part of a broader collection of public history – usually of a particular community, place, or group of community members – offering a "powerfully emotive by-product of oral history" that can "offer an insight [in]to our collective social history" (Klaebe 2006a: 10). For instance, Tuggeranong Community Arts' "First Person" project, located in the Australian Capital Territory, facilitated, produced, and collected the digital stories of elderly Hungarian-born locals who had migrated to the area. The purpose of the project was to contribute to a public history of the city by putting a "spotlight on the Hungarian contribution to Canberra's rich cultural legacy."[8] Slightly differently, Canada's Centre for Independent Living in Toronto offers the "Envisioning New Meanings of Disability and Difference" program. This contributes to public history, but aims to do so critically. Specifically, it encourages its participants to approach their own stories as a challenge to existing representations of people with a disability or other physical difference.[9]

One of the best known historical digital storytelling programs is "Stories of Service," which began in 1998 and is run by the Digital Clubhouse Network. The Digital Clubhouse is a major USA digital storytelling umbrella organization that has produced hundreds of digital stories, contributing more than three hundred of them to the National Museum of American History (permanently contributing to American public histories). "Stories of Service" is their most prominent program, as well as one of their longest running; specifically, the program collects the stories of "men and women who have served" the USA "and our communities" through military service.[10] The program is probably the most internationally prominent historical digital storytelling program currently operating in the USA, at least since selections of its stories began to be broadcast by the History Channel in 2005, including a special international broadcast to celebrate US Veterans Day.

*Aspirational* programs articulate digital storytelling as an empowering experience that can qualitatively change the lives of its storytellers, often focusing on marginalized community members (see Klaebe 2006a: 9–10). Like traditional community development projects, aspirational programs seek to "improve" the "social and economic circumstances" of its participants through their participation in, in this case, digital storytelling programs (Midgley et al. 1986: 17). Consider, for example, the "Outta Your Backpack" program run by Indigenous Action Media in Flagstaff, Arizona. This seeks to empower indigenous youth through access to media production, improving not only the lives of its participants but also the unequal access to and representation of indigenous people in mainstream media. Similarly, Queensland

University of Technology's "Finding a Voice" project, led by Jo Tacchi (and discussed in her chapter 11 in this volume), aims to "empower poor people to communicate their 'voices' within marginalized communities" through media access and training, including in digital storytelling.[11]

Indeed, while it is not the case with the examples I have cited, aspirational programs are much more likely than recuperative programs, and slightly more likely than historical programs, to link "empowerment" through media access and training with the idea of "bridging" the "digital divide." And aspirational programs are a likely bedfellow with issues of media access, given Lisa Servon's argument that the digital divide is ultimately a "symptom of a larger and more complex problem – the problem of persistent poverty and inequality" (Servon 2002: 2; see also Mehra, Merkel, and Bishop 2004).

*Recuperative* digital storytelling is an emerging subset of community digital storytelling programs. Typically, recuperative programs are an extension of aspirational programs, but with a primary focus on digital storytelling as a healing, even therapeutic process, which is usually approached through personal reflection and story sharing in a safe space. Philip Neilsen argues that digital storytelling, like life writing, is "well-established as a therapeutic and healing tool, especially for those in distress – parents of a dying child, children coming to terms with divorce and so on" (2005: 2). One of the most compelling programs of recuperative digital storytelling is the Israeli "Kids for Kids," which uses digital storytelling as "narrative therapy" to "provide a platform" for youth "traumatized" by war "to find their voice."[12] Probably the longest-running recuperative program, however, is "Silence Speaks," which uses digital storytelling "in support of healing and violence prevention."[13] Originally set up by Amy Hill of the CDS in 2000, "Silence Speaks" aims to provide "survivors, witnesses, and prevention advocates" with the access and training to "create original multimedia pieces of courage and healing."[14]

Consistent across all historical, aspirational, and recuperative programs is a central ideological commitment, typical of community media, to "free expression," "enhancing community relations and promoting community solidarity" (Howley 2005: 2). Indeed, as a community media practice, digital storytelling is "rooted fundamentally in the notion of democratized culture that was the hallmark of the folk music, re-claimed folk culture, and cultural activist traditions of the 1960's" (Lambert 2006: 2). As such, its prevalence in community settings is part of a straightforward trajectory from its community-based origins.

*Cultural institutions and government, business, and religious hosts*

"Community co-creation programs," like digital storytelling, are also "increasingly used by cultural institutions" to increase both audience size and engagement (Watkins and Russo 2005c: 2). To be precise, approximately one-sixth of the digital storytelling programs surveyed (51 of 300) were hosted in or by cultural institutions, meaning publicly funded institutions dedicated to the preservation, production, and/or distribution of cultural artifacts. Cultural institutions are, in short, the "custodians of cultural content" (Russo et al. 2006: 1). Of the 51 digital storytelling programs based in cultural institutions, 40 were hosted in or with libraries, 6 with media centers and/or film boards, and 5 with museums.

Almost all of these programs, as is to be expected of public institutions, are publicly available to local residents (42 of 51). Of those that are not available to the public, the programs targeted, in the main, cultural institution staff, as in the Marcus Digital Education Project for Texas Museums, which aims to teach the staff of Texas art museums how to "tell media-rich stories about the museums' collections and exhibitions."[15] Hence, those that did not target the public as participants were usually targeting a public benefit, such as improved public service. Perhaps unsurprisingly, most (36) programs located in cultural institutions are framed as *historical* digital storytelling programs, or about collecting digital stories as part of the public history of a community and/or place, like the historical programs hosted by community organizations. For example, six Californian public libraries – in Benicia, Covina, Hayward, Orange County, Sacramento, and south San Francisco – participated in the "California of the Past" digital storytelling umbrella program in 2007.[16] Each library ran workshops for local residents to collect digital stories that collectively contributed to a public history of the state, through the memories of its residents. Similarly, the Norwegian Digitalbridge's "Urban Echoes" program ran a workshop in Malmö for local residents, so as to collect a public history of the city.[17]

Historical programs are also the most popular program among public broadcasters, which fall into the final category of "host" in this survey: government, business, and religious hosts. Government, business, and religious hosts, including those funded by government or business, of which there are 55 in all, comprise companies or consultancies (27), public broadcasters (15), governments or government departments (10), health organizations (2), and a church (1). While companies or consultancies are the largest category

**Table 3.5** Survey of DST online: cultural institutions

| Title | Host | Continent | Country | State/Region | City | Year began |
|---|---|---|---|---|---|---|
| DST Express | Powerhouse Museum | Australasia | Australia | New South Wales | Sydney | ? |
| | Australian Centre for the Moving Image | Australasia | Australia | Victoria | Melbourne | 2007 |
| Train the Trainers | Australian Centre for the Moving Image | Australasia | Australia | Victoria | Melbourne | 2001 |
| DST Workshops | Australian Centre for the Moving Image | Australasia | Australia | Victoria | Melbourne | 2001 |
| DST at Stoke-on-Trent Museums | Stoke-on-Trent Museums | Europe | England, UK | Staffordshire | Stoke-on-Trent | 2007? |
| Life Stories | National Film Board of Canada | North America | Canada | British Columbia | Vancouver | 2006 |
| Marcus Digital Education Project for Texas Museums | Edward and Betty Marcus Foundation | North America | USA | Texas | | 2006 |
| Million-Youth-Life-Stories Movement | Museu da Pessoa (Museum of the Person) and Aracati | South America | Brazil | | São Paulo | 2006 |
| Finding a Voice | Agyauli Community Library and QUT | Asia | Nepal | | Agyauli | 2006 |
| Finding a Voice | Jhuwani Community Library and QUT | Asia | Nepal | | Jhuwani | 2006 |

(cont'd)

**Table 3.5** (cont'd)

| Title | Host | Continent | Country | State/Region | City | Year began |
|---|---|---|---|---|---|---|
| Queensland Stories/ Acacia Ridge and Algester Stories | State Library of Queensland and Acacia Ridge Community Library | Australasia | Australia | Queensland | Brisbane | 2004 |
| Queensland Stories/ Bits, Boots and Bulldust | State Library of Queensland and Aramac Shire Council | Australasia | Australia | Queensland | Brisbane | 2004 |
| Queensland Stories/ Between the Bougainvilleas Stories | State Library of Queensland and Barcaldine Shire Council | Australasia | Australia | Queensland | Brisbane | 2004 |
| Queensland Stories/ The Jundah Sheep Industry | State Library of Queensland, Barcoo Shire Council, and Jundah Library | Australasia | Australia | Queensland | Brisbane | 2004 |
| Queensland Stories/ Community Book Project | State Library of Queensland and Barcoo Shire Council – Windorah Library | Australasia | Australia | Queensland | Brisbane | 2004 |
| Queensland Stories/ Words from the West | State Library of Queensland and Bendemere, Roma, Bungil, Booringa, Waroo Shires | Australasia | Australia | Queensland | Brisbane | 2004 |
| Queensland Stories, Music and Urban Virtuolygles | State Library of Queensland and Brisbane City Council | Australasia | Australia | Queensland | Brisbane | 2004 |

| Queensland Stories/The Keeping Place | State Library of Queensland and Bwgcolman Community School | Australasia | Australia | Queensland | Brisbane | 2004 |
|---|---|---|---|---|---|---|
| Queensland Stories/School Days New Ways | State Library of Queensland and Caboolture Shire Council | Australasia | Australia | Queensland | Brisbane | 2004 |
| Queensland Stories/Yarning in Caboolture | State Library of Queensland and Caboolture Shire Council | Australasia | Australia | Queensland | Brisbane | 2004 |
| Queensland Stories/Mooroobool's Folk Tale | State Library of Queensland and Cairns City Council | Australasia | Australia | Queensland | Brisbane | 2004 |
| Queensland Stories/Finding the Thread | State Library of Queensland and Caloundra City Council | Australasia | Australia | Queensland | Brisbane | 2004 |
| Queensland Stories/Cherbourg Stories | State Library of Queensland and Cherbourg State School | Australasia | Australia | Queensland | Brisbane | 2004 |
| Queensland Stories/Woorabinda Stories (Cherbourg) | State Library of Queensland | Australasia | Australia | Queensland | Brisbane | 2004 |
| Queensland Stories/Walls can Speak | State Library of Queensland and Jondaryan Shire Council | Australasia | Australia | Queensland | Brisbane | 2004 |
| Queensland Stories/Liv-e-zine | State Library of Queensland and Livingstone Shire Council | Australasia | Australia | Queensland | Brisbane | 2004 |
| Queensland Stories/Loving Logan | State Library of Queensland and Logan City Council | Australasia | Australia | Queensland | Brisbane | 2004 |

(cont'd)

**Table 3.5** *(cont'd)*

| Title | Host | Continent | Country | State/Region | City | Year began |
|---|---|---|---|---|---|---|
| Queensland Stories/ My Neighbourhood: Loganlea, Kingston, and Woodridge | State Library of Queensland and Logan City Council | Australasia | Australia | Queensland | Brisbane | 2004 |
| Queensland Stories/ Stori Blong Yu Mi (The Story is Mine) | State Library of Queensland and Mackay City Council | Australasia | Australia | Queensland | Brisbane | 2004 |
| Queensland Stories/ Echidna Creek: the Story of a Creek and its Community | State Library of Queensland and Maroochy Shire Council | Australasia | Australia | Queensland | Brisbane | 2004 |
| Queensland Stories/ RememberWhen | State Library of Queensland and Maryborough City Council | Australasia | Australia | Queensland | Brisbane | 2004 |
| Queensland Stories/ Murweh P.O.P Point of Presence | State Library of Queensland and Murweh Shire Council | Australasia | Australia | Queensland | Brisbane | 2004 |
| Queensland Stories/ The Nature of Noosa | State Library of Queensland and Noosa Shire Council | Australasia | Australia | Queensland | Brisbane | 2004 |
| Queensland Stories/ Timber-Getters and Woodworkers on the Pine: A Film History | State Library of Queensland and Pine Rivers Shire Council | Australasia | Australia | Queensland | Brisbane | 2004 |

| | | | | | | |
|---|---|---|---|---|---|---|
| Queensland Stories/Redcliffe Remembers: The War Years 1939–1949 | State Library of Queensland and Redcliffe City Council | Australasia | Australia | Queensland | Brisbane | 2004 |
| Queensland Stories/Stradbroke Stories: North Stradbroke Island Oral History Project Stage 2 | State Library of Queensland and Redland Shire Council | Australasia | Australia | Queensland | Brisbane | 2004 |
| Queensland Stories/Eureka! Unearthing the Stor | State Library of Queensland and Thuringowa City Council | Australasia | Australia | Queensland | Brisbane | 2004 |
| Queensland Stories/Picture Poles-Telling Townsville Stories | State Library of Queensland and Townsville City Council | Australasia | Australia | Queensland | Brisbane | 2004 |
| DST and Animation for Primary Schools | School Library Association of Victoria and Victoria Information Technology Teacher's Association | Australasia | Australia | Victoria | Carlton | 2008 |
| The New Frontier: Digital Storytelling | Pima County Public Library | North America | USA | Arizona | Pima County | 2007 |
| California of the Past | Benicia Public Library | North America | USA | California | Benicia | 2007 |
| California of the Past | Covina Public Library | North America | USA | California | Covina | 2007 |
| California of the Past | Hayward Public Library | North America | USA | California | Hayward | 2007 |
| California of the Past | Orange County Public Library | North America | USA | California | Orange County | 2007 |

(cont'd)

**Table 3.5**  (cont'd)

| Title | Host | Continent | Country | State/Region | City | Year began |
|---|---|---|---|---|---|---|
| California of the Past | Sacramento Public Library | North America | USA | California | Sacramento | 2007 |
| California of the Past | South San Francisco Public Library | North America | USA | California | South San Francisco | 2007 |
| Sunnyvale Voices | Sunnyvale Library | North America | USA | Illinois | Sunnydale | 2000 |
| DST | Media Resource Centre | Australasia | Australia | South Australia | Adelaide | 2007 |
| Bristol Stories | Bristol Museums and Watershed | Europe | England, UK | Avon | Bristol | 2006 |
| DST | MediaLinx Habitat, Canadian Film Centre | North America | Canada | Ontario | Toronto | 2001? |
| DST Station | Escondido Public Library and Media Arts Centre of San Diego | North America | USA | California | Escondido | 2007 |

of government, business, and religious hosts of digital storytelling programs, it is comparatively insignificant within the larger context of the survey of 300 programs. Indeed, despite Dana Atchley's early pioneering consultancy work in the 1990s with a number of multinationals, the majority of the surveyed companies only began their programs in the early 2000s, showing the relatively slow international takeup of commercial applications of digital storytelling. Moreover, most of those applications are still directed at educational or community participants, continuing to emphasize digital storytelling's overwhelming popularity in those select areas of the public sector. For example, Duckworth Design, a company that specializes in providing professional development, training programs, and online branding and is based in Colorado, USA, runs a program called "Tell Your Story – Technical Training in a Narrative Context," which draws on the expertise of the CDS to run digital storytelling workshops. The program is one course among a suite of courses targeting teachers interested in professional development, highlighting the ever-increasing educative applications of digital storytelling, across both the public and private sectors.[18]

Even so, when programs are run by either public broadcasters (of which there were 15 examples) and governments or government departments (of which there were 10), the focus tends to be consistent with community-based applications, but particularly historical digital storytelling. This is the case with both the "Sharing Stories" program run at Australia's Kelvin Grove Urban Village and the BBC's various programs, but most notably its "Capture Wales" program (both of these programs are discussed at length in this volume: see Chapter 10 on the former, and Chapter 5 on the latter). This makes historical digital storytelling the overwhelmingly most popular focus of digital storytelling programs around the globe. However, what is perhaps most interesting about trends among "cultural institutions" and "government, business, and religious hosts" of digital storytelling programs is the West's complete dominance. No non-Western sites were surveyed in either of these categories of host, signaling not only the different levels of cultural "embeddedness" and institutional acceptance of the practice, but perhaps also offering a clue that entrepreneurial innovation originates in the public sector – where digital storytelling has now been growing in popularity in the West for more than a decade and a half – before being developed in the private sector. In a comparison of Canadian public- and private-sector innovation, for instance, Louise Earl found that public-sector organizations introduced substantially more change than their private counterparts, while scholars like Tom Ling have noted that the private

**Table 3.6** Survey of DST online: government, business, and religious hosts

| Title | Host | Continent | Country | State/Region | City | Year began |
|---|---|---|---|---|---|---|
| Telling Lives | BBC | Europe | England | | Various | 2007? |
| Mundo/Digitales (Europe) | YLE/Digi-Tales (Europe) | Europe | Finland | | Helsinki | 2004? |
| Rum för Berättande (Space for Storytelling) | UR | Europe | Sweden | | Kundtjänst | 2006 |
| DST Workshop | BBC Northern Ireland | Europe | Northern Ireland, UK | | Various, Northern Ireland | 2005 |
| Highland Lives | BBC Scotland | Europe | Scotland, UK | | Various, Highlands | 2007 |
| Capture Wales | BBC Wales | Europe | Wales, UK | | Various | 2008 |
| Breaking Barriers | BBC Wales | Europe | Wales, UK | | Various | 2007? |
| Coleg Sir Gâr | BBC Wales | Europe | Wales, UK | | Various | 2008 |
| Dimension 10 | BBC Wales | Europe | Wales, UK | | Various | 2007 |
| Rhondda Lives! | BBC Wales | Europe | Wales, UK | | Various | 2007 |
| Sarah's Stories | BBC Wales | Europe | Wales, UK | | Various | 2005? |
| School Shoebox Stories | BBC Wales | Europe | Wales, UK | | Various | 2008 |
| Shoebox Stories | BBC Wales | Europe | Wales, UK | | Various | 2007 |
| Basic DST Workshop | KQED | North America | USA | California | San Francisco | 2007 |
| Train the Trainers | KQED | North America | USA | California | San Francisco | 2005 |

| Project | Producer/Organization | Region | Country | State/Province | City | Year |
| --- | --- | --- | --- | --- | --- | --- |
| The Hero Within | tallstoreez productionz | Australasia | Australia | South Australia | Adelaide | 2005 |
| Digitale for Tellinger | Flimmer Film | Europe | Norway | | Various | 2007? |
| DST | Daryll Bellingham | Australasia | Australia | Queensland | Brisbane | 2004? |
| Mobil Workshop for DST | Sonja Wessel | Europe | Germany | | Munich | 2006 |
| DST | Ingrid Weidig/Renate Schütz | Europe | Germany | | Essen | 2005 |
| CKV Project DST | Judith Bach | Europe | Netherlands | | | 2007 |
| Adisa Stories | Project Adisa/Dani Landau DST | Europe | England, UK | Avon | Bristol | 2008 |
| Knowle West Stories | Knowle West Media Centre/Dani Landau DST | Europe | England, UK | Avon | Bristol | 2007? |
| Pilgrim Projects and Patient Voices | Pilgrim Projects | Europe | England, UK | Cambridgeshire | Landbeach | 2008 |
| Durham Digital Stories | Digistories/BBC Tees | Europe | England, UK | Yorkshire | York | 2007 |
| uToo Malta | uToo young parents group/Dani Landau DST | Europe | England, UK | Wiltshire | Swindon | 2007 |
| Our Community | Teyfant Community Primary School/Dani Landau DST | Europe | England, UK | Avon | Bristol | 2005? |
| DST | Noisybrain Productions | North America | USA | Massachusetts | Waltham | 2008 |
| DST Workshops | Creative Narrations | North America | USA | Washington | Seattle | 2007 |

(cont'd)

**Table 3.6** (cont'd)

| Title | Host | Continent | Country | State/Region | City | Year began |
|---|---|---|---|---|---|---|
| DST | Will Boyd Media Solutions | North America | USA | Georgia | Macon | 2007 |
| DST Program | Local Productions | Australasia | Australia | Victoria | Melbourne | 2005 |
| DST | Calgary Regional Consortium | North America | Canada | Alberta | Calgary | 2005 |
| Digital Pictures Speak | LEARN: Leading English Education and Resource Network | North America | Canada | Québec | Laval | 2007? |
| Technical Training in a Narrative Context | Duckworth Design and CDS | North America | USA | Colorado | Aurora | 2004? |
| Davis DST Workshop | Davis Publications, Digication.com | North America | USA | Massachusetts | Worcester | 2006 |
| DST Workshops | Dr. Helen Barrett – electronic portfolios.org | North America | USA | Mobile | Mobile | 2005 |
| DST Workshops | Dana Atchley Productions | North America | USA | California | San Francisco | 1999? |
| DST | Midwestern IU IV Learning Centre "Global Classroom" | North America | USA | Vermont | Burlington | 2007 |
| Everyone Has a Story to Tell | Innovative Teaching Concepts | North America | USA | | | 2008 |

| Name | Organization | Region | Country | State | City | Year |
|---|---|---|---|---|---|---|
| David DST Workshop | Digication | North America | USA | | | 2007? |
| DigiTales ST Camp | DigiTales | North America | USA | Colorado | Denver | 2008 |
| DST Bootcamp | Mass Impact | North America | USA | Massachusetts | Boston | 2007 |
| DST | Hampshire City Council | Europe | England, UK | Hampshire | Various, Hampshire | 2007 |
| DST | Country Areas Program Professional Learning | Australasia | Australia | New South Wales | Various | 2005? |
| Intro to DST | Govrnmnt of South Australia, Department of Education and Children's Services | Australasia | Australia | South Australia | Adelaide | 2008 |
| DST | Youth Central and Victorian Government | Australasia | Australia | Victoria | Melbourne | 2007 |
| DST | Connecticut Education Network, State of Connecticut | North America | USA | Connecticut | Willimantic | 2007 |
| DST | Maine Learning Technology Initiative, State of Maine | North America | USA | Maine | | 2005 |
| DST | Assistive Technology Partnership, Nebraska Government | North America | USA | Nebraska | Cozad | 2005 |
| Sharing Stories | Kelvin Grove Urban Village/QUT | Australasia | Australia | Queensland | Brisbane | 2005 |

(cont'd)

**Table 3.6** (cont'd)

| Title | Host | Continent | Country | State/Region | City | Year began |
|---|---|---|---|---|---|---|
| IDTECH500.1 DST | Arizona Department of Education, IDEAL | North America | USA | Arizona | Phoenix | 2004? |
| DST | The Lakes Area (and CDS) | North America | USA | Iowa | Lakes Area | 2006 |
| Our Stories | Vancouver Coastal Health SMART Fund and Aboriginal Health Initiative Program | North America | Canada | British Columbia | Vancouver | 2005 |
| DST Advocacy and Education Project | California Obesity Prevention Initiative and Santa Barbara County Public Health Department | | | | | 2007 |
| DST | Church of Norway | | | | | 2008 |

sector potentially has much to learn about innovation from the public sector (2002; see also Halvorsen et al. 2005). In other words, it might be entirely expected that countries in the West, which have hosted public-sector digital storytelling programs for a number of years, are more likely than countries that have embraced digital storytelling less readily to now be developing private-sector applications of the practice. And perhaps that is where the most significant innovations in digital storytelling practice around the world will occur in the next fifteen years and/or over the next 300 programs to be launched. As Richard Florida says, "human creativity is the ultimate economic resource" (Florida 2004: xiii). At the very least, this chapter, the first to attempt an evidence-based global mapping of digital storytelling, provides a starting point to compare such developments.

## Notes

1   See www.storycenter.org/stories/
2   For a discussion of the difference between "specific" and "generic" digital story-telling, see McWilliam (2008).
3   See www.nextexit.com/dap/dapframeset.html
4   teachers.santee.k12.ca.us/lauderbach/Important%20Dates.htm
5   See www.carmarthenshire.gov.uk/index.asp?locID=8112&docID=14209
6   See www.digitalstories.org/
7   Toronto School of Art: www.tsa-art.ca/Courses/Discipline/View_All/273; Phoenix College: www.dist.maricopa.edu/cgi-bin/curric.pl?crs=art150&trm= 20056&host=www.pc.maricopa.edu
8   See www.tuggeranongarts.com/Docs/DigitalStorytelling.doc
9   See www.cilt.ca/Lists/News%20Items/DispForm.aspx?ID=327
10  See digiclub.org/sofs/
11  See www.findingavoice.org/en/about
12  See kidsforkids.net/Page318.aspx
13  See www.silencespeaks.org/
14  See silencespeaks.org/about.html
15  See www.pachyderm.org/news.html#marcus
16  See www.library.ca.gov/pressreleases/pr_070509.html
17  See www.digitalbridge.nu/
18  See the other courses here: www.duckworthdesign.com/misc_training.php

# Part II

# Foundational Practices

# 4

# Where It All Started
## The Center for Digital Storytelling in California

## *Joe Lambert*

### Looking Backward

In August 1997 I wrote an overview article about our four years of practice in digital storytelling, linking our work formally with self-proclaimed practices of community arts. The article started with the following premise:[1]

> Many, many people in the world have spent the last century in a conscious effort to examine how story makes us human. We have accepted that oral transmission has been and remains our principal form of cultural exchange as a species, while also gaining a better understanding of how mediated culture, printed or electronic, has greatly affected the way we use and rely on our oral cultural transactions.
>
> In twentieth-century societies, numerous artistic movements developed drawing on aesthetic principles that celebrated the creative expression of "common folk" – that is, the creativity of the non-professional artist. Those aesthetics were manifested in an art of social commitment, an art of public education, an art of therapeutic recovery, an art of memorializing the common victim of historical/social tragedies, among many others. Oral history, art therapy, community spectacle, multicultural arts-in-education activism, arts practice as community economic development, are all examples of how these aesthetics have evolved. In the USA, these approaches come under many names, but for the sake of this chapter, we will refer to these art processes as community arts.
>
> Shared by all of these artistic practices is the central value of personal experience and memory. Artists adapted the organizing principle of countless varieties of psychological, cultural identity, and social change movements, which had demonstrated that the reciting and coming to terms with

one's own past, you build "self-esteem" or "personal empowerment." For the contemporary social activist, personal empowerment and emotional recovery become the basis of a larger civic project of social change and the basis for self-determination of a community's, or large sections of the society's, political and economic future.

In revisiting the article ten years later, I am struck by how much we are still fighting for ways to understand the dilemmas of the current cultural moment. We are still reaching for ways to explain the widening gulf between cosmopolitanism and fundamentalism in our culture. This gulf, and the resulting stalemate in political and cultural dialogue, has become unsettling, and in many ways dangerously disabling for our society as a whole.

## Digital Storytelling Searches for its Own Story

The principles we were trying to expound, by linking our work to the values of the historical and contemporary community arts practice, were part of our early efforts in self-definition. While we were part of the new media revolution, our appropriation of "storytelling" had positioned us as heirs to the folksy populism of the oral tradition. And while we had many legitimate links to the community of traditional storytellers, folk-music culture and other forms of cultural populism, neither Dana Atchley, nor myself and my principal collaborator Nina Mullen, considered ourselves protectors of that heritage.

In my own journey from political activism to cultural activism, and then to contemporary experimental performance and digital media, I had come to appreciate a balance between a radical populism and increasing stances of cultural iconoclasm. Like many reconstructing Marxists, I had lost faith in essentializing tendencies in the battle for economic democracy and multicultural equity. As soon as communities long marginalized had found their political muscle, it seems they were creating new myths that called for lockstep conformity. Artists from those communities were often the defenders of popular traditions, even as they poked fun at, or directly confronted the self-importance or self-righteousness of their newly installed cultural and political leadership. My theater company in San Francisco, "Life on the Water," succeeded in presenting community-based artists who built their work on strong identification with their communities (see Lambert 2006). They made approachable, entertaining work, as well as presented artists that were experimenting with forms that challenged their audiences, and included sexual, political, and cultural content that meant to assault dominant culture, as well as community expectations.

I also was facing consumer capitalism's essential victory in the Cold War. I felt my choices were to self-isolate within the subculture of political dissidence, or cross over into some aspect of the mainstream. My joining the digital media revolution was an attempt at looking beyond my socialist legacy to a hybridized future – with one foot in the emergent commercial world of new media, and one foot still maintaining a sense of purity and integrity within the politicized arts community. So when I wrote about the intersection of the emerging digital arts field and the contemporary community arts field, I was trying to accomplish several things. First was to reclaim my own political legacy, and the legacy for our methods and approach to teaching people to make digital stories. The other was to place our work and its particular discourse within the nascent digital media arts community.

Digital media were creating many new genres of practice, but the dominant approach to the practice was a cool conceptualism, 1990s cyber-chic, very much within the traditions of modernism. We wanted to provide an alternative to this style of arts practice. And finally, we saw ourselves as providing a political viewpoint to the digital arts community. Some artists had entered the field as a form of escape from the messy politics of cultural equity. The new field of art and technology in the early 1990s, and the resulting bubble of activity and funding, was described by one of my colleagues, artist Keith Antar Mason, as the newest form of white flight. This critique stung precisely because … well, he was right.

So I wanted to bring our work out of the suburbs and back downtown, where it belonged.

## Being in the Present

In 2007, the challenges for the community of practice around digital storytelling, as diverse and expansive as it has become, seem to call for a similar reclamation project to restate and reinstil core principles. While diversity and plurality are inevitable and important in any emergent practice, it seems that various attempts to situate the work outside a social change framework – the languages, attitudes, and principles of educators, social service professionals, or community artists committed to social change are essentially the same – is to miss the point, almost entirely.

The expansion of the digital storytelling moniker into broadcast, into the greater field of educational technology, into practices as diverse as its use as a tool for evaluation and research, or for marketing purposes, has stretched the concept and values of our work to a thin, superficial veneer. And of more concern, the situating of the brand as concomitant with general media literacy projects, such as teaching kids to make videos that imitate the content and milquetoast perspectives, the empty-headed bling of commercial television, coopts the concept. Suddenly our efforts to have people consider their stories as fundamentally acts of self-discovery, and a means to localize and control the context of their presentation, becomes just another tool to be used against us: "America's Most Heartfelt Videos, see it on YouTube."

We are absolutely committed to freedom of expression; the work is participant-centered and people are encouraged to find their own path in their story. In this way we are not dogmatically tied to a perspective where people are challenged to address social issues as part of their stories. We agree with Ivan Illich (1973: 24) that providing people with convivial tools, such as the methods of digital storytelling practice (as opposed to mass media's "industrial production"), enables "autonomous and creative intercourse among persons," which is a precondition for promoting social change.

But we do not believe in treating this as the basis for total neutrality in our approach to story gathering. At the Center for Digital Storytelling (CDS), we understand that the choices we make in sharing stories as examples, in how we guide the considerations of meaning, of making connections to the social construct, are not meant to be balanced. We start with point of view, because we believe everyone should know that they have one. Even if our efforts are just showing people a way to take responsibility for their own lives, their own stories, as the first step to larger awareness, all our choices are informed with a touch of the subversive. It is a subtle, or not so subtle, an indirect or not so indirect confrontation with the dominant culture and representative authorities which is driving the bus of our planet off the precipice. We cannot afford to be naive or pluralistic to the point of pointlessness.

## The Field of Community Arts

In 2007 we joined with Mass Impact, Narrative Creations, and a community of practitioners around the country to create StoriesforChange.net.[2] This is a wonderful accomplishment for the digital storytelling community in the USA because it offers a portal to the work being done by many of our most committed community-based facilitators. While the digital storytelling facilitative community is certainly dominated by people with formal creative training, very few would define themselves as community-based artists, as in having been introduced to the larger field that includes practitioners across many disciplines.

So what are community-based arts? To begin, I will borrow from colleague Jan Cohen-Cruz's definitions of this field of practice. She defines a community-based project as "usually a response to a collectively significant issue or circumstance. It is a collaboration between an artist or an ensemble [group of artists] and a 'community' constituted by virtue of a shared primary identity based on place, ethnicity, class, race, sexual preference, profession, circumstances or political orientation" (Cohen-Cruz 2006: 2).

Most people think of community arts work as essentially involved in either the politics of inequity or the politics of identity, or both. An oral history theater that involves the respondents in the performance, participatory murals, community processions, a multigenerational dance performance, and a spoken word concert with multicultural youth; all come to mind when we think of community arts projects. We think of the facilitators as social issue-focused artists/activists creating work to help agitate and advocate for change in policy. Cohen-Cruz (2006) mentions that the single largest reference for many of the artists is Paulo Freire's work in popular literacy (see Freire 1972). It is not surprising that many of the educators drawn to digital storytelling have Freirian backgrounds as well.

But in its evolution over the last century, the nuance of community arts practice has evolved to include a number of other strategies. In my and others' observations, community artists are now more directly engaged in learning and training processes. They are actively reclaiming space within communities that has been lost or threatened by redevelopment and gentrification processes, in providing life skills to people in economic development processes, in sustained dialogues as cultural diplomats to address and negotiate substantive conflicts within communities, as scenario planners helping communities to conceive their futures, and finally, as spiritual and healing forces within communities.

In the USA we have several models of community-based art practice that are worthy of our examination in thinking about how to develop successful digital storytelling work in communities. In our own general area of media arts, there is the work of Appalshop in Kentucky,[3] Wendy Ewald and others at the Center for Documentary Studies,[4] and Dave Isay's radio work in New York (SoundPortraits).[5] In theater, Los Angeles-based Cornerstone Theater has taken both traditional theatrical scripts and community-created texts to perform ongoing cycles of work on countless community topics, receiving accolades from community leadership, art critics, and their peers.[6] There is the work of Anna Deavere-Smith,[7] or Culture Clash's performance investigations, Bread and Puppet's processions and pageants,[8] and all the organizations connected to the AlternateROOTS network based in the South.[9] In visual arts, Judy Baca and her SPARC collaborators in Los Angeles have turned community "muralism" into vast projects that have engaged broad sections of the public.[10] In dance, Liz Lerman's Dance Exchange in Washington, DC has created groundbreaking work with elders, and evolved important general principles for community arts practice through countless small- and large-scale, long-term community residencies.[11] These artists have made a point of sharing the lessons and experiences of their work in countless case studies through publications and online communities such as the Virginia Tech's support of Art in the Public Interest's Community Arts Network.[12]

## Digital Storytelling in the Big Picture

The more complex and commercial the society, the more people experience a loss of agency, a decline in spontaneous connection, a tendency for consumer activities to supplant other social relationships and a strong pull toward isolated pursuits. Yet as these tendencies have come to light, the will to resist them has grown stronger, expressed in countless ways, such as the locally based "slow food" movement, remarkable growth of do-it-yourself approaches, burgeoning interest in craft and other traditional practices and a great awakening of the impulse to seek spiritual meaning. The feelings that animate this growing refusal to succumb to corporate vales also enspirit those who work for community cultural development. (Goldbard 2006: 23)

There seem to be two broad arguments for the specific strength of community arts practices for contemporary culture. The first was connected to Jan Cohen-Cruz's definition mentioned above, as a tool to address the continued construction and reconstruction of identity. But the community arts field has also successfully positioned itself to address the issue of cultural dislocation in contemporary society caused by unbridled consumer capitalism – a k a globalization.

In her book, *New Creative Community*, Arlene Goldbard (2006) suggested six areas where community arts practices can respond to social concerns, including the proliferation of mass media, mass migration, the environment, the recognition of cultural minorities, the process of negotiating difference (the "Culture Wars"), and the general rubric of Development; as in eliminating poverty and economic inequity. I would add to the list of globalization's ills the increase in violence within our families and communities, the failing efficacy of educational institutions to prepare students for their future, and the never-ending fetishism for technological innovation.

When I think about the meta-argument for digital storytelling as a community arts practice, my thinking has not changed much in a decade. As our culture becomes more digitized, we have responded to each of these social concerns within the digital environment. The ability to express oneself in digital media, in our case using digital video editing, has become a central literacy for full participation in society. And as we started this work, we recognized that unlike some other forms of community arts activity, there would be barriers of access; the penetration of digital culture to virtually all sectors of society has mitigated this critique.

But perhaps the largest argument for the digital storytelling approach as a community arts practice in addressing social issues (and as a tool in education) is its multi-modality. Digital storytelling, like other community- or activist-based film and video projects, speaks a language that is attractive to vast numbers of people raised on screen culture. The baby boomers and their Nintendo-generation children see screen representation as synonymous with civic participation. The battle for hearts and minds has been fought for decades in audiovisual media, but the digital tools and distribution mechanisms have leveled the playing field.

As Appalshop educator Mimi Pickering said about their work in the American South:

> The Digital Storytelling Workshops were perhaps most successful at providing a glimpse into the power of local stories told by local people as a

cultural and community development tool, and at whetting an appetite to do more. Participants learned that current communications technologies are not beyond their reach, that in many cases there are digital resources they can access locally, and that they can make use of digital technology to widely disseminate their powerful and important stories. (Pickering 2007: n.p.)

## Principles and Methods

Our work borrowed from the general participant-centered perspective of progressive education and community cultural development. We had faith in the power of story, but we also knew we had to set standards for our practice that would make our facilitators increasingly self-aware about how they work with people, in group process, and one-on-one. Historically we have discussed five general principles that inform the methods of our work. In summary:

1.   Everyone has a story to tell, but most people do not feel that their story has meaning or significance. The work of digital storytelling focuses on individual authorship in order to address this problem.

2.   People open up and share their stories when they are provided an environment where they feel that their ideas will be valued, their stories have resonance, and they feel safe. There is a quality of focus and listening in doing story work in a group process that requires utmost attention by the facilitators.

3.   We all perceive the world differently, and so our sense of story, of how to construct meaning through a narrative process, is different. While understanding rudiments of effective communication is useful, there is no formula for making a great story. Even as we provide a framework that assists with organizing people's story ideas, we need to respect the diversity of potential approaches.

4.   Creative activity is human activity, but many people are taught that creativity is the province of experts. Confronting a sense of inadequacy, even among people who have training and describe themselves as artists, is a critical part of the process.

5.   Computers are poorly designed, but massively powerful tools for creativity. Most people blame themselves for technical inadequacy, but

often the problems lie in how the hardware and software are designed. Digital literacy begins with a faith that people can work around the never-ending complexities of their computing devices.

While these principles relate broadly to story work, and working in a digital environment, they have resonance with many similar principles informing other areas of creative community work.

## Assessing our Work in Digital Storytelling

Like any field, we are competing for limited social resources. The same social issues are being addressed by strategies led by equally social change-oriented communities of educators, traditional arts organizations, social service providers, environmentalists, community organizers, and researchers. So a critical question for both the community arts field, and for our emergent field of digital storytelling, is how to argue about what defines the success of our efforts. Our approach to digital storytelling has been accepted as a useful tool, taking the form of our work, but not the content, by many other fields and disciplines. But our goal is not simply to argue for our methods as a way to learn software and hardware; we are working toward people adopting the total package of principles, approaches to process with participants, methods of teaching, and connection to communities.

One stumbling block is the dearth of research and analysis of the work comparing our work to other practices, but the field itself needs to define broader principles. Evaluating the work has always been problematic. The constructive and fluid nature of the work, the never-ending debate about process versus product, means that metrics that might serve the art critic, the media theorist, the educator, or social-service provider do not suffice. The CDS has suffered from criticism from the arts community that our participants' products lack the design integrity and technical fluency of more formal video and film arts training. From the educational community, we are criticized for fully explicating our methods, and from the social-service community, we are criticized for failing to maintain professional distance. We defend ourselves as best we can, but we have lacked a more complete framework for assessment that would allow us to maintain what we intuitively recognize as a successful practice, and meet the requirements of these distinct disciplines and discourse models.

Arlene Goldbard offers one potential framework for evaluating community arts that I believe is quite relevant to our model in digital storytelling. To paraphrase her (Goldbard 2006: 154), a successful project would demonstrate:

1.    Mutually meaningful collaborations with the community, not just aiding, supporting, or entertaining the community members, but useful and instructive reciprocal learning between all of the participants, artist, and community members alike.

2.    Participants being seen as full co-directors in the process with the artist/facilitators.

3.    Participants experiencing broadened cultural knowledge, including a greater mastery of the arts media used to execute the project.

4.    Participants feeling they have successfully expressed themselves and communicated through the project.

5.    Participants feeling that their local aims have been addressed, as well as their aims to bring their work to an external audience.

6.    Participants feeling confident about taking on social and cultural projects and action in the future.

What I appreciate about Goldbard's model is that the evaluative criteria do not require that the work have an overt political agenda. The model is placed within an ethos that could be embraced by people whose agendas could vary widely, but who nevertheless share a commitment to democratic civic participation. In reference to these criteria, there are several principles we have used to distinguish our work.

1.    Our work always places the sharing of tools and the direction of the participant as ultimate creative arbiter.

2.    We distinguish our work from other forms of media or educational practice through a deep concern for genuine collaboration.

3.    Because of the focus on personal stories, people often leave feeling that the opportunity for self-expression is the most important part of the experience.

4.    We are not focused on the artist-expert at the centre of the process (the master lecturer/teacher in the education model), but on a community of learning that situates the story circle at the heart of the practice, with everyone having an equal opportunity to receive and provide feedback.

5. We attempt to view each workshop, or process of working with a group, as unique and adjust our practice accordingly.

6. If literacy levels (or other causes) preclude participants writing their own stories, we do interviews and work with them to edit the interviews. If time, resources, or circumstance prevent us from allowing the participants to learn the basics to operate the computers, we strive to have the participants direct the *artistic* process, or have the "final say" on its editing and distribution.

I do not think we have been as conscious about how we could structure our experiences with the possibility of our own discovery about the issues or stories allowing us to work with participants to reshape the process. We have been very concerned about completing work, and often working with limited time constraints, but we need to look more closely at the limits of our model. We could shift our work to make it more explicitly about reviewing the pieces, and finding appropriate social contexts for sharing the work that would enliven the individuals and their communities to their potential for action.

Our three-day workshop process is greatly limited with regard to instilling a sense of social agency. Those projects that allow for ongoing work with participants, in after-school or community-based projects that take people from their personal stories to other more broadly defined projects, like our work in "Storymapping" and "Silence Speaks," tend to build the kind of cohort structure that supports self-agency and broader social awareness.[13]

# Conclusion

I would put myself out on a limb and say that there really is something extraordinary about our best and wisest community artists, and our digital storytelling facilitators. Something about the depth of engagement with other humans, not just listening but acting with and alongside people, the use of every conceivable aesthetic tool and cultural reference, the fluidity and improvisational complexity of the production processes, and the never-ending humbling of one's expectations and senses of authority, make this work a profound journey for an individual.

I am slightly hesitant about fusing social, pedagogical, and spiritual aims, the establishment of norms of professional conduct and the quest for enlightenment, but we story-midwives are playing with some heavy juju.

It has changed me.

Short of enlightenment, I hope your journey at least leads you to some good stories.

I look forward to hearing yours.

## Notes

1   See the entire article at www.storycenter.org/memoryboxnew.html
2   See Mass Impact, www.massimpact.org
3   See www.appalshop.org/
4   See cds.aas.duke.edu
5   See soundportraits.org
6   See www.cornerstonetheater.org
7   See the Wikipedia entry for Anna Deavere Smith.
8   See www.breadandpuppet.org
9   See www.alternateroots.org/
10  See www.sparcmurals.org
11  See www.danceexchange.org/
12  See www.communityarts.net
13  For more on Storymapping, see www.storymapping.org; and Silence Speaks, see ww.silencespeaks.org/.

# 5

# "Capture Wales"
## The BBC Digital Storytelling Project

## *Daniel Meadows and Jenny Kidd*

DANIEL:
### Multimedia Sonnets from the People

In the autumn of 2000, in the School of Journalism, Media and Cultural Studies at Cardiff University, I began developing a Californian model of digital storytelling as a new broadcast television form. I believed that the new tools of digital production could and should be used to open up the airwaves for a wide range of new users; in short, to give a voice to all of us who are accustomed to thinking of ourselves – in a broadcast context, anyway – only as audience. Digital storytelling – the way *I* like it – is an elegant and economic means of self-representation based on personal collections of still photographs coupled with a voice-over narration. It can be done on the kitchen table using off-the-shelf software and home computers. It is an engaging, rich, short media form which can be mastered by people of differing abilities and from all walks of life. In time I would come to think of the stories facilitated by my BBC Digital Storytelling team in workshops delivered across Wales as beautiful things – multimedia sonnets from the people – but in early 2001 when, at the instigation of Professor Ian Hargreaves (my head of department), I began offering seminars on the subject in our school's digilab for executives, editors, web producers, and other members of staff at BBC Cymru Wales, most of what I talked about was still just theory.

This chapter tells the story of what happened when, following those seminar sessions, I was seconded to BBC Wales to help build a team to test out the theory in practice, and how Jenny Kidd (hired on a PhD scholarship to work in my university department) then applied some fresh theory to what we were doing in order to find out what had been achieved. In this chapter I relate why and how the BBC team did what it did, while Jenny describes the processes she used for evaluating our work and the conclusions she was able to draw.

But first you should sample some digital stories on the BBC Wales website.[1] The following is a representative selection:

*Memories Written on my Face* by Giorgia Carpagnano
*A Night at the Dog & Duck* by Rhiannon Morgan
*A Quest for Understanding* by Richard Pugh
*Elvis Died in my Bedroom* by Paul Cabuts
*Something On My Heart* by Doris Cole
*Pinky, Baby and Me* by Anita Badhan
*A Dog's Life* by Allan Jeffreys
*Two Families* by Dai Evans
*My Picture* by Samiya
*Pink* by Jessica Jones

And in Welsh:

*Mam* by Abigail Elliott
*Seren Wîb* by Shirley G. Williams
*Gweld Llun, Clywed Llais* by Vivian Parry Williams

The objective of the "Capture Wales" team, right from the start, was to make this work sustainable and, happily – as a result of our efforts and the efforts of a great many people working in the community – a vibrant digital story-telling culture has now started to grow up in Wales, with more than thirty groups across the country running their own projects.

JENNY:

# Locating "Capture Wales"

The British Broadcasting Corporation (BBC) articulates its vision as achieving status as "the most creative organization in the world" (BBC Wales 2006/7: 1). In achieving this vision it upholds the following values: trust as the key, audiences at the center of everything, delivering quality and value for money, being creative, respecting others and celebrating diversity, and working together (BBC Wales 2006/7: 1). At the core of these values is an insistence on the importance of dialogue with audience members and/or license payers. This "dialogue" has, according to Dan Gillmor, been better achieved by the BBC than any other major journalistic organization, although for the most part, "While news companies make it their mission to inform the public, few have made it a mission to arm them with tools they can use to make a public ruckus" (Gillmor 2006: 125). "Capture Wales," as will be seen, puts the tools of production in the hands of the public, and in so doing perhaps represents a step toward the "conversation" which is touted by many as framing the future look, focus, and values of journalism (Gillmor 2006, Bowman and Willis 2004, Kovach and Rosenstiel 2001). Until now, opportunities to enter (let alone instigate) genuine two-way communications with(in) media corporations have been minimal and often tokenistic. Perhaps a ruckus is on the cards.

The BBC has endured a volatile relationship with both the British public and the various political climates within which it has operated since its inception. The Corporation, at times unstable, at times critical to the state of "nation," has survived on the premise that public service media provision benefits viewers and listeners, giving them something that would be obsolete in a purely market-driven commercial media environment. This "something" has most frequently been encapsulated in the buzzwords "inform," "educate," and "entertain." For John Reith, the first Director-General (1927–38), this philosophy was crucial if public service broadcasting was to prove itself to be a vital, indispensable means of media distribution: "I wonder if many have paused to consider ... the incalculable harm which might have been done had different principles guided the conduct of the service in the early days" (Reith 1922: 34, quoted in Franklin 2001: 19).

This maxim has remained core to the BBC's understanding of its function within a society that has changed monumentally since its launch (see, for example, the current Agreement and Charter). Within a phenomenally effervescent media landscape in transition, the BBC has sought to remain central to our notions of truth, honesty, quality, nation, and culture. But that transitory broadcasting ecology has in many ways eroded the requirement for public service media provision and rocked the BBC on its axes. The rise of digital provision and consequential demise of the reality of spectrum scarcity, rising competition from an increasing number of alternate media and leisure sources, the decline in audience "share," and increasing importance of audience "reach," have necessitated a repositioning of the BBC as a democratic, responsive, accountable service with "community" at its core. Greg Dyke recognized these shifting trends and the need to connect more closely with communities during his time as Director-General (2000–4), and the concurrent shift in focus to "new" media exemplified a reappraisal of where and how much audience autonomy should be valued. The rise of supposedly interactive technologies and mechanisms for feedback made digital and internet services the natural home for activities which involved more creative relationships with license-payers. "Capture Wales" is an example of one such activity. In 2001, with Charter renewal around the corner, Menna Richards (Controller, BBC Cymru-Wales) gave the go-ahead for a project that would give license-payers new responsibilities and opportunities for participation, but also, reciprocally, "enrich the BBC's services" in a way that was "fresh and exciting, and different from anything else happening in broadcasting" (Richards 2003).

DANIEL:
## The Electric Engagement

The first time I saw a digital story I didn't even know that that was what I was watching … and, very likely, "digital story" is not what its author would have called it. But, without doubt, as I look back on the projects which influenced me, Pedro Meyer's *I Photograph to Remember*, about his parents in old age, *was* a digital story and it was also beautiful.[2] Using digital desktop tools, Pedro had created something entirely new: a disk on which still pictures had discovered the talkies. Although long (over 35 minutes), its emotional impact was considerable and, as an example of a brilliant first-person multimedia narrative made "on the kitchen table," it set the bar very high indeed.

It was on Meyer's ZoneZero website that, in October 1995, I first came across the term "digital storytelling" – in an article about a digital storytelling festival held in Crested Butte, Colorado. Even so, it wasn't until the early summer of 2000 when I discovered the astonishing NextExit website of Dana Winslow Atchley III who, with his wife Denise, had co-founded that Crested Butte festival, that I made the connection which led me to the Center for Digital Storytelling (CDS) in Berkeley, California.

Atchley may not have invented digital storytelling, but his work (for me anyway) defined it absolutely. His compelling two-minute narratives, particularly "Home Movies" and "Redheads," with their brilliantly written and delivered voice tracks, were both innovative and compelling. I learned that at CDS in the mid-1990s – together with Joe Lambert and Nina Mullen – he had begun teaching this form to others in three-day "boot camps."

In Cardiff we were intrigued. Would this kind of scrapbook television have a part to play in the new world of interactive journalism? Could anyone do it? Ian Hargreaves wanted me to find out and, with money raised from the Welsh Development Agency, he encouraged me to go to California to make my own digital story on a CDS boot camp and also to accept Atchley's invitation to address his autumn festival, the proposed "DSF 6," about my photographic work.

Over the previous five years I had been revisiting a set of portraits I had made back in the 1970s on the streets of England from my Free Photographic Omnibus.[3] Assisted by local newspaper journalists, I had traced people all over the country whom I hadn't seen for a quarter of a century and rephotographed them. This work, in part an exploration of the active relationship we have with our personal picture archives, was by now the focus of my PhD, and the photographs (known as National Portraits) were being increasingly published and exhibited. I was also building a website for this work.

To feed this experience back into the classroom I had begun teaching an undergraduate module (devised in 1998), "Digital Storytelling and Photography." Students were required to collaborate with a stranger to tell a story based on that person's own personal archive of pictures. The work was delivered not as what we now think of as a digital story (i.e., a film-like considered narrative), but as published web pages of text and pictures (although, occasionally, the more enterprising students would slip in a clip of video or audio). This work drew some international attention and, in Finland (October 1999) and Italy (April 2000), I delivered workshops in the use of these emerging techniques.

My hope for the digital revolution was that it would enable me to do better what I had always tried to do anyway, that is, look at the world "from the common man's point of view"; one of William Stott's definitions of documentary practice.[4] Indeed it seemed to me – both from reading about the social history of broadcasting and from a lifetime of listening to BBC Radio – that the work on which I was now embarking had a well-established tradition. Broadcasters who wanted their audiences to "hear the voice of the people" in all its vernacular wonder – Olive Shapley in the 1930s, for example, or Charles Parker in the 1950s – had frequently used new technologies to enliven the electric engagement between themselves and those with whom they worked. (Shapley experimented with a seven-ton recording truck; Parker used the EMI Midget tape recorder.) And now here was digital storytelling.

In an email, Atchley expressed his delight at my new Photobus website. What he didn't tell me, though, was that he was seriously ill; so ill in fact that, by the time I arrived in California in November 2000, he had been admitted to an intensive care unit. Lambert and Mullen ran the boot camp without him but his illness cast a shadow and, when we left the Bay area at the end of that week to attend an international "gathering" – a seminar-style event held over three days at Ben Lomond in the Santa Cruz mountains which Lambert had arranged at short notice to make up for the now cancelled DFS 6 – there was much concern.

At Ben Lomond I met several people with whom I would later form friendships, people who were able to articulate many of the ideas around which the digital storytelling "movement" was beginning to gather. People like Derek Powazek of *Fray*: "Authentic media is what happens when the mediators get out of the way and give the mike over to the people who actually have something to say." And Ana Serrano of the Great Canadian Story Engine and Habitat (the Canadian Film Center's media lab): "Digital Storytelling has a lot to do with economic and cultural development … it's about changing the way citizens behave … it's about how art, media, and culture impact on society in our time … it's about the development of a participatory culture." These were ideas I liked, ideas which I reported back to colleagues in Cardiff and to my students.

Ian Hargreaves defined his own version of these ideas in a short digital storytelling bid document which we presented to BBC Wales executives in January 2001. Our project would be "a major piece of social enquiry" that would also "generate highly entertaining material." It would make "an original and sustainable contribution to community self-expression … a new way for the BBC in Wales to connect with communities, not in a top-down corporate manner but through a project which depends for its delivery and success upon action within communities." We were to reach out, give people a voice, build an archive of stories, break new "talent" – and make the whole thing sustainable. Wow.

Back in California, however, on Wednesday, December 13, 2000, Dana Atchley died.

JENNY:

# The Research

Coming from a background in television production with a view to "media for democracy," discovering an opportunity to research a media form that was touted as being "wonderfully democratic" (Lambert n.d.) was intriguing, to say the least. When the PhD scholarship was advertised in 2002 I was working for a London company (dktv – a different kind of television), piloting the use of upcoming interactive technologies in order to provide entertainment, education, council, and housing services through people's television sets. At a time when digital takeup was low and skepticism about audiences' willingness and ability to "interact" was high, we were feeling our way in the unknown. This research project, however, proposed to delve into the world of the "user," exploring their response to and feelings about opportunities for interaction being offered by a known cultural institution. Following a competitive selection process, I took on my first responsibility as researcher, participating in a "Capture Wales" workshop.

It was not until completing this initial workshop in Ammanford in June 2002 that I began to think about how best to research the "Capture Wales" project and its participants. In this way, I was able to experience the emotion, mood, group dynamics, technology, and "Capture Wales" team in the same way as any other participant in the course of the study.

It was decided that data collection would involve participant observation and ethnography, both within the workshop environment and at the BBC Wales offices in Cardiff, administering a questionnaire to workshop participants, interviewing workshop participants and BBC staff, and also carrying out archival research of documentation around the setup of the project and application and feedback forms for all of the storytellers. To the best of my knowledge I was given uncensored access to all of the above. A total of 116 workshop participants articulated their experiences of "Capture Wales" (a significant proportion of all storytellers at the time) through questionnaires and/or interviews. The mixed-method approach to data collection was crucial to any understanding of the lived experience of those working on and taking part in the "Capture Wales" project.

Crucially, at no point in the research has any one person's narrative of the workshop process been valued over and above another or become the standard against which all others are measured. As will be seen later in this chapter, "Capture Wales" means many different things for the tellers whose stories form the lifeblood of the project.

DANIEL:

## From "Boot Camp" to "Workshop"

On Monday, April 2, 2001 Menna Richards launched the BBC Digital Storytelling project at *Platfform*, an international multimedia conference held at Broadcasting House in Llandaff. Before introducing me she told the audience: "We want to look at the way digital technology can enable people in the smallest communities to be digital storytellers … It is a tremendously exciting and ambitious project and a collaboration which is unique in the United Kingdom … Over the next few months we'll be piloting schemes in Wrexham, in Blackwood, and in Cardiff."

I explained the project, and screened Dana Atchley's "Home Movies" and also *Polyfoto*, a new digital story of my own.

We had liftoff.

That summer – between July 17 and 27 – 22 invitees were engaged as boot camp participants during a fortnight of digital storytelling training in mid-Wales, led by Lambert and Mullen from CDS. Participants were chosen for their diversity of interests and skill. There were artists: three musicians, two photographers, three painters, and a performance artist. There were community workers: a local authority arts development officer and two IT tutors. There were BBC employees, some to provide technical support, others because they had editorial and organizational skills: a script editor, a researcher, and two online producers. There was an unemployed teenager from a youth project, and a university professor. Community Action Network (CAN), a charity we hoped might help us to find future workshop participants, was also represented.

Karen Lewis was the project's coordinator and she organized some evening question-and-answer sessions. These were hosted by Mandy Rose, BBC Wales's newly appointed Head of New Media. (As one of the co-founders of the hugely successful Video Nation shorts on BBC2 television in the 1990s, Rose's experience of community broadcasting was invaluable.) We were, of course, all keen to learn as much as we could and Rose, Maggie Russell (Head of Talent), Hargreaves, Adele Blakebrough (national organizer of CAN), Lewis, and I would sit in a back kitchen after dinner and interrogate Lambert and Mullen on their classroom methodology and business practice. They were generous in their responses and everything was minuted. Later, without Lambert and Mullen, this group became formalized into our steering committee.

We had a new lab to break in and, over the months immediately following the boot camp, we learned a lot … mostly that if something could go wrong it would. Here, in no particular order – for that *was* the order – are some of the other things we learned. That the Apple Macs we were using were good for digital storytelling and that the Sony Vaios we were using were not. That cross-platform working doesn't. That networking the machines is time-consuming and, ultimately, unnecessary. That everyone in a team of facilitators needs to be on top of all the jobs, including the technological jobs (one moment you'll be driving the van, the next moment you'll be showing someone how to activate an alpha channel with the motion tool in Adobe Premiere). That only facilitators who have made at least one digital story unaided should be allowed anywhere near a workshop participant's computer. That participants could, by turns, be generous, kind, bad-tempered, cantankerous, selfish, caring, obstreperous, willful, outrageous, brilliant, rude, late, inventive, funny, careless, incompetent, inspiring … but they were never, ever wrong and that, as facilitators, our principal task was to see that they all had a great time (in fact, it was only when we eventually realized that the best way to deliver the workshops was as an entertainment that everyone really began to enjoy themselves). That the boot-camp approach was not a good one because it set up counterproductive competition between participants (there were no more "boot camps" after that, only "workshops"). That three days per workshop was simply not enough time in which to produce stories of broadcast standard (our workshop model quickly changed from a three-day into a five-day experience). That it was absolutely vital that everyone finished their story. That without a story there was certainly no digital story, which meant that at least two days of the participants' workshop time needed to be allocated to script development. That participants tired quickly when asked to do repetitive processes like scanning and sizing images (so, gradually, that job became one for the facilitators to do outside of workshop time). That the digital storytelling form was like a sonnet or a haiku and should be adhered to strictly (you can do a lot in two minutes in the first person with 250 words and a dozen pictures). That we had to trust the digital storytelling form to contain the story but that the process by which we helped the storytellers should never reduce it to a mere format or, worse, a formula. That music can be iffy because of the many interpretations listeners bring to it (my favorite tune is probably your least favorite tune). That copyright law exists to drive us mad but that it must be observed to the letter. That the inclusion of video – except for clips from home movies (something which surprisingly few people had) – nearly always threatens a story's scrapbook aesthetic, rendering an otherwise good digital story as bad television. That you have to work very hard to get the best quality voice-over recordings. That there are Welsh-language workshops and there are English-language workshops, but bilingual workshops were more than we could manage. That none of us understood the terms of the contract our legal department wanted participants to sign (Lewis immediately embarked on a process of whittling it down to a single page written in plain English – a brilliant feat, which took her almost a year). That workshop leaders (I was on my own in this category for the first two years) needed to teach from their own training film and not from one made by someone else. That we would have to output seven different versions of every story in order to accommodate all the possible ways in which the BBC might screen them – dv, .mov, .rm, .wav, mini-dv (and/or DV-8), CD and VHS (or later DVD), and digibeta – and that this would mean assigning post-production as a big part of someone's job. That we needed to collate all our tutorial notes between one set of covers, a manual; something that we knew would be out of date as soon as it was done. (Even so, the *Digital Storytelling, How We Do It* manual I finally completed in the autumn of 2002 was, bar none, the single most useful source of reference we had.)

All this we learned and much more. We also learned that we couldn't do without Gilly Adams. Adams came to us from the BBC Writers' Unit. She had had a long history of working in the community, producing plays and developing scripts for radio. She had joined the BBC only comparatively recently and after a long spell as artistic director of the Made in Wales Stage Company. Now she was to run our story circle sessions. She had for some time also been Chair of Welfare State International, the legendary "engineers of the imagination" who, since the 1960s, had done so much to inspire arts workers everywhere. (I had worked as a photographer for them in the north of England over a number of years. Indeed it still tickles me that, when I visited CDS in the autumn of 2000, the first book I saw in the classroom there was the Welfare State International handbook. Who said this wasn't a movement?) As the pilot stage drew to a close, Lewis busied herself with setting up the project's rollout: its systems, its workflow, its budgets, and the recruitment of a team. In between fitting in my university teaching I worried away at the impossibilities of the technology.

As 2001 turned into 2002, with two pilot workshops under our belt, Lewis and Rose completed the extensive documentation required for our funding pitch to BBC Nations and Regions. We kidded ourselves that we were ready to roll ... and waited. On Friday, January 18, 2002 the BBC Director-General, Greg Dyke, visited Cardiff and we screened some of our digital stories for him. He loved them and, within a month, we had the go-ahead. For the first time in the history of broadcasting, a mainstream player was putting the tools of both production and editing into the hands of the audience. It was a landmark moment and we savored it. And our project was given a name: "Capture Wales."

Our team of full-timers and part-timers – 12 in all – lined up as follows: Mandy Rose, executive producer; Karen Lewis, project producer; Daniel Meadows, creative director; Gilly Adams, script facilitator. Gareth Morlais, our bilingual web producer (and veteran of the boot camp) doubled up as a trainer (in 2005 he would take over Lewis's producer role). Huw Davies, a community artist who had been a participant on our pilot workshop in Blackwood, shadowed me as workshop leader, post-production expert, and minder of the equipment (roles which he, in due course, made entirely his own). He also made us laugh ... a lot. There were two researchers, Lisa Heledd and Carwyn Evans, both of them Welsh speakers. Their principal job was to recruit participants and set up the workshop venues but, of course, they were also workshop trainers – and very good ones too, in fact, the best. (Initially Jody Abramson had done this job but, when she returned to her native USA in 2004, we restructured.) Heledd was a recent graduate from Cardiff University where she had taken my digital storytelling module. Evans had arrived at the BBC as a trainee and, like Heledd, learned quickly. In no time, these two were at the heart of everything. And they were brilliant. The project coordinator who perused all the stories with a fresh pair of eyes after each workshop looking for infringements of copyright and compliance (she had a law degree) and who also devised the schedules, booked the accommodation, the hire cars, and the catering, and did much of the secretarial work, was Lisa Jones. In 2004 Melanie Lindsell joined the team with the principal task of liaising with commissioning editors and program producers to get our stuff screened on TV and aired on radio. Dafydd Llewelyn, a Welsh-speaking script editor, would also join us from time to time to work on script facilitation when workshops were delivered in the Welsh language. One final team member was Simon Turner, a musician and audio wizard. Turner had made himself indispensable during the boot camp and we contracted him to attend the workshops, sit with participants, and (when they wanted it) compose music for their stories, something he did with amazing commitment and ingenuity. We also put him in charge of all the voice-over audio recording sessions.

Every month we took out our van with its portable computer lab and, over five days in a location somewhere in Wales, we showed ten participants how to make digital stories, facilitating everyone's progress as they wrote scripts, created images, recorded their voices, and edited their stories on our Apple PowerBook computers. Our venues were language centers, hotel conference rooms, IT units, village halls, centers for the physically disabled, miners' institutes and libraries, arts centers, colleges, schools, leisure complexes … community centers of all kinds. For training-the-trainers sessions we used our Llandaff digilab.

Our remit was to reach parts of the community normally outside the reach of television and to represent as broad a cross-section of people as possible, including those who had never before used computers (which, in 2001, was a lot). For two weeks in advance of each workshop, our researchers would knock on doors, phone-bash and generally do what they could to summon as many people as possible to a presentation evening where the thing would be explained. Over the years we had as few as ten people turn up for this event and as many as ninety. Even so, recruitment was always a struggle. People had to take time off work, find babysitters, commit time.

Two weeks after the presentation evening we held the "gathering," when the ten participants could get to know each other. We would screen and deconstruct some stories and explain the various stages of the process. We explained the rules of copyright ("don't use other people's stuff unless you absolutely have to and then only with their express permission"), and we played a storytelling game or two to get everyone in the mood.

A week later came the "story circle." In the mornings we would play games – word, picture, and memory games: the love/hate game, the favorite toy game, the pick-a-picture-and-tell-us-what's-going-on-in-it game, the match game – where you had only the time it takes to burn a match to say your piece. These games (smoke detectors permitting) changed and developed as time went on, as we discovered how participants reacted to them and as team members became more confident and inventive. The process was designed to support participants, to put them at ease, to show them that, although they might be nervous and uncertain, it was still possible – by working together in a structured way – to enjoy the business of agonizing over a script.

In the early days Adams took charge of the story circle but in time everyone took their turn. Story facilitators have to work hard at listening, trying to hear what participants sound like; how they speak when they aren't being formal; their use of language; their relative abilities when speaking and telling, reading, and writing (statistically, in the UK one in five adults experiences a "literacy skills deficiency"). Facilitators also need to be keen observers of the group dynamic, to see if anyone is becoming uncomfortable or getting upset, for (unlike the American model) it was never an objective of "Capture Wales" to provide therapy. In fact we were always keen to point out that this process is *not* a "safe" one, for the stories told were destined for publication, to be shared with strangers.

Ultimately what makes a digital story compelling – as Adams would constantly remind us – is the storyteller's handling of specifics. The many games

**Figure 5.1** "*Capture Wales*" story circle: match game, Rhayader. *Photo courtesy BBC Cymru-Wales*

**Figure 5.2** "Capture Wales" story circle: story-in-a-picture game, Butetown, Cardiff. *Photo courtesy BBC Cymru-Wales*

we devised functioned principally to get people to bring their experiences freshly to life; for the essence of a story is always that it needs to be clear, with the order in which its significant stages are revealed being carefully considered. And – although it is never anyone's business to suggest story ideas or put words into another's mouth – it is vital that participants should be encouraged to be ambitious for their stories, to do them as well as they possibly can, better even than they themselves could imagine.

The afternoon of the story circle was spent listening to story ideas – one at a time.

The story day was followed immediately by a day of image capture, when each participant could attend for as long as it took to get their pictures scanned into the computer and/or some movie captured. While waiting for a scanner or a picture-editing session, they might also try out their script ideas on one of the facilitators (there were always at least four facilitators present on image-capture day).

Then followed a period of five days during which, with the facilitators back in Cardiff, the participants could work on their own to perfect their scripts. During this time they were encouraged to email or telephone members of the team to discuss the various draft stages. Then, finally, we would all reconvene for the intense three-day production workshop. In the morning of day one the participants all read their scripts and tweaked them into a final version. After lunch (we always arranged catering) we did a Photoshop tutorial and then voice-over recording commenced. Day two was all about learning Adobe Premiere and the aim was to have everyone complete a rough-cut. This meant that voice-over recording would have to be completed by lunchtime. On the final day everyone learned fancy things with Premiere: zooms, pans, transitions, and the like. Production would finish by mid-afternoon, anyway, early enough to allow the team to output the stories to tape (or later, DVD) and prepare for a screening.

At 4 p.m. the films would be screened. And, without doubt, the screening was always the best part. Mums, dads, cousins and aunties, friends and neighbors, all would attend. Refreshments were served.

JENNY:

# On the Road with "Capture Wales"

While it was important in the research to understand something of the workshop process through observations and as recorded in field notes, the

**Figure 5.3**     "Capture Wales" production tutorial: the eye of Daniel, Harlech. *Photo courtesy BBC Cymru-Wales*

real story of the project should be told by the participants. In a bid to give voice to those experiences, all workshop participants were given a means for feedback both to the BBC (through feedback forms) and, possibly more impartially, in contributions to the research project. Participants were asked to reflect on their experiences of the workshop as much as three years after the event, and the response rate of 71 percent attests to their willingness to talk about associated memories, experiences, and feelings. This was highlighted in the letters, cards, and notes that I received alongside completed questionnaires.

I was interested in learning more about participants' experiences and how they chose to articulate them, especially in relation to the group dynamic, the technology, the BBC, and their ongoing relationship with all three. I had not anticipated I would learn so much about what it meant personally for people to be involved in this kind of creative endeavor, and was surprised by the number of people who professed to have found the experience of therapeutic value and to have renegotiated their notions of "self" as a result. As Daniel has outlined, this was not an intended phenomenon; at the same time, it was a completely unavoidable outcome.

Before articulating something of those narratives, it is crucial to note the diversity of people involved in the "Capture Wales" project as participants. This undoubtedly impacts not only upon the range of stories told, but often on people's motivations for being involved in the first instance and for choosing to tell their particular story.

Issues of representation and "cultural diversity" are of concern in any public service media provision. In Wales, stereotypes and under-representation have problematized traditional output (Osmond 1995, Cameron 1999) but, as Diane Davies says – and I would add, especially in light of the affordances of new technologies – this must undergo change: "there is no future in imagining an artificial Wales, but only in engagement with the real nation in all its diversity" (Davies 1999: 25). A demographic analysis of the first 191 workshop participants reveals "cultural diversity" in evidence. Participants are more or less 50 percent male and female, and from mixed age ranges. They are more likely to be from South Wales than North or Mid-Wales, but this is in keeping with the overall population bias. Notably, significantly higher proportions of ethnic minorities take part in workshops than make up the total population of Wales, although 87 percent of participants are white British (73 percent white Welsh, 14 percent born elsewhere in the UK). There are also a higher than representative number of stories made in the Welsh language. Thus, we see a number of active biases in place in order to represent previously "voiceless" segments of the population.

What follows is a brief discussion of some key findings from the research, and the issues they raise for wider debates about media.

### The workshop dynamic

By the end of workshops, an almost tangible connection between group members has been facilitated through the process' various constituent parts. In questionnaire and interview responses, participants attest to this connection, articulating it in a number of ways, a selection of which appear below:

"The group workshops were for me one of the best and most valuable experiences of making my story."
"The participants were social like bees in hives."

"A good mix of strange folk telling urgent things to one another."
"You have all this empathy with people that last week you did not know or care for, you really felt something … I don't want to dramatize it too much, but it is a really good feeling."
"Great atmosphere, felt part of a team. The first time I have felt like that really."

The group "get on well" (52 respondents), "bonded" (18), were "friends" (12), "supportive" (11), and constituted a "team" (10), even a "beeb family." For some, these relationships intensify beyond the workshop walls and prove in themselves to be productive and joyous long-term outcomes of the process.

Positivity is also evident in language describing the "Capture Wales" team, who are "helpful" (47 respondents), "friendly" (38), "excellent" (16), "professional" (13), and "supportive" (12). The team's contribution is seen as simultaneously easygoing and enthusiastic, but also as fulfilling a compassionate role. Phrases such as "shoulder to cry on," "sympathetic," and "listening" hint at the therapeutic nature of the workshop for some, and the flexibility required in team members' responses to individual needs and anxieties.

Perhaps crucially for the BBC, it is evident in the majority of responses that opinions of and feelings toward the Corporation have been positively impacted upon. This has much to do with that particular group of BBC representatives outlined previously: "The BBC Wales team was an interesting lot – they are clever people who have the cleverness to appear ordinary, so that after a short period of time no one was in any way in awe of the 'Great BBC Entities.'" We all became part of a team.

There is a sense among respondents that this indicates something of a shift; that for too long there has been a gulf between a faceless "BBC" and an amorphous "public" that is only now being subject to scrutiny. As such, the kind of dialogue engendered through "Capture Wales" workshops is seen as long overdue and potentially barrier-breaking.

## The story

Respondents testify to telling their particular stories for a variety of reasons. Frequently, storytellers are passing on a message born of experience, self-medicating, commemorating a life, celebrating a passion (human or otherwise), describing childhood events, or reciting family or local histories. These motivations perhaps reflect the emphasis on photographic elements and thus often a sense of "the past."

The content of the stories gives yet more away about the participants: their tone, theme, length, and pacing give the viewer (and researcher) insight into storytellers' motivations and priorities. Common themes include family and memory, journeys (literal and metaphorical) and "overcoming," history, and childhood. Given the opportunity to tell one story (and only one), "self-defining memories" take precedence (Singer and Blagor 2004: 118).[5]

After the workshop, 76 percent of respondents got some ongoing use-value out of their stories (where use-value is crudely measured as viewing/display):

> I show the film at every opportunity.
> Yes, to groups I teach to show them what technology is capable of.
> To a few. Others contacted me after seeing it on the Web. A long-lost friend contacted me from the USA.
> Relatives, friends, anyone else I could rope securely to a chair for long enough.

Others however, have not "aired" their story for a whole complex of reasons, again relating to personal motivation, and even self-image:

> I have enough criticism from "brainless """heads" without a double dose from what I created.
> No, more keen on using skills.
> I have not showed the film to many people because it is not a subject I care to dwell on.
> Do not show, but proud.

Interestingly, those people who do not desire "others" to see their story do not equate this wish with their ready availability on the Web. The story is seen as an intimate and personal expression or achievement, and the "global stage" enabled by its Web presence does not appear to frustrate this perception. It is not recognized that any Web audience could potentially consist of those people who exist within the locality of the storyteller's everyday "non-virtual" life.

In discussion with participants after the workshop, it became clear that their ongoing relationship with their story, the form, and the technology was sometimes complicated by their own, and others', perception of this kind of "memory work." Watching the piece was an act of self-indulgence, or something to do on occasion when the individual needed self-affirmation:

> Life has been rather difficult/hectic/problematic during the last six months or so and the inclination to indulge myself wasn't there. Things are OK now so I may drag it out.

> [W]henever I am feeling useless or something I'll think "Oh yeah, I did that, and that was all right" ... I use it in that way. When I think that I am lacking anything.

Rather than being an act of "responsibility" (McAdams 1993), society teaches us that the creation of self-narrative is a narcissistic mission foregrounding a concern with the "self" over and above "community." Older people in particular have often been discouraged to talk openly in this way (Kamler 2001).

This led some participants to understate their achievement, or indicate embarrassment by it, even though their overall experience remained very positive. As we see increased use of participatory media forms and interest in "real life," however, it is entirely possible that we will see a shift in people's perceptions of and comfort with personal narratives, and an increasing sense of "legitimacy" attached to them.

### *The technology*

Looking at participants' responses in relation to the technology and its use is integral to any discussion of media democracy and possibility for change. Both skills growth and comfort with the technology have been assessed as a part of the research project. In BBC feedback forms, 91 percent of respondents professed to have gained IT skills through their participation in the "Capture Wales" workshop, but when followed up by the researcher, it appears the situation is more complex than this perhaps indicates.

Here is a sample of responses relating to the technology – some positive, and some negative:

> The opportunity to use the BBC's technology was what attracted me to the project.
> I jumped into the pool and it wasn't deep at all.
> [F]ascinating and straightforward.
> My first introduction to technology. Fantastic. Thanks to them I have

since had the confidence to do more.
Fine, but I got obsessed.
I think I am literate but I found it overwhelming and stressful.
My weak area.
Thank God for the team!
Struggled with most of it – previous experience in the 1970s.
I was nervous of messing things up, not getting it right ... They ... allowed my son to come in and help me.

There was a great deal of overlap in responses, indicating that some found navigating the technical aspects both challenging and rewarding. Tellingly, only 51 percent had experimented with the technology in some form since their workshop. Those who had not cited costs, limited time, and problems of access as factors inhibiting their ability to do so; others fully intended to in the future, but had not done so to date:

No, unfortunately; do you know how much it costs?
No equipment, but would love it.
Sadly no, acquired the software but need a more reliable computer; as soon as that is dealt with, I will have a few more tales off my chest.
No, I'm not computer-minded.
No time or need. As time goes on, I am less confident.

Surprisingly perhaps, many of those who do continue to use the technology are older respondents who had struggled with it in the first instance.

The extent to which respondents are using the technology, however, is hugely varied:

I enjoy trying to reproduce the experience on my own home computer using the down-to-earth notes of Daniel Meadows.
I can now turn on our PC and am able to use it.
Myself and one other formed a company film/TV/video production with a humanitarian perspective as a result of meeting each other.
Used Photoshop and going to get Premiere – and will use it!
A little, I have an iMac but no expensive software.

Only a handful of respondents to the research had gone on to make more stories or teach others the technique:

I've been building my skills (and my own workshops) ever since. Their help has enabled me to establish digital workshops … which has meant people in the Wrexham area who have missed the BBC workshop have been given the chance.

This number is growing, as Daniel will outline later. However, it must be noted that workshop participants do not constitute a nation of digital storytellers at the current time. For many, this is simply not a viable or even attractive option, since (as the following section outlines) the workshop has often fulfilled other, not insignificant, individual needs.

## The self

Of the respondents to the research project, 79 percent felt that the workshop had had, or would continue to have, a lasting impact upon them. This "lasting effect" was expressed in a variety of ways.

For some, resultant changes in working lives were directly credited to the workshop process:

It has progressed my work/career.
[I]t has brought me closer to my community and inspired more work.
Without a doubt it has changed my life. I went out and got a grant, set up my own project.
Yes, I work on the project as a result of the workshop. Get more lasting than that!

A number of respondents felt that the experience had in some way impacted upon their sense of self or resulted in attitudinal change:

It allowed me to be proud of myself and who I am.
I learnt a lot about myself and the BBC.
I found I had something to offer despite my disability.
It was uncomfortable initially to be so open about yourself … but it was an incredibly beneficial, self-developing experience.

Even one respondent who regretted having changed the subject of her story over the course of the workshop had learnt something about herself: "I thought I would have been stronger and would have stuck to my story the way I wanted to have it made."

Some also highlighted the therapeutic nature of the workshop as having lasting influence:

> Telling my story felt as though I had lifted a heavy burden from my back. The slate was clean and I could move on. That period of my life now had a line drawn under it.
> Telling and making the story was a kind of a catharsis.
> Personally I gained a lot emotionally from my experience because of the story I told. It was therapeutic for me and my family.
> In a way I won't go into detail over, it has helped to lay a personal ghost.

This complex and hard-to-measure outcome is a natural byproduct of any creative endeavor whereby people are encouraged to think about events in their lives in such a way (Kamler 2001, Dwelly 2001, Crossley 2003, Lambert 2002, 2004), but is notable for its prominence as an outcome (articulated by 31 respondents). Narrative psychologists see great benefit in ordering events and expressing feelings through a coherent "story" in order to achieve personal peace and unity. It appears that given time and a chance to engage with their own archives and "histories," the desire to tell a story that will reflect or engage with that history takes prominence. This is perhaps no surprise, given that workshop participants are, for the most part, making a one-off intervention into the media, the technology, or even their own (mental or physical) archives.

Thus, engagement with a digital storytelling workshop in the "Capture Wales" model is an intricate and ongoing personal negotiation of relationships within and between various communities, the technology, the BBC, the self, and the personal archive. No two narratives of the workshop process I have encountered have even approached concordance, the threads leading in so many different directions that establishing the potential for democracy could become an exercise in creative thinking.

DANIEL:

## Spreading the Word

The only promise we made to our participants regarding publication of their work was that we would post their stories on the BBC website. The "Capture Wales" site launched on Friday, May 2, 2002.

Working out of the New Media department, we had no remit to reach a television audience. However, we were determined that digital stories would appear on TV and eventually it happened, the first one being broadcast on at 9.15 P.M. on Tuesday, November 5, 2002. It was number one in a series of 20 topped, tailed, and contextualized stories shown in their own commissioned, mid-evening, five-minute slot on the new Welsh digital television channel BBC2W. As time went by, the number of stories broadcast as well as the number of broadcast opportunities for them increased so that, by the calendar year 2006 (the most recent full year for which figures are available), 45 were shown on BBC2W, 1 on BBC2 (Wales), 40 on the Community Channel, 26 on BBC Radio Wales, and 273 on BBCi (on the digi-satellite interactive service *Your Stories*). The total airtime for digital stories in 2006 was approximately 23 hours – slightly more than one story per day.

The project also won a number of important awards, including a BAFTA Cymru in 2002.

Our work expanded. We recruited and trained two digital storytelling teams in BBC English Regions – one in Hull (Yorkshire) and the other in Blackburn (Lancashire). (This project, Telling Lives – which Rose and I mentored for its first six months – ran for two years until March 2005.) We ran (and I led) a dozen or more training-the-trainer workshops, each one for between six and ten participants. We ran a seminar for educators and Lewis was permanently on the case with officials from the basic skills, examinations, and curriculum agencies, government departments, quangos, local authorities, the Arts Council – every organization she might hope to engage to help make digital storytelling catch fire as a community activity.

The list of those with whom we eventually collaborated to make this project sustainable – supplying training support, teaching materials, and advice on funding – is a long one. We worked with staff and students in the further education sector at Yale College in Wrexham (where their project won a Beacon Award in 2004) and also at Coleg Sir Gâr in Llanelli. We worked with the youth ICT project CREDU – hosted by Canllaw Online and supported by Fujitsu – which has over 100 digilabs scattered across Wales, a lot of them in YMCAs. We worked with the Scarman Trust, Aberystwyth Arts Centre, the eCommunities initiative of the Welsh Development Agency (WDA), and the Welsh Assembly Government's social inclusion project Communities@One. We worked with local authority arts development units like the one in Monmouthshire, and also in the Miners' Institute at Blackwood, where the hugely innovative Breaking Barriers digital storytelling project run by Caerphilly County Borough Council soon set a standard for others to follow.

In 2006 Kate Strudwick of Breaking Barriers – a veteran of our 2001 boot camp – became Chair of a newly formed organization, DS Cymru, the association for digital storytellers in Wales which, that year, raised funds for and organized DS1, Wales's first Digital Storytelling Festival which was held at Aberystwyth Arts Centre.

As DS1 approached, we counted up the number of digital stories which had been made in Wales since the project began. The total was more than 1,000 but, to our delight, it was clear that only about half of these had been made by those on BBC workshops. The remainder, though produced on projects instigated as a result of the "Capture Wales" initiative, had been made by community groups working on their own.

The baton was passing.

JENNY:

# Reflective Conclusions

In terms of representation, we have seen that something new is exemplified by "Capture Wales." Indeed, those voices being heard through the project leave a more varied and "real" archive than exists elsewhere in the media. However, it must be remembered that representations, whether constructed by the "mass" media or "ordinary" people are just that: constructions. They are also, by the nature of the project, the voices of those people who wish to step forward and talk about their experiences. As Valerie Yow says of the practice of recording oral history, "it is the articulate who come forward to be participants" (Yow 1994: 7). In the case of "Capture Wales," they volunteer not only a story and their voice, but their time, energy, and commitment to the project. This presupposes a level of interest in artistic endeavor, "new media," "community," and/or the BBC as "Corporation." We must be careful before asserting it that more voices being heard within the media will naturally lead to a more democratic system of representation for all.

As outlined previously, the coming of new Internet and multimedia technologies was heralded as the dawn of a more democratic media system where the public would become "empowered." To assert that a public is empowered (in terms of media) is to assume not only that they have access to the means of making and distributing media, but that they are actively engaged in seeking that empowerment (not just using those avenues opened up to them). As Hamelink asserts: "Human rights imply both entitlements and responsibilities … empowerment cannot be passively enjoyed, but has to be actively achieved and guarded" (Hamelink 1995: 12) This does not seem to be the case for the majority of people who take part in "Capture Wales" workshops, whose interventions remain one-off and whose experience of "interactivity" cannot be re-created elsewhere in "the media."

Although we might imagine interactive texts/projects to offer increased opportunity to assert control and creative influence over media output, for the most part, "interactive" possibility currently operates within boundaries that are set and maintained by an authority. In this respect, the creative opportunity on offer is pre-scripted and necessarily limited. According to Hockley, "Interactivity is actually about power. It is about persuading users that they are powerful when in fact they are powerless" (Hockley 1996: 10). Interactivity as we currently know it relies on "users," not "creators," of authored environments (Murray 1999: 152). In this respect we have moved forward very little from Raymond Williams's view of interactivity as mere "reactivity," voiced in 1974: "Nearly all equipment that is being currently developed is reactive; the range of choices, both in detail and in scope, is pre-set" (Williams 1974: 139).

"Capture Wales" perhaps hints at a more genuinely interactive proposition. For the lifespan of the workshop at least, members of the public, story creators, are in genuine open dialogue with those who exist at the sharp end of the BBC's digital storytelling initiative. And the BBC also gains from the interaction; the acquisition of content, the creation of a living archive, and the intangible profit that is the connection with participants. A positive, respectful exchange is occurring benefiting both the public (or those members of the public who are chosen to take part) and the BBC. Knowledge exchange is thus two-way, and perhaps indicative of changing trends within (multi)media that position "users" or "consumers" in a much more inspiring and creative role. For the moment though, as we have seen, storytellers do not go on to have wholly redefined relationships with the Corporation, or with "the media" at large.

DANIEL:

# Video Postcards

As Jenny has pointed out, the big ideas of the digital age currently changing our mediascape assert that mass media are becoming (1) a conversation, (2) democratized, and (3) interactive. The promise for those of us formerly known as the audience is that we will be recast as the viewer/producers of a new participatory culture.

Nothing would please me more than to see Wales become a nation of digital storytellers, but the BBC model provides only one new media form of the participatory culture. The challenge for the future is to have many more forms for people to use – video postcards, if you like – forms which are less difficult to master. Outside of the monthly workshops, the "Capture Wales" team has never stopped experimenting with new approaches: the one-day "taster" session; the audio-only option; Davies's Shoebox Stories; Heledd's and Evans's audio slideshow project In the Frame; the three-day option; the iMovie option; the four-day option. Unless this restless search for new forms continues, the transformation of our mediascape into one where we can all assume the viewer/producer role will happen only slowly. Too slowly.

Just now, the three big obstacles are:

1.   Too many media workers behave as though their professional status gives them the right to be gatekeepers of the airwaves.

2.   Most of the digital tools available to citizen producers (PCs, video, and still cameras, mobile devices of all kinds) are difficult to learn, unevenly distributed, always in need of updating, and horribly expensive.

3.   Big media facilitators deny the lessons of our "Capture Wales" experience and continue to assume that giving people the tools to make their own media means giving them kit: computers, gizmos, gadgets. OK, well sometimes it does. But mostly the tools that people need are the tools of empowerment – confidence, self-belief, and assistance with scriptwriting and skill acquisition – and these are things you can only learn by attending a workshop of some kind. You cannot expect people to join the conversation if you won't teach them the language.

"Capture Wales," in its seven short years, has generated interest far and wide, as I know only too well, for – by invitation – I have made five trips to America and four to Australia explaining the project, delivering lectures, giving presentations, and leading workshops. I have also attended a great many UK and international conferences and seminars. In November 2003 we hosted our own international conference at BBC Wales in Llandaff sponsored by the WDA (Jenny played an important role in organizing this). It was a huge gathering of the participatory media clans. The Chair at that conference was Professor Ian Hargreaves from the School of Journalism, Media and Cultural Studies at Cardiff University – which was of course where, for me, this long journey began … and the place to which, in the spring of 2006, I returned to pick up the loose ends of my career as an academic.

## Notes

1　BBC Cymru Wales Digital Storytelling at www.bbc.co.uk/wales/audiovideo/ sites/galleries/pages/digitalstorytelling.shtml

2　*I Photograph To Remember*: the "world's first commercial CD-ROM with sound and images," published by Voyager, New York, in 1991.

3　See www.photobus.co.uk

4　W. Stott, *Documentary Expression and Thirties America*, Chicago: University of Chicago Press, 1973, p. 49.

5　Characteristics of self-defining memories make them vivid, affectively intense (even at the point of recollection), and repetitively recalled as reference points. They often present unresolved conflicts or enduring concerns (Singer and Blagor 2004).

# 6

# Digital Storytelling at the Australian Centre for the Moving Image

## *Helen Simondson*

Frida Kahlo once said, "I paint self-portraits because … I am the person I know best" (see Cruz 1996). Kahlo's statement reinforces the notion that we each have unique, powerful, and evocative stories that only we have the power to tell. This is the central premise of the digital storytelling program at the Australian Centre for the Moving Image (ACMI). We have assisted hundreds of people to tell their own stories using the powerful mediums of their own voices and the rich archives of personal images that memorialize their lives.

ACMI's journey with digital storytelling represents a significant period in the organization's history and, more broadly, in the history of digital storytelling in Australia. Consequently, understanding ACMI's origins is one way of understanding digital storytelling's development in the country. Originally the Victorian State Film Centre, which was established in 1946, the (then) VSFC's broad aims were to maintain a collection of documentary and educational films for public consumption. Over the following decades, there were numerous developments: by the 1970s, the VSFC exhibited noncommercial films and collected student films and independent work; by the 1980s, the VSFC had established a major education program, which provided a valuable interface between the VSFC and the secondary school curriculum and represents a key precedent for our current digital storytelling program. Perhaps the key change, however, occurred in July 1997 when work began on designing Australia's most ambitious civic, cultural, and commercial precinct at Federation Square in the heart of Melbourne, Victoria. The VSFC had begun its transformation into a new cultural institution: the Australian Centre for the Moving Image, opened in 2002.

When ACMI opened there was little or no precedent for a cultural institution dedicated to the moving image in all its forms. Yet, in an age where the development of digital technologies had significantly shifted the way people related to and consumed media, it was critical for an organization to recognize this shift and implement an institutional space that would allow people to directly interact with increasingly innovative moving image content. Part of this shift has been in changing our own relationship to the public; instead of perceiving of them as passive receivers, ACMI views its public as creative partners in the production of moving images. And digital storytelling is one of ACMI's key programs in its active engagement with individuals and communities as creative partners.

I joined ACMI when the building was under construction; at that time, the programs we were devising were also informing the internal spaces of the new building in a way that was intended to innovatively connect the production, exhibition, and collection of the moving image. We wanted to build on the strong education program of the VSFC, and digital storytelling was one of the ways we decided to do that. In 1998 I became aware of the Center for Digital Storytelling (CDS) in Berkeley, California. The CDS's work had a strong resonance with what we were already developing for ACMI, so we invited Joe Lambert and Nina Mullen to share their methodology with our team, including the now standard model of delivery: the three-day training workshop. We have spent the years since then revising that model of delivery to refine its translation to ACMI, as both a cultural institution and an Australian media organization.

Of course, revising that model of delivery was far from our only challenge. Pioneering a user-generated content program in a cultural institution required considerable thought and planning and we faced a range of initial and ongoing obstacles. It was immediately clear, for example, that no other cultural institution at the time had embarked on a program of a similar scale, which spanned production, exhibition, and the long-term collection of user-generated media. In order to exhibit these works in a public institution, we recognized that ACMI had obligations and responsibilities to the storytellers and to the broader public. ACMI was in uncharted territory, so we looked to other leading international programs to see how they managed the exhibition and collection of digital stories. At the time, the CDS did not publicly exhibit or collect the stories it produced, while the BBC's "Capture Wales" program had the significant (and unique) support of its broadcaster to exhibit its stories. ACMI, however, hoped to collect and exhibit digital stories on both our website and in the Memory Grid, an onsite interactive exhibition space I describe later. To do that, our first challenges involved negotiating image copyright, music licensing, digital story licensing, and classification guidelines.

While many digital storytellers draw on their own personal archives, we make not only our production facilities but also our stock image library available to our digital storytellers so that they can augment their digital stories with these images. However, while facilitating basic image copyright clearance was easily managed, music licensing was more complex. We worked closely with APPRA and AMCOS, the Australian music copyright and licensing bodies, to identify the context and scope of this style of media production in a non-broadcast environment. Where standard broadcast or theatrical licensing fees would have been prohibitive, ACMI actively negotiated a blanket license fee for the ongoing exhibition and collection of community-made digital stories. Licensing of the digital stories themselves also needed to be carefully negotiated. In the traditional media environment, content producers ask copyright holders to assign copyright to the producer or distributor. As an agency that also collects user-generated content, however, ACMI has to manage the cultural sensitivities, moral rights, and ownership issues that are inherent in user-generated media. At ACMI, the copyright of digital stories stays with the storyteller and ACMI seeks an ongoing license to exhibit and collect the work. We also manage the partners and community groups involved in projects on behalf of the storytellers. And if a storyteller no longer wishes ACMI or the sub-license organizations to have access to their content, then ACMI is responsible to ensure that all parties relinquish their screening and collection rights. This licensing arrangement is clearly a complex one, but it honors the personal nature of the content and allows the individual to have ongoing control over their story.

As a cultural institution we are also required to adhere to classification guidelines: impartiality, fairness, privacy, truth, and decency are crucial. It would be impossible to submit every digital story produced at ACMI to the Office of Film and Literature Classification (OFLC) for formal clearance to exhibit the work. Nevertheless, classification is a necessity for the work exhibited in a public building where people are able to wander in and view this content as part of an on-demand exhibition system. ACMI did not have a self-classification status, which is usually the domain of the broadcasters, so we embarked on the long and rigorous process with the OFLC to apply for this status. Our status will be ratified in federal parliament in the near future, which will make us the first cultural institution in Australia with a self-classification status. In effect, this status means that trained staff at ACMI will ensure that our content complies with all classification require-ments, as part of the production, exhibition, and collection process of – among other moving image content produced at ACMI – digital stories. This status will make ACMI an important precedent for other Australian cultural institutions.

Understanding digital storytelling in a context beyond more traditional mainstream media formats was also critical when it came to developing a space to exhibit this kind of "less expert" media. The Memory Grid is ACMI's interactive exhibition space, which functions as a repository for these kinds of moving image memories, encouraging people to view these works sympathetically. It contextualizes and preserves the diverse stories produced by the public and, in so doing, gives ownership to the public of the stories they produce. However, sometimes criticism is leveled at digital storytelling, particularly with our support of people with little or no media background to produce autobiographical content. While this is one of the cornerstones of the digital storytelling movement, it has been a challenge to encourage some members of the wider audience to accept user-generated content as having a legitimate place in a cultural institution. The use of sentimentality, the subjectivity of content, and the confessional style of many digital stories are criticized, as are stories which might be viewed as nostalgic or otherwise unsophisticated. However, it is precisely the rawness of digital storytelling that can be surprisingly powerful (see Figures 6.1 and 6.2).

And curatorial decisions are still made: there is a high expectation for quality screening material, so decisions of inclusion and exclusion are made at ACMI every day. We carefully manage the balance between process and product in the production workshops and, in our experience, we have found that it is the screen literacy and facilitation role of digital storytelling trainers that is key to assisting people to produce the best story they can. The ACMI public programs team are experienced media makers and edu-cators who support an extraordinarily diverse range of people to create their own story. Thus, it is significant that digital storytelling and other user-generated content seem to have found their audience at ACMI. Thousands of people a month view the Memory Grid, and many more view digital stories online. Many of the other media forms that are produced and exhibited at ACMI are invariably more professionally produced, more interactive, more structurally sophisticated and innovative, but we have no doubt that our digital storytelling program deserves its flagship status within the organization. It is an award-winning program that continues

**Figure 6.1** *GP Express 01*, from ACMI's Memory Grid. *Courtesy ACMI*

**Figure 6.2** *Hong Kong*, from ACMI's Memory Grid. *Courtesy ACMI*

from strength to strength, with ACMI currently holding one of the largest collections of digital stories worldwide.

Beyond our own exhibition of digital stories, our creative partnerships with the public and with community groups offer some of our most profound applications of digital storytelling. We have worked with many communities and individuals to capture important memories that have become personal and powerful advocacy tools. In the Alzheimer's Australia project the process of constructing memory was profound and vital for the participants and their families. The stories of survivors of the Gippsland, Victoria bushfires assisted others in coming to terms with the harsh reality of rural Australian life. Breast Cancer Network Australia screened a selection from their digital storytelling project on the big screen at half-time at the Melbourne football ground as part of the Field of Women campaign to raise awareness of breast cancer. The Yorta Yorta elders shared stories as a process of knowledge transfer between the indigenous elders and the younger members of their community. We have also facilitated many stories that capture the courageous journeys of migration and the impacts of settlement. All these stories speak to the power and possibility of digital storytelling in its search for meaning and justice. Despite the fallibility of memory and the subjectivity of first-person accounts, digital stories reframe traditional notions of Australian identity and history by representing diverse lives.

Inside each digital story is a profusion of ideas and emotions that are edited together into meaningful sequences. It is exactly this montage principle inherent in a moving-image story that reflects how memory itself works. We do not live our life as a linear sequence but we piece together, edit, and reflect as a way to shape our own memory. Our challenge as facilitators of digital storytelling is to create an environment for participants that evokes memory and engages the senses, intellect, spirit, and heart and at the same time sparks curiosity and imagination. The great irony in doing this kind of work is that even though we have crossed the digital divide we find ourselves moving backward to ground ourselves in the oral tradition of storytelling and we adapt this to the potential of every new technology as a way of understanding narrative.

In an age when the accessibility of digital toolkits means that more and more people have the capacity to become a multi-platform publisher, it is an ongoing, but interesting challenge for large organizations like ACMI to stay responsive. Perhaps it will be our systematized collection of these stories that will represent our greatest contribution in the future as a unique source of user-generated material. No matter, ACMI believes that is the creative partnership inherent in programs like our digital storytelling program that best celebrates technology's facilitation of our understanding sharing of diverse stories, which ultimately allows cultural institutions like ACMI to better engage with the public it serves.

# 7

# Radio Storytelling and Beyond

## Marie Crook

The BBC first began using digital storytelling in their work with communities with the project "Capture Wales" in 2001 and later with "Telling Lives" in the north of England. Digital storytelling was not just a means of eliciting engaging and innovative content, but it also enabled the public service broadcaster to connect with communities in unprecedented ways and proved to be transformative for many of the people who took part. Radio storytelling was first piloted in the BBC in 2003 as a means of enabling more people across the UK to share their stories and to facilitate delivery of a greater number of workshops by using local radio stations as both the venue for workshops and the broadcast outlet.

Radio stories are two- to three-minute audio stories made in the same way as digital stories, but without images. They can be made more quickly, fewer resources in terms of staff and equipment are required, and because of this radio storytelling presents a lower-cost option for storytelling in the BBC. Working as project producer of the first BBC Radio storytelling project ("Inside Lives" at BBC Radio Stoke), the challenge was to adapt the digital storytelling model without diluting its impact.

Radio storytelling workshops involve a three-step process. As with digital storytelling, the first step is the story circle, where participants work on the script of their story, focusing on what will work well for radio. The subsequent workshop gives participants a chance to finalize their scripts before recording the stories, where possible using the recording studio in the radio station. In the final workshop, participants learn how to edit their own audio and produce a complete, broadcast-quality version before celebrating their achievement by listening to the "world première" of the group's stories. The editing process is usually straightforward, and it's possible for people with little or no experience of IT to learn how to edit their audio in the space of a one-day workshop.[1]

The pilot was successful: other BBC local radio stations developed their own versions of it and an early sample of "Inside Lives" stories attracted a Sony Radio Academy Award. Like digital storytelling, radio storytelling has proven to be transformative for many participants, building their confidence and stimulating a desire to further develop the skills they have gained.

Although several BBC local radio stations continue to work with radio storytelling based on the pilot model, I have been involved in further adaptations of the model and have witnessed some interesting developments. In 2004–5, for example, the BBC joined the Learning and Skills Council and the National Institute of Adult Continuing Education to develop a pilot project, "Tell Us Your Story." The pilot aimed to determine the extent to which radio-storytelling workshops could be used to widen adult participation in more formal learning programs. The hope was that a personal storytelling "hook" would help education providers to engage "hard-to-reach" learners – that is, people living mostly in deprived communities and not engaged in formal education owing to a lack of confidence, negative experiences of education, and other barriers.

In the early stages of the pilot, I trained adult education tutors across the North-West of England to facilitate radio storytelling workshops. They then worked on incorporating the story-circle techniques into their existing programs. A good example of how this worked was a project in Salford, where a local college joined forces with a voluntary community organization to work with refugees and asylum seekers who were not accessing free ESOL (English for speakers of other languages) courses at the college. ESOL tutors who had been trained to deliver workshop techniques went on to embed ESOL teaching into a 10-week radio storytelling course. Crucially, the course was not delivered at the college, but at a small, informal community center which the learners felt comfortable attending. All stories were recorded at the community center and later edited for broadcast on local radio. We lacked the resources to teach participants how to edit their own audio, so in this project the focus was very much on the sharing of stories and the use of informal story-sharing as a language-teaching device. At the end of the course, participants requested a further creative writing course, which was delivered at the local college. This was considered an excellent result, demonstrating how storytelling had functioned as a first step to more formal learning.

In 2005, I worked with some of the participants in the "Tell Us Your Story" project to produce a 20-minute radio play based on their stories. This was broadcast as part of the North-West launch of the BBC's literacy campaign RaW (Reading and Writing). Storytelling has since become central to the RaW campaign, which aims to encourage "emergent readers" to improve their literacy skills. Sport fans have learnt how to craft and share stories about their passion; men and women in prisons have learnt how to write stories for their children; writing competitions have been supported by informal writing workshops: these are always very much based on the digital storytelling story circle. I have delivered several national programs of "train the trainer" storytelling workshops where partners in the RaW campaign – mostly library staff and others working in the community, heritage, and education sectors – learn how to use storytelling as a way to engage "hard-to-reach" learners in literacy activity.

These workshops – the outcome of which is often simply a written story – take us a long way from the digital storytelling model that first inspired the BBC to get involved. But there are several features of the digital storytelling model (as I have experienced it) that, I feel, are essential to retain:

1.   There should be no agenda on the part of the facilitator regarding which story the participant should tell. For radio storytelling, this could sometimes be difficult; one of our aims was to elicit compelling material for broadcast, and at times a participant with a great story that fit perfectly with the news agenda would choose to tell one that did not fit so well. But however apprehensive participants might feel about aspects of the workshop (writing, performance, IT), they are experts in their own story and need to feel that way.

2.   Participants should tell their story in their own way. The facilitator's role is to enable this process and to help participants to recognize and feel confident about using their own expressions and accent and to learn how to write the way they speak. Knowing their stories were likely to be broadcast on BBC radio, participants would sometimes feel they lacked the "right" voice, vocabulary, and grammar. Helping them to see the value of their natural speaking voice and its relationship to their story often proved liberating.

3.   Participants already have the tools to enable them to tell their own stories well, but might not recognize their skills as such. I have developed an exercise where participants construct their own "Guide to Good Storytelling," based on their observations about what works in other stories

they hear and read. They can then use the guide to help them in their own writing. The facilitator's aim is to draw out existing knowledge and skill and to feed it back to the group *as* knowledge and skill, rather than "teaching" writing skills.

4. The story-circle process is important and should not be cut short; this is where the group forms the bond that will enable them to confidently share stories and offer affirmative and constructive feedback to each other. It is crucial that participants feel comfortable, respected, and safe and that the atmosphere is kept light-hearted and fun.

In training partners in the BBC RaW campaign to deliver storytelling workshops, I am confident that they can adapt the workshop model in whichever way they choose, according to the resources that are available to them and the outcomes they seek. But by retaining some of the ethos of the digital storytelling story circle, they will be able to offer a workshop experience that amounts to more than the sum of its parts – that is, transformative and confidence-building, and which will inspire participants to continue to learn and develop their skills.[2]

## Notes

1 We used Adobe Audition, then Cool Edit Pro.
2 The BBC digital storytelling workshop model that was adapted for radio story-telling projects is itself very much based on the US model founded by Dana Atchley and Nina Mullen and continued by Joe Lambert.

# Part III

# Digital Storytelling Around the World

# 8

# Narrating Euro-African Life in Digital Space

## Sissy Helff and Julie Woletz

Perhaps without being much noticed yet, Euro-African life is increasingly present in digital space.[1] This presence materializes in, for example, digital stories told by African-Welsh living in Wales, UK in the BBC's "Capture Wales." We will analyze two such videos by drawing on an interdisciplinary approach that connects insights into storytelling from computer science, cultural anthropology, and narratology with concepts from transcultural and postcolonial studies.

Storytelling is a key form of cultural expression. Authors self-reflexively invent and collect story elements, structure them, and finally narrate them in a particular mode. Accordingly, the act of storytelling becomes a cultural practice. In the context of digital storytelling, this practice is even more complex. Digital narratives easily overstep generic borders by playing with fact and fiction, and documentary and imaginary modes of representation, while producing new compositions of media, genres, and narrative practices.[2] In times of globalization, new spatial and cultural complexities are also reflected within narratives. Thus, stories do not solely reflect authors' backgrounds, their ethnic and cultural experiences and upbringings, but are increasingly formed by story elements that can be neither located in a specific narrative tradition nor in a singular national context. Against this background, we introduce the term *digital life narration* as a new, contextually situated cultural practice of storytelling on the side of the authors, including a distinct usage of the movies on the side of the users.

# Digital Storytelling

Looking at digital movies from an interdisciplinary perspective, the historical and intellectual origins of digital narration demonstrate that digital storytelling, while neither being clearly defined nor commonly used as a term in the humanities, has a long history within computer science (Woletz forthcoming). Still, one has to bear in mind that in the 1970s, when computer scientists started an early interest in narratology, neither personal computers nor the concept of personal digital media existed.[3] Research concentrated mostly on the field of artificial intelligence (AI), of which an increasing interest in narratology was mainly a byproduct. Up to this point, AI had mainly dealt with mathematics and formal logic, but in the following two decades, narrative theories became increasingly popular.[4] In this context, narratives were perceived as "less formal forms of knowledge" (Davis and Travers 1999: 3), and not much interest was paid to media or cultural practices.

This situation changed when Brenda Laurel (1986) received the first PhD in interactive narrative for designing a computer-based interactive fantasy system. Laurel's study combined her personal experience as a computer programmer with expertise in theater, and transgressed the boundaries of computer sciences at the time. A similar approach was introduced by Marc Davis and Michael Travers, founders of the Narrative Intelligence reading group (NI) in 1990. The NI group broadened scientific discourse on narratology by integrating disciplines such as literary theory, narrative psychology, and art in computer sciences (Mateas and Sengers 1999: 3–5).

In contrast to these stories deriving from high-tech laboratories, a movement arose in the early 1990s promoting "bottom-up" digital storytelling that puts its emphasis on *personal stories*.[5] This shift toward more personal topics in digital narrations can be seen in early applications like Abbe Don's *We Make Memories* (Don 1989–95), or the digital magazine *Fray* (Powazek 1996),[6] and is also indicated in the work of multimedia performer Dana Atchley. With the support of the programmer Joe Lambert, Atchley designed the first digital autobiography *Next Exit* (Atchley 1990–2000). In 1994 Lambert, Atchley, and Nina Mullen founded the San Francisco Digital Media Center, which later became the influential Center for Digital Storytelling (CDS), and started offering workshops on video-based personal stories. Our selected movies have been produced in such a workshop of the BBC project "Capture Wales" (BBC 2006a), following the workshop methodology of the CDS (Atchley, Lambert, and Mullen 1994, Lambert 2003). The BBC (2006b) describes their idea of digital storytelling as follows:

> Digital stories are "mini-movies" created and edited by people like you – using cameras, computers, scanners and their own photo albums. Everyone has a story to tell and new technology means that anyone can create a story that can show on a website like the ones you see here. The idea is to show the richness of life in Wales through stories made by the people of Wales. It's you who decide what those stories are.

In a much broader sense than this focus on movies, computer sciences distinguish between two categories of story systems: First, generic story systems that build a whole new story, and second, storytelling systems that interactively narrate a predefined story (Spierling et al. 2002: 32). The latter category includes digital storytelling and our selected movies.

Interestingly enough, the criteria for these categories are not technical, but are addressing questions of where to locate "interactivity" in the context of computer-based stories, and how exactly the user's interactions affect a narrative. That is because there is a considerable difference between user involvement in story generating or user involvement in storytelling. In the former case the reader becomes a coauthor by creating new stories out of given possibilities every time she or he "reads" the story, e.g., in hypertexts with multiple authoring, in role-playing games, or interactive drama. In the latter case the interactive telling relies on a predefined and pre-authored story, where the user only influences the storytelling, but cannot influence the plot or change the story goal (ibid.). Innovative examples for this category are educational stories, which need to be preauthored and have a defined end or peak in order to achieve their educational objectives. Marie-Laure Ryan (2004a) argues:

> If digital media can be said to create new forms of narrativity, this novelty does not concern semantics, but, rather, *presentational strategies* (that is, discourse) and above all, *pragmatic factors*: new modes of user involvement; new types of interface; and new relations between the author (or, rather, system designer), the plot (or plots), and users. (p. 333, emphasis added)

Digital storytelling offers combinations of media – respectively *modes of presentation* – in various configurations (Paul and Fiebich 2005) such as single media, multiple media (two or more types of media used separately), or multimedia (two or more types of media in a seamless presentation). Users are involved, e.g., by their choice over these modes of presentation. By calling such an influence on the story "participation," this term seems to be more precise than "interactivity," because the user's influence is restricted. Furthermore, digital storytelling allows *multi-modal communication* (ibid.), which not only works in one direction, from the author to his or her audience, but in several directions, e.g., by submitting feedback on a given story, or by providing a forum for discussion with other recipients. Such activities and communication represent "social interactions," as they are mutually interdependent.

Thus we can summarize the following characteristics: Digital storytelling excludes the generating of new stories, but includes explicit means of influencing the telling of a given story. Such means comprise participatory modes on the level of presentation and interactive modes on the level of communication, which in turn lead to specific interfaces and new relations between the author, the story, and the users. However, the means of influencing the storytelling vary according to the chosen media formats and technical artifacts, as do presentational strategies and communicative modes. Furthermore, the contexts of the storytelling practice, that is, the intentions and motives of authors and readers, have to be taken into account.

## Digital Life Narration – A New Cultural Practice?

Encompassing all these aspects of communication and social interaction, technical and media artifacts, the conceptualization as cultural practice seems particularly appropriate. By digital life narration, we are referring to "digital" from a non-technically determinist point of view highlighting the utilization of new modes of presentation and communication. "Life narration" in this context illuminates the personal level of storytelling based on private archives.

The premise for determining digital life narration as a common cultural practice is the general increase of easy-to-use editing systems for private publishing. Because technical and media artifacts are relatively easy to access, anybody could become the author of a digital story and distribute it over the Internet. And because just about everything can be photographed, scanned, imported, or sampled, private media archives are being used more and more to document and represent individual lives. These practices perform a "bottom-up" movement of storytelling (Woletz forthcoming) by creatively using and recombining easy-to-access elements of "traditional" or common media such as photographs, films, music, or text. Stories are produced with the lower technical standard of a common personal computer and are distributed over the Internet for everybody's use. In contrast to a high-tech approach on digital storytelling in media labs, private publishing based on personal archives shifts the content of narratives from institutionalized knowledge transfer toward personal life narration. So telling individual life stories or at least playfully claiming that stories are "true" mark the author's intentions and central motives within a particular practice of digital storytelling. While none of the content is revisable, the use of presentation strategies such as homodiegetic narratives and the integration of private archives nevertheless creates credibility (Helff 2007). Because of the highly personal content and the documentary character, such stories offer the audience a possibility of identification – if not always through the theme, at least through the fact that potentially every reader could narrate their story in the same manner.

As a result, the use and reception of such stories are predetermined. It is important to note that in the same way that educational storytelling cannot give up its educational aim, digital life narratives cannot let the user create another plot and still claim the authenticity of a true life story. Hence, within digital life narratives the explicit means of influencing the storytelling are restricted to participatory modes on the level of presentation and interactive modes on the level of communication. Thus, the modes and strategies of representation on the author's side and participatory and interactive modes on the user's side finally come together within the distinctive cultural practice of digital life narration, where digital media are used to express individual lives.

## Mapping Digital Video Stories

Our selected Euro-African videos cover a family story of four generations of migrants and a transcultural performance of a poet who represents his cultural heritage as a constant amalgamating process of merged cultural traditions, influences, and practices. Both storytellers were supported by professionals of the "Capture Wales" workshop in creating their storyboards and in the digital production of their videos. Therefore, the digital life narratives seem to be more advanced and rather semi-professional compared to most products of private publishing. Nevertheless, neither the technology used for the production of the movies nor their distribution is "high-tech" in the sense of professional film technology and composition.[7] The three-minute movies are in fact slideshows made of private media artifacts. In addition to such filmic narration, each video uses a rather dominant voice-over narration.

Although all the stories are first-person narratives, the videos never show the actual telling of the story. Yet it is obvious that the voice-over is always spoken by the author/producer, as language particularities in pronunciation or small mistakes are not corrected. Both the use of personal archives and the "authentic voice" of the narrator seem to guarantee the trueness and authenticity of each story. Furthermore, the voice-over narration is also provided in a transcript of each video. Within these transcripts small errors remain uncorrected. And while this might all be part of an intended aesthetics, it adds to the credibility of the stories, nevertheless.

All the video stories are streamed on demand on the BBC websites. Through this form of distribution, accessing a story is the choice of the user. To some extent, then, the user's choice of their preferred media to view the story might be read as them participating in the storytelling: the hyperlink "View movie" starts a visual presentation in a video, whereas "Read the transcript" navigates to a textual version of the narrative including still images. Besides this choice over the modes of presentation,[8] no other influencing of the storytelling or the story plot is possible. The *interactive modes* of this particular storytelling comprise additional channels of communication. The hyperlink "Interview with the storyteller" navigates viewers to a separate "background" site with additional features. Here, interviews with the narrators present further information, such as an introductory note by the storyteller, a synopsis of the video, and comments on the workshop, and thus support the overall documentary character of the stories. Additionally, a standardized feedback mode is integrated and invoked by "Please let us know." Besides communicating about a particular life narrative, users can also contact the workshop organizers. The hyperlink "Do you have a story to tell?" on the permanent navigation bar of the BBC websites gives information about further workshops and invites users to participate. These features demonstrate that the *modes of communication* work on multimodal levels and transgress traditional "one-way" forms of mass communication.

In addition to organizing the stories by theme, the navigation bar also offers browsing by area, reconnecting the digital movies to local places in Wales. In this way all digital narratives become locations on the map of Wales and are translated into topographical units and physical spaces. It can be argued that within these digital narratives spatial practices work on different narrative levels, namely in the narrated border crossings of the protagonists as well as on a formal level in the interactive fabrication of new narratives. The anthropologist Nancy Schmidt (1981: 8–18) describes the general and basic outline of mapping devices in literature as a conscious predominance of cultural information within a text. The cultural information provided by the videos is strongly reflective of topographical and cartographical realities and thus points to several functions of maps.

The emerging literary and digital mapping of these texts can be linked to what the postcolonial scholar Graham Huggan referred to as "literary cartography." According to Huggan (1994: 31), literary cartography "not only examines the function of maps in literary texts, but also explores the operations of a series of territorial strategies that are implicitly or explicitly associated with maps." While examining digital life narratives, this approach should be taken even further, because "the process of matching map to text, or text to map, involves the reader in a comparison that may bring to the surface flaws or discrepancies in the process of mimetic representation" (22). The digital life narrative presents a friction between mimetic representations of people's lives and the translation of places into a digital cartographical map. This friction confronts the users with "the relativity of modes of spatial (and, by extension, cultural) perception" (Huggan 2008: 30). In this respect, the idea of an authentic story located on a digital map encourages us to reflect on digital reality, a reality which becomes real neither in a mimetic representation of an individual story nor in a place. It is a life story in flux that materializes in its constant negotiation with multiple interactive spaces. Since the user decides how to read or watch the material of the same story, these stories keep changing their form and narrative structure.

The project "Capture Wales," with its range of Euro-African experiences in a multicultural Welsh society, seeks to represent individual stories against the backdrop of local communities. Interestingly, the representations show Euro-African life in Wales from an uncompromisingly affirmative point of view. In this context, Heide Safiza Mirza's critical analysis of the social and cultural texture of British society with regard to belonging to or being excluded from an imaginary Britishness based on ethnicity seems not to be an issue in the affirmative multicultural makeup presented in the videos. Whereas Mirza (1997: 3) points out that racism is still an integral part of today's British identity politics, these digital life narratives introduce notions of Britishness that do not directly address racist realities. Instead, they reach far beyond the color line to celebrate movie themes of family (*Aftaag Family*) and culture (*Culture Vulture*). However, the emerging discursive gap also has problematic edges, because it installs a cultural reality that, in part, defines the frames through which African-Welsh are rendered legitimately visible; it is the mode of representation which matters, and the motivation that gives the stories their narrative drive.

## Proud to Be from Cardiff: Said Dualeh's *Aftaag Family*

In the first video (BBC 2005a) Said Dualeh, the homodiegetic narrator, strives to establish a digital family archive in order to honor his grandfather Aftaag and put the family's history on the (digital) map of Wales. This motivation propels his story – a story that could be read as a reflection on the collective history of the ethnic minority of Somalis living in Wales.

Whereas most parts of the movie are presented as a digital slideshow, the story is framed by two brief video sequences shown in the beginning and the end presenting Dualeh and his two sons on a local playground. This filmic technique creates a recurring moment within the plot that reconnects the life of four generations with Dualeh's present family situation and their Welsh hometown. The exceptional use of music, underlying the dedication to Aftaag in the end slide, creates an emotional moment that mounts in a homage to his grandfather. The voice-over serves the purpose of telling about the successful integration of the Aftaag family, because Cardiff is explicitly referred to three times as the home of Said Dualeh's father Ibrahim, the home of Said, and the home of the entire family. The quoting of Ibrahim, who "feels like a Welsh man and [is] even able to speak Welsh" (ibid.), underlines the family's feelings toward their Welshness. Their identification with Wales through the use of its ancient language only confirms their will of becoming and being fully integrated Welsh citizens. The storyteller's motivation is also indicated in the interview supplied on the site: "[My story] is about four generations of my family living in Cardiff. I wanted to tell this story to educate people in Wales about the history of ethnic minority in Cardiff. This story is dedicated to the memory of my grandfather" (BBC 2005b).

The central sentence of the video is therefore placed above the hyperlink to start it: "My father stayed in Somalia, but longed for his home back in

Cardiff" (ibid.). In the course of the video, viewers learn that the narrator-protagonist married a local girl and has two sons, meaning that the home-coming of the Dualeh family in Wales has become reality. This video is not only a miniature family archive, but also a personal story which eventually materializes in this digital life narrative. Thus the narrator's comment, "In three years time we will celebrate 100 years of Dualeh family in Cardiff and we are looking forward to another 100 years in the city we call home" (BBC 2005a), brings the narrative full cycle. In his attempt to reconstruct the past and its moments, the narrator comes face to face with his four-generation family history of Somali experiences in Britain. With this mapping strategy the author seeks to territorially appropriate his chosen home, the city of Cardiff, and thus seeks to include himself and the collective Somali migrant community within British historiography.

## An "Afric-Cymric Rhythmic Poet": Nicky Delgado's "Culture Vulture"

The second video in our analysis is a poetry performance by Nicky Delgado, who describes himself as an "Afric-Cymric rhythmic poet" of African, Portuguese, Arabic, and Welsh heritage (BBC 2002). In his digital story, we learn about his upbringing and his later travels through Europe and North Africa as well as his more recent experiences as a teacher, poet, and script-writer.

Part family history, part travelogue, it is also a poetry performance in digital space. Delgado mostly uses photos of himself and his family, of impressive architecture, and cultural symbols in order to generate his narrative identity. In its introductory sequence the video presents a special combination of visual and sound effects: An animated clay figure of Nicky Delgado is accompanied by voices talking in different languages. Delgado's cultural heritage is furthermore reflected in his pseudonym "Culture Vulture," an expression describing somebody who is hungry for culture. Not only is he hungry for culture, he is "made up" of many different cultures: Delgado's background of mixed cultures is mentioned not only at the beginning of his performance, but is also visually expressed in a series of portrait photos depicting him wearing six different hats. It is a transcultural identity that is celebrated in this digital life narrating. Delgado's perform-ance is not concerned with the task of making the past of black people in

Wales visible to a wider audience, nor is Delgado interested in creating a cultural archive. Instead, he seeks to use his past as a fertile ground for the invention of a fresh, individually organized self who perceives his cultural background as an integral part of his transcultural personality. In this context the mapping of the various places he has visited can neither be understood as an attempt to reflect on the places' cultural heritages nor to narrate the stories of people living there. The different geographies and cultures, however, culminate in Delgado himself, who credits the different people along the way, with inspiring him to write and perform poetry about humanity.

His experiences come alive in a brief travelogue sequence. Here Delgado's cosmopolitan lifestyle is rhythmically narrated in a romantic tone. Delgado's performance, however, represents the Black Welsh poet as a transcultural author who narrates his individual story by utilizing story elements representing neither assimilation nor mimicry (Bhabha 1995). Thus in his position as a traveling cosmopolite, he is talking in a transcultural, but not in a postcolonial "language." In this respect his vivid tone, carrying some wistful moments, controls the narrative, but without investing any thought on responsibilities of a colonial past, postcolonial and transcultural present, or the challenging trajectories of future.

The motivation for culture once more becomes narrative reality in Delgado's rhyme, "At sixteen I ran away to London town seeking stimulation of cultural gratification" (BBC 2002) and the visual translation of a photo depicting him with his arms around the shoulders of two friends. The young men seem ready to experience life, thus the following sentence, "[t]wice I hitch hiked across the European Nation" (ibid.), which is told while a photo of mountains is shown, only illuminates the adventurous attitude of the young man. His spiritual voyage is reflected eventually in "then journeyed through North Africa," which he remembers as his "most spiritual uplifting adventure so far" (ibid.). The distance between Africa and himself becomes explicit in the word "adventure," thus his visit is not meant to be read as a homecoming to some of his ancestral roots. Instead, Delgado's poetry combines travel memories and experiences with his present life in Wales. The emerging perspective corresponds to what critics of travel literature have called memoirs of the self-ironic figure of the "English gentleman traveller" (Holland and Huggan 2000: 27–47). Like this figure, Delgado's modern Welsh tourist holds the ambivalent position of an adventurer who, with his plea for human compassion, at the same time laments and celebrates his own imagined obsolescence (ibid.). Thus when

Delgado finally, in a self-parodying manner, addresses viewers (using a voice-over with echo effects) with the words "am I mad, afflicted by such attraction to difference, cursed with the taste for humane dignity, foolishly believing we are all unique in that we are all different?" (BBC 2002), viewers find themselves confronted with an ideal of humanity which narrows the gap between reported facts and invented tales. Delgado's digital poetry performance connects a vibrant middle-class habitus and taste by renewing the Victorian makeup of the gentleman traveler with shiny layers of a nostalgic affirmative multicultural and transcultural black Britishness. In this respect, Delgado's performance and its distribution through the BBC website with its "call" for interaction highlight the invention and creation of self and identity as an appropriate narrative means for generating modern transcultural Britishness (Helff 2007).

However, after initial indulging moments, his represented ideal of human compassion across cultural differences seems somehow irritating. Owing to the almost naive narrative voice and his utilized visual style, Delgado, in the manner of a true transcultural salesman, performs a perfect marketing show that seeks to sell, next to his ideals and books, himself as a storyteller. All in all, the represented multicultural and transcultural reality serves as canvas against which the poet invents himself. In the movie's endeavor to demonstrate Delgado's "hunger" for culture, the digestion of the culturally overstated images is entirely left up to the viewer.

## Conclusion

Private publishing based on personal archives shifts the content of narratives from institutionalized knowledge transfer toward personal life narration. The usage and reception of such stories, however, is bound to the specific fabric of the digital narrative. Thus within *digital life narratives* the explicit means of influencing the narration are restricted to participatory modes on the level of representation, and interactive modes on the level of communication. In this respect participation creates increasingly dynamic stories that do not encourage a distinct narrative closure, but rather represent constant flux and furthermore let viewers connect with the narratives. The specific strategies of representation, such as homodiegetic narration and the use of personal archives, underline the "authentic" and "true" life underlying every digital story. In this way the established "trueness" and reliability of each story frame the socio-historical experiences of the authors while seeking to emphasize their right to participate in Welsh society. Driven by the will to demonstrate an affirmative attitude toward British life, the videos focus on ultimate human experiences, such as discovery and home-sickness (Dualeh family), as well as the more recent phenomenon of self-invention (Delgado's performance). All narratives engage in the process of defining or stating a cultural space on the map of Wales, because the narra-tive is not only indicated by the digital map, but more directly by the virtual and very real physical presence of the narrators within Welsh society. Such representations on a digital map, furthermore, demonstrate fresh practices of storytelling by including new relations between authors, stories, and the audience, thus creating social and fictitious cartographies of Euro-African life within digital space.

## Notes

1   In order to challenge the commonly accepted understanding of Eurocentric description of identity formations, we have deliberately chosen to switch around the more commonly used term "African-European" and use the term "Euro-African" instead.

2   The genre of computer-based digital media not only establishes new forms and genres such as literary hypertext, weblogs, or narrative computer games, but also leads to extensive discussions about if and to what extent new media pro-duce new structures and modes of storytelling (Ryan 2004a). Accordingly, some critics claim that interactive multimedia narratives present the future mode of storytelling (Murray 1997).

3   The first personal computer was the ALTAIR 8800 from 1975. In 1977 Alan Kay and Adele Goldberg (1977: 31–41) introduced the concept of personal dynamic media with the "Dynabook."

4   E.g., Schank and Riesbeck (1981) developed a theory on "story understanding" concerning knowledge structures that are necessary to understand textual narratives and tried to model the processes.

5   It has been argued that the field of digital storytelling can be divided into two main positions: first a "top-down" approach deriving from institutions or high-tech laboratories and implying the use of advanced technology, where storytelling is utilized as a means of knowledge transfer; and second a "bottom-up" approach to personal stories, where user-generated content is published on the Internet. Each approach follows its specific way of digital storytelling in relation to media utilization and technical standards, modes of communication, and user involve-ment, as well as the intentions of authors and users (Woletz forthcoming).

6   Powazek (1996, emphasis added) introduces *Fray* as "a magazine about *true stories* that's been publishing since 1996, and a place for people who believe that the Web is about *personal expression* and a new kind of art."

7   In fact programs like Microsoft Office Publisher or Movie Maker are part of a common office packet for personal computers.

8   This differentiation is based on the assumption that the same (transmedial) narrative can be presented in different media, e.g., in a video with voice-over narration and a textual transcription of the voices as in the presented case studies. For a discussion of "narrative media studies" or "transmedial narratology" see Ryan (2004b: 1–40).

# 9

# Developing Digital Storytelling in Brazil

## Margaret Anne Clarke

> For me, both as a participant and lay historian of many social and political
> movements, I always thought of our work in Digital Storytelling as what we
> used to call "movement building." That is, we wanted to motivate people to
> change their behaviour, to change the distribution of power and relations. As
> such, Digital Storytelling for us was more of an idea than a product, more
> affecting social behaviour than consumer behaviour. (Lambert 2000)

According to Joe Lambert, digital storytelling, both as a practice and as a
genre, has been conceived from its inception as a means of agency and
empowerment for individual participants and creators. The "assemblage of
cultural practices" (Selber 2004: 81) created by the affirmation of individual
voice, and mediated through workshops, video, and multimedia, may
enable citizen-creators to recognize, name, and challenge their own position in society, and their relations with others and with established political
and social orders. If digital stories are integrated further within other movements or organizations promoting democratic participation, the practice
may indeed hold the potential for personal transformation, community
activism, and social change envisaged by the movement's founders. Thus
Joe Lambert's original vision of digital storytelling as "knowing in practice"
has provided a powerful springboard for the development of digital storytelling projects in diverse social, educational, activist, and community contexts. Yet, while acknowledging the fundamental premise behind Lambert's
definition of digital storytelling as "movement building," the particular
tenets and methods informing the practice must necessarily adapt, transform, and acquire new dimensions as digital storytelling traverses national
boundaries, and is established and disseminated at an international level,

through comprehensive programs for learning, social action, and citizens' empowerment, and within diverse communities of practice.

This study, then, will trace the background, evolution, and development of the movement founded in Brazil in 2006, "Um Milhão de Histórias de Vida de Jovens" (One Million Life Stories of Youth).[1] The movement is based on the creation and recording of short, first-person narratives in video, audio, and multimedia by Brazilian citizens aged between 15 and 29, and the archiving and dissemination of the stories within other performance, communication, and media networks. Once a critical mass of narratives has been created, the young participants, or "story agents," will be responsible for embedding the stories within multilevel frameworks of national, municipal, and community institutions and organizations. The stories, giving a human face to the numerous problems, challenges, and aspirations of the nation's youth, will enhance the potential for meaningful participation and inclusion in the reconstruction and building of the nation.

The movement, then, has national reach, and its ultimate aim and purpose is to integrate and mobilize a million individuals for the explicit purpose of democratic evolution across a country characterized by the geographical and human diversity of its five major regions, "likened to islands in a huge archipelago" (Levine and Crocitti 1999: 3). The process of confronting and overcoming the formidable challenges involved in a project of such scope must both raise new questions and develop further the central tenets and practices of digital storytelling established by the movement's founders. Some of these have been addressed in the recent literature on digital storytelling, which has focused on the organization of the practice, its potential for transformation within sociocultural, community, and media networks, and the relation of both the stories and their narrators with the production, distribution, and ownership of knowledge in society as a whole. According to Jean Burgess, "The mere fact of productivity in itself is not sufficient grounds for celebration. The question that we ask about 'democratic' media production can no longer be limited to 'who gets to speak?' We must also ask 'who is heard, and to what end?'" (Burgess 2006a: 204).

Another theme recently addressed is the means by which the pedagogical, training, and dissemination aspects of digital storytelling practice may increase access and participation for those on the wrong side of the "digital divide": low-income groups, youth, and seniors. Digital storytelling has been particularly identified with youth participation and projects in all educational sectors, but particularly as a developmental resource for youth outside the economic, educational, and ethnic mainstream (Kajder 2004, Hull and Katz 2006, Snyder and Prinsloo 2007). This question is of particular relevance in Brazil, a "young" country in its demographic makeup. In 2000, the median age of the Brazilian population was 25.8 years (Luna and Klein 2006: 162), and the age group encompassing the years 15–29 comprises 50.5 million of the population of Brazil.[2] The marginalization of much of Brazil's youth in general from the nation's economy, employment, and social frameworks is also reflected in their situation of "digital exclusion," the highly unequal access to computers, information and communication technologies (ICTs), and the new media which affects the majority of young people in Brazil,[3] and the population as a whole;[4] for example, as of June 2007 only 13 percent of the nation's households owned a PC and just 3 percent of the population had broadband access. In addition, the ICT infrastructure of Brazil is extremely poorly distributed, with virtually no connectivity in rural areas (Woudhysen 2007)

> [I]t is important, on the one hand, to discover channels through which the members of these communities (even the youngest) can master digital technology. But it is equally essential to be aware of the form in which this new media can be incorporated in a consolidated process of oral transmission of values … allowing such projects as these to be self-sustaining. Public resources for digitisation initiatives are extremely rare in Brazil, and it is important that this type of initiative does not become just one more element in the domination and dependency of certain cultural communities. (Worcman 2002)

This chapter will consider three related questions.

1.   First, how must digital storytelling, initially developed in the relatively resource-rich environments of North American educational institutions, be improvised and adapted to a million diverse participants residing in an entire subcontinent? And how can the disparity in the availability of resources within Brazil, as compared to North America, be addressed?

2.   Second, in what way can the workshop, training, and pedagogical aspects, on which the construction of the stories is based, best be adapted to encourage the acquisition of literacies, cultural awareness, and the capacity for independent action by young people contributing to the movement?

3.  Third, how may digital stories, once created and amassed, be embedded and disseminated within other systems of communication and technological media? Of particular relevance here are flexible and adaptable technologies, including open-source platforms which support and encourage as far as is possible the effectiveness of the stories, their circulation, and their potential to form new social and community networks through the addition of forums, discussion, and other relevant material. This is a key element in the capacity of digital stories to function as a base and means of creating sustainable knowledge, and a possible means by which the digital divide – the alienation of citizens from the communication technologies that increasingly create their world – may at least be partly bridged.

## Brazil: The Transition to Democracy, Information Technology, Citizens' Memory, and Voice

The concept of "digital inclusion" has never been defined in Brazil in terms of the installation and access to computers, but has been inextricably linked to broader public goals of social and civic inclusion, one part of wider programs encouraging citizens to take on more active roles in their community. Programs for digital inclusion are thus inextricably linked to social or civic participation, and the harnessing of technology to combat social exclusion and marginalization (Worcman 2002). The impetus for the establishment of ICT initiatives for broader social aims has mainly come from Brazilian nongovernmental organizations and municipal networks, supported by charitable and corporate foundations, who have taken up the cause of access to ICTs as a civic right (Albernaz 2002: 6). It is against this background that an independent tradition of recorded stories, episodic memories, and life narratives created by Brazilian citizens has evolved in Brazil. The largest and most comprehensive collection of recorded stories, the virtual museum and oral history archive Museu da Pessoa (Museum of the Person),[5] based in São Paulo, has provided the expertise and base to support and create a project of the scope of A Million Life Stories, in collaboration with the nongovernmental organization Aracati, which is dedicated to youth participation and mobilization. But Brazil's autonomous tradition of digital storytelling has also evolved from a far longer history of oral narrative tradition in the country; and has acquired new roles and dimensions within the metamorphosis in the nation's public, political, and social institutions, and the construction of democratic frameworks enabling greater participation on the part of the majority of Brazil's citizens. This transition accelerated with the *abertura*, or opening, of the nation in 1985 after the final demise of the military regime implanted in 1964. This was the most oppressive example of a political culture established since the nation's independence in 1822, characterized by "a long electoral history but little democratic tradition," which had served, throughout the twentieth century, to marginalize the vast majority of Brazil's populace from autonomous political participation and full citizens' rights. The requirement that a citizen had to be literate to vote, which was only finally revoked in 1988 with the advent of direct presidential elections, greatly exacerbated this exclusion in a country which, even up to the year 2000, still had a functional illiteracy rate of 60 percent. Thus the broader political and social aims of grassroots social movements, independent trade unions, and nongovernmental organizations, and the hard work of shifting the axis of power in Brazil to a new equilibrium, have been inextricably linked to popular education, pedagogy, and the acquisition of literacies in a broad sense. This is summed up in the expression "formação": Brazilian citizens' awareness of the circumstances which have given rise to the situation, and the development of their innate potential as part of a conscious process of social change: "the striving for access to knowledge that is due them as citizens and yet not given to them by the state" (Ghanem 1998). A crucial component of "formação," then, must be the development of the means to assert Brazilian citizens' voices in their full plurality, the insertion of these voices in spheres of public life and democratic institutions, and the recovery of memory, both individual and collective, hitherto suppressed or forgotten under authoritarian regimes and "official" versions of history. Digital technologies and virtual networks, then, may provide public spaces and act as focal points for the "gathering of voices": "[I]nasmuch as the members of communities acquire digital technology, they themselves can also become producers and keepers of their own history, integrating it or not with the social history of other communities" (Worcman 2002).

One example is the website Favela Tem Memória (The Favela Has a Memory) supported by the nongovernmental organization and web portal Viva Rio,[6] which collects the stories and memories of the older residents of five of Rio de Janeiro's longest-established favelas. The websites and virtual spaces supported by Viva Rio are the spaces which enable the construction of "circular histories of the past in order to reinforce identities in the present," and are a sustainable focal point for the community's collective memory, knowledge of itself and its past.

The Museu da Pessoa (Museum of the Person) was established in 1992 with the objective of recording, collecting, and archiving the personal stories, memories, and life narratives of Brazilian citizens, within diverse frameworks and programs designed to recover numerous community and social memories, formerly marginalized or submerged within "official" narratives of the nation's history. The recorded narratives assert the primacy of the personal experiential knowledge of all Brazilian citizens and the plurality of voices as the building blocks through which constructivist concepts of the nation's historical formation and ongoing development are built:

> Each human being is a library, a singular fount of knowledge. To know how to listen to each one, integrating and composing different visions, is a basic exercise of citizenship – an essential part of human learning and development ... we can envisage a future in which historical narrative of society can contain many "voices" including, without any form of hierarchy, life stories from all individuals from all sectors of society and where the history of each person will be a point in our social framework. (Worcman 2006: 10)

## Project Aracati: *A Million Life Stories of Youth*

The "Million Life Stories," the Museu da Pessoa's most ambitious project to date, was established in 2006 in partnership with Aracati. It consists of the amassing and dissemination of first-person stories drawn from young people's observations of life, their experience, and their memories. Its methodology has been partly adapted from the central tenets of digital storytelling practice as established by the California-based Center for Digital Storytelling.[7] The workshop-based construction of three-minute narratives based primarily on oral performance is particularly suited for the project, combining as it does ease of use, flexibility, and economy of expression and based on everyday communicative practices and performance skills acquired, instinctively or not, from other media. The fundamental aim of the project, then, is to enable and assist young people to convert themselves into both reflective and active subjects in the construction of their lives, their life stories, and the ongoing history and building of the nation.

The pervasive media images of marginalized and dispossessed young men on the peripheries of Brazil's urban areas, defined as both the agents and victims of violence, have become the most visible face of Brazil's youth in the national and international media. It is certainly true that the violent disparities in income, and in access to employment and educational opportunities, impact particularly hard on this age group (Dell'Aglio et al. 2007).[8] Before 2003, there were no dedicated polices either at national or federal level to integrate young people into these sectors. But Brazil's youth is also a reflection of the highly plural, ethnically mixed, and regionally diverse nature of Brazil's population as a whole, "a category in permanent social and historical construction" (Sposito and Carrano 2003: 19).

Informed by the slogan, "one story is a story, a million stories are a movement," digital storytelling is a key component of this social and historical construction: the means "to offer opportunities for young Brazilian people to develop their potential and participation in the construction of a better and different country for everyone."[9] The Aracati website also makes clear the inextricable link between youth participation and broader pedagogical aims: "Participation is the right of young people. But no one is born a participative citizen. Participation is something that is learned throughout life."[10] The hope, then, is that the process of creating, recording, and disseminating the stories will enhance the young participants' literacies and skills, and create a heightened sense of agency, confidence, and interaction with others. The creative expansion of the stories, in new directions and new ways, will enable the million young people to pursue on their own account a process of community participation and community building, in ways that will benefit their peer groups, local communities, society in general, and the nation, through "a synthesis of individual and collective change" (Page and Czubba 1999). But the process of change is two-way and reciprocal. The expansion and dissemination of the stories in new directions and through different outlets may also change stereotyped perceptions that the population as a whole may hold concerning the youth of their districts, communities, and society in general and enable the insertion of youth perspectives within the framing of specific economic and social policies and municipal, federal, and national level.

The methodologies adopted by the project, then, must take two fundamental considerations into account: the methods through which the movement can become both sustainable in its practice and also expansive: acquiring its own momentum and converting the collections of stories already created and collected into a self-supporting focal point for community, transformation, and education.

Several principles have been established which underpin the practices of the project as a whole. First, in order to ensure the maximum degree of agency and participation, the workshop process, the creation and recording of stories and their dissemination, is the responsibility of the young participants at every point from the inception of the preliminary "story circle" to the dissemination of the stories in multiple outlets. Key to the movement are the activities of the young "story agents" who, once trained through the workshops provided by the Museu da Pessoa, create new story circles of their own, and pass on their knowledge to their peers, creating ever-widening groups and networks in the process. It is, then, the responsibility of the story agents to collect and research common themes and connections in the stories they collect; and to use these as a basis for social and cultural activism within their communities. Thus the original concept of the "story circle," envisaged as a base for mutual collaboration and inspiration in the preliminary creation of the stories (Lambert 2002; and see Chapter 5, this volume), has been extended to dissemination of the stories and their potentially numerous uses for future activism, forming a huge chain of transversal contacts, extending ever outwards, of emerging social structures and communities which the young people themselves help to create.[11]

Some examples of the way this might work in practice are given in the project's training manual, the *Diário de Bordo*: if the story agent has a group of stories describing a moment of first love, or some other romantic encounter, these can be placed on a CD-ROM and transmitted from a community radio station, helping to alter whatever stereotypes may exist of young people in the district as violent or aggressive, presenting an alternative view of young people who are romantic, sensitive, and give value to personal relations. Or, problems recounted by participants concerning difficulties with local services or exclusion in a community context could be placed on a CD-ROM and given to the local deputy or elected representative of the district at municipal or federal level, giving a direct and human perspective to "political" or social problems.[12]

Any possible barriers to development of the stories must also be lowered through the adoption of a high degree of versatility, adaptability, and flexibility in the format and practice of creating the stories. The process of ongoing development of the stories, their expansion and dissemination, and the mutual exchange and participation created by the embedding of the stories in diverse media and communication networks, is enhanced by the use of free software with open-source code which can be adapted throughout. The project's dedicated site, the virtual platform iREDES,[13] which was specifically designed for sustainable social development, has enabled the original story agents to group the stories together, taking on the form of concentric circles as more stories are added. Thus a complete map of the accumulated stories has been created on the platform, which also permits the insertion of documents and comments, and the creation of new forums by any participant. This expands the concept of the "circle" still further to include the constant interactions between virtual and public space, within which the continuous expansion of shared and diversified communication between participants, and the transformation of their stories, can take place. In addition, the stories are also put on easily circulated and adaptable technologies such as CD-ROM, in order to encourage and promote the highest degree of remediation and recycling. They can then be distributed to community radio, or local television stations which function outside hegemonic national television and media networks. "What is important," says Carol Misorelli, the coordinator of the project, "is that the stories are heard."[14] That point is also made on the Project's website: "What is as important as telling the story is making sure that it is heard and used. What is produced socially ought to be appropriated by society. Public access and the use of historical narratives should be guaranteed."[15]

The stories of the first group of story agents first trained by the Museu da Pessoa in northeastern Brazil in 2006 illustrate a common feature of digital stories, which Hull and Katz (2006: 42) have defined as "turning points" in the narrators' lives. In this particular context, these "turning points" are linked with the young activists' engagement with hip-hop communities, youth theater, and other activities; or the participants' struggle, often against considerable odds, to acquire educational qualifications or new skills. In either case, the epiphany, or turning point in the stories arises from the transformation of the participants' abilities through their newly realized or heightened self, and the subsequent development of a new type of social commitment which Beck terms the "reintegration dimension" (Thompson 2007: 83–4).

One example is the story of Paulo Roberto de Lima, from the northeastern state of Pernambuco, who describes his personal transformation through the skills he acquired with a training scheme in information technology, SERTA: Paulo's story not only contributes a critical reflection on his identity and selfhood, but also illustrates the way this has enabled him to create new spaces for knowledge, communication, and interaction within the society of which he now feels fully a part:

> In truth, my story took a clear direction and path with those fifty computers, all of them broken. With them, we learned to repair, to configure, in other words, to understand how a machine works. From that time, my work stopped being work and became my desire, my dream, and my fulfillment. From those fifty machines we managed to set up four training schools and give a future to future efforts; today, actions and activities are multiplying, new projects are coming into being. Many people have participated and are participating. I thank God for my teachers and technicians who fight and fought for what is right … and who changed the lives of many young people, including mine. That concludes my story.

## Conclusion

The tenets and practices of digital storytelling have been established in Brazil within wider movements directed toward social goals of full participation on the part of the nation's citizens. Although the projects described in this chapter are still at a relatively early stage, they have already demonstrated the ways in which the stories and narratives created by Brazilian youth could play a part in the long movement toward the construction of fully democratic frameworks absent for so long in the nation's history. Directly relevant to people's lives and communities, digital stories which recover memory and foster collective and individual awareness may also enhance the sense of ownership of knowledge and voice which is crucial to further participation. They may also act as a bridge and mediator between networks and communities of all kinds engaged in building and transforming Brazil.

## Notes

1 The movement, jointly supported by the NGO Aracati and the Museu da Pessoa, is hosted by the Museu da Pessoa website (www.museudapessoa.net/ MuseuVirtual/home/resources/homesPublicadas/MVHM_23.html).
2 "2Tesouro da juventude," *Correio Braziliense* (DF), June 2, 2007 (www.uff.br/ obsjovem/mambo/index.php?option=com_content&task=view&id=293& Itemid=9).

3   In a national survey of 8,000 young people in Brazil aged between 15 and 21, 50.2 percent had never accessed a computer. The Internet appeared as the third principal means of communication used by youth from the A/B classes and as the eighth most used means of communication for youth from the D/E classes.

4   With regard to Internet access, as of the latter part of September 2007, 13.3 percent of the entire population of Brazil were Internet users, or had access to the Internet, a figure which is projected to rise to 22.1 percent by 2011 (Internet World Stats, Brazil: Internet Stats and Telecom Market Report, www. internetworldstats.com/sa/br.htm).

5   See www.museudapessoa.com.br

6   See www.vivario.org.br

7   See www.storycenter.org/memvoice/pages/cookbook.html

8   According to this study carried out by the World Bank, young people aged between 15 and 24 account for 47 percent of the total numbers of unemployed in the nation, and 40 percent of the total homicides; but only account for 6 percent of total government spending on social welfare.

9   See www.aracati.org.br/portal/aracati/articulacao_politica.htm

10  See www.aracati.org.br/portal/aracati/projetos_educacao.htm

11  Carol Misorelli, interview, August 10, 2007.

12  "Diário de Bordo" (www.museudapessoa.net/ummilhao/diariodebordo.pdf).

13  See iredes.rits.org.br/iredes/viewIndex.do

14  Carol Misorelli, interview, August 10, 2007.

15  See www.museudapessoa.net/MuseuVirtual/home/resources/homesPublicadas/ MVHM_23.html

# 10

# Digital Storytelling as Participatory Public History in Australia

## Jean Burgess and Helen Klaebe

The model of digital storytelling first developed by Joe Lambert and others at the Center for Digital Storytelling (CDS) has been adopted and variously transformed for use in an ever-increasing number of mainly institutional contexts, many of which are represented in the present volume. In most forms of digital storytelling understood in this way, everyday storytelling, life narrative, and the domestic archive of biographical images are re-mediated through the production and distribution of digital stories, transforming them from one-to-one, private forms of communication and translating them into contexts where they can potentially contribute to public culture (Burgess 2006a, Burgess, Klaebe, and Foth 2006). Despite this, it is now clear that there is no "one" thing that is digital storytelling; in practice, it is shaped and reconfigured to fit the goals and ideologies of each of these contexts – from public service broadcasting to community activism and education. However, there are (at least) two core elements of both the form and method of digital storytelling that appear to remain consistent: first, the collaborative workshop; and second, the first-person narrative.

In both of these two core elements – the participatory workshop and the first-person narrative – the digital storytelling movement has parallels in the tradition of oral history, especially when it is used as an element of public history projects. In this chapter, we discuss the potential of digital storytelling as a methodology through a detailed reflection on an applied research project that integrated both participatory public history and digital storytelling in the context of a new master-planned urban development: the Kelvin Grove Urban Village (KGUV) "Sharing Stories" project in Australia.

## The Idea of Participatory Public History

The term "public history" was first used in the USA in the 1970s to describe the employment outside universities of trained historians; in other words, scholarly history practiced in public, rather than within the academy (Liddington and Ditchfield 2005). Here we use it in a way that incorporates the multiple meanings of the concept "public," in line with the definition used by the New York University (NYU) program for public history, as well as scholars such as Frisch (1990, 1997) and Glassberg (1987), who position the development of "public history" both past and present in relation to the progressive democratic agendas in the USA. The NYU public history program provides a useful and comprehensive lay definition that captures the idea of public history as a democratic practice and its relevance to lived experience: "Public history is a set of theories, methods, assumptions and practices guiding the identification, preservation, interpretation and presentation of historical artifacts, texts, structures and, landscapes *in conjunction with and for the public*" (NYU Public History Program 2007, emphasis added).

Public history understood in this way often uses oral history as a research method. Traditionally, however, few public history projects approach the authorship of history as a process undertaken *with* the public; that is, an activity in which the public participate as co-creators of some or all of the content. When the practice of public history moves beyond merely "accessing" or "harvesting" vernacular histories and engages the public directly as co-creators, it is transformed into something we might properly call participatory public history. To the definition of public history as "history that is seen, heard, read, and interpreted by a popular audience" (NYU Public History Program 2007), we would add "created."

This ethic of participation is common to all branches of the digital storytelling tradition: one of the core aims of the practice is to provide people who are not necessarily expert users with an opportunity to produce an aesthetically coherent and interesting broadcast-quality work that communicates effectively with a wider public audience. In comparison to Web 2.0 platforms like YouTube or Flickr, which are driven by relatively autonomous participation and informal, peer-led learning rather than "top-down" training (Burgess 2006b, Perkel 2006), digital storytelling works to broaden participation by articulating everyday vernacular experiences and practices (such as oral storytelling) with professional expertise and institutional support. The comparatively small scale of a local history project allows for this kind of direct and intensive participation. This explicitly participatory approach is especially useful in projects that seek not only to document history, but also to reconstruct the impact of change on communities, or to engage communities in the process of change, as was the case with the redevelopment of Kelvin Grove. For these reasons, the digital storytelling workshop appeared to be an ideal vehicle for an experiment in participatory public history.

## The "Sharing Stories" Project

The Kelvin Grove site, which sits at the edge of the Brisbane Central Business District, had housed iconic educational and military institutions – including an army barracks – for nearly a century. When the barracks closed in 1998 the Queensland Department of Housing and Queensland University of Technology (QUT) went into partnership to redevelop the site to include a high-density mix of residential, commercial, institutional, and retail land use. The "Sharing Stories" public history project was a vehicle through which to stimulate community engagement as the area underwent this redevelopment and was transformed into the KGUV. The project produced two books representing the history of the area from the first European settlement (Klaebe 2006b), and a website, which includes community oral history, visual artworks, and digital stories produced as part of the project (www.kgurbanvillage.com.au/sharing/).

The project produced a collection of 18 digital stories in two workshops. The digital stories were screened publicly and were also published on the Sharing Stories website, where they attracted significantly more visitors than any other creative content housed there. Methodologically, the digital storytelling workshops functioned to examine how new media techniques such as digital storytelling could be successfully employed to remember personal experiences in relation to a community public history project (Klaebe and Foth 2006), as well as in exploring the affordances of digital storytelling as an effective remediation of "vernacular creativity" (Burgess 2006a) in the service of cultural citizenship, particularly for older, less computer-literate people. The digital stories produced for the project primarily took the shape of anecdotal reminiscences – about childhoods, work experiences, or military service in the area. They use stock narrative devices – the humorous anecdote, the memorial to loss, and the recounting with pride of past achievements; and old photographs drawn from personal, public, and organizational archives. Taken as a body of work, the stories re-mediate "public" history in subtle, associative ways: they connect representations of storytellers' present "selves" with personal memories of the past, even while focusing on a "public" place and referencing major historical events and shared memories, such as World War II.

## Reconfiguring the Digital Storytelling Workshop

The first of the two workshops was held in a university computer lab, facilitated by a three-person team with the additional support of two young people who volunteered to help the older participants to use the computers. This was an intergenerational and cross-institutional workshop: it included students, educators, retired military personnel, and nearby residents. In this first workshop, the intention was to adhere as closely as possible to the model that had been introduced to a group of QUT researchers by Daniel Meadows in an earlier "train-the-trainers" workshop, and which had been used successfully, with minor adaptations, in the Youth Internet Radio Network project (Hartley et al. 2003, Notley and Tacchi 2004). While providing as much assistance as necessary, we expected the participants to write their own scripts, record their own voice-overs, and to participate actively in scanning, editing, and assembling the digital images and video.

However, it quickly became clear that the participants' primary goal in taking part in the workshop was to contribute to a public history project rather than to "express" themselves or to share their life experiences. While they participated enthusiastically in the workshop at a social level, they did not represent themselves as being motivated or engaged by the many technical tasks involved with the digital production of the stories. This contrast between the apparent interests and motivations of these participants and those who had taken part in other digital storytelling projects meant that the process had to be quickly and significantly adapted "on the fly" in order to ensure both timely completion of the stories and an enjoyable experience for the participants.

In the first workshop, the activities that form part of the story circle day – the "games" designed to lower the barriers to collaboration and trust, as well as to encourage and reward "self-expression" – were met with a polite but lukewarm reception. However, once the conversation turned to what was clearly perceived as the "real business" of the workshop – the history of the Kelvin Grove Urban Village area – the atmosphere became charged with enthusiasm. Once the "production" part of the workshop began, the top-down, step-by-step "teaching" of how to use the software was abandoned in favor of a more collaborative and ad hoc approach, with older participants who were reluctant to use computers teamed up one-on-one with trainers or younger volunteers. The most significant finding from this first phase of the research was that for these participants, the motivation to make digital stories as part of this project was not primarily "creative," but rather it was oriented toward the preservation of memory, social interaction, and the sharing of knowledge.

In the second workshop, which involved mostly older people who were either current or past residents of the Kelvin Grove area, we deliberately departed even further from the production-oriented workshop model – partly based on insights gained from the first workshop, but for other reasons as well. Several participants had health and literacy difficulties that made it impossible for the workshop to proceed in strictly the "usual" way. For example, one of the participants had Parkinson's Disease, another, very poor eyesight, and another, very basic formal literacy skills. Accordingly, we experimented in several significant ways with the workshop model. Three group workshop days were held, where the focus was placed on getting all the participants together to share their stories, talk about their memories of the KGUV site, and ensure that they all participated in the storyboarding of their individual digital stories and made, or were consulted on, decisions around the selection and ordering of images to illustrate the scripts. Some of the stories were unscripted. This meant that the outcome of the story circle process for some participants was something like an interview schedule – a roadmap for a chat – rather than a script that they then read out aloud. These interviews or conversations were recorded, and the resultant audio files (in some cases, 20 minutes in length) were edited down to two-minute voice-overs by the production team. In this workshop, while the participants were consulted and ultimately had control over the content of their stories, it was the production team (which included experienced digital storytellers, a researcher, and a semi-professional video producer) who scanned, edited, and assembled the images and soundtracks.

One longstanding local resident who participated in this group had previously been interviewed as part of the oral history collection and had become an invaluable source of information that was not available in the archives. While a gifted storyteller, she had limited formal literacy skills. It was important that these literacy issues – and her strong desire to conceal them – did not exclude her from producing a digital story. Rather than preparing a written script, which she would then read aloud, we prepared a set of questions to prompt the retelling of a number of the engaging and humorous anecdotes that she was extremely well-practiced in performing. The recording was then cut and edited into a coherent voice-over by the production team. The colloquial language used by this participant is very engaging, and reveals glimpses of the changes that the socioeconomic composition of the Kelvin Grove community had undergone from the immediate postwar period to the present day.

Another participant, Teresa, was the full-time carer for her partner Igor. The couple had emigrated to Australia as refugees from an Italian internment camp after World War II. Teresa's digital story was based on an extended interview recorded directly to a laptop over tea and cake in her kitchen. The appropriate images to accompany the story were selected as part of a conversation over the photo album – effectively, an informal and collaborative storyboarding process. The digital assembly was undertaken entirely by the production team back at QUT, in consultation with the participant. Additionally, we held a private "screening" in the couple's home, as Teresa's care responsibilities meant that she was unable to attend the initial participants-only screening and focus group. When we showed her the completed story, Teresa watched it once and instantly phoned her neighbors, asking them to come over immediately to view it. Teresa and her son were able to attend the public screening at the Creative Industries Precinct, which is part of the KGUV, and once again her neighbors came along to support her. Teresa's story, which recounts the couple's experience as refugees and new residents of Kelvin Grove, has proven to be one of the most engaging and discussion-provoking of all the stories produced in the Sharing Stories project.

## Reflection and Evaluation

The main evaluation instruments used in the project were focus groups and informal feedback at the public screenings. The focus groups were used to discuss and evaluate the stories that had been produced, as well as to assist us in evaluating the fit between the workshop process, the goals of the stakeholders, and the benefits of participation. The responses to the question of whether the workshop had benefited the participants in any way were characterized by two clear themes. First, the participants were enthusiastic about the preservation of memories in a form that can be easily passed on to others (mainly in the family) and that would be appealing to wider audiences, especially audiences who were not especially "interested" in history. For example, one man told us that he saw the digital story form as a good substitute for his "red book" of photos – which he said friends and family members tended to "complain about" rather than engage with when he brought it out to show them. Another said that he could see digital storytelling being very useful in his family, as his children were "always at him" and his wife to document their lives for the benefit of future generations. A third also focused on the potential for the preservation of family memories, lamenting the difficulties of reconstructing history when artifacts have been lost and little has been written down. Beyond the focus on family history, the participants clearly identified the benefits of encountering new or diverse perspectives on shared memories of historical events. In the focus group, these discussions repeatedly and animatedly became sidetracked into more sharing of memories and stories. Whenever the conversation was not explicitly being directed elsewhere, it turned to history – potential crossovers between family trees, arguments about the exact locations of buildings in the area at a particular time, and personal memories or amusing anecdotes produced in response to the digital stories on screen. This enthusiasm around sharing and comparing historical information and memories was the most marked dynamic of social interaction across all three of the group sessions at the workshop.

The second primary theme that characterized the focus-group discussion clustered around social interaction, community engagement, and encounters with difference. For example, following the screening of Teresa Mircovich's story, which narrates her journey with a young family from a refugee camp in Italy to her eventual home in Kelvin Grove, the other participants remarked that hearing about the "Italian immigration" experience was "interesting." This led to a discussion about how the names of southern European immigrants were often Anglicized upon settling in Australia, and then to the significance of the connotations of Scottish, Irish, and English names in the interwar and postwar period, memories of the cultural clash between Protestants and Catholics, and in turn to stories about "past" prejudices against "colored people" in Brisbane.

Similarly, when asked to critique the digital stories and evaluate the way we had edited them, the participants were overwhelmingly concerned with assessing the historical accuracy of the texts that had been produced. In some cases, participants asked us to change or add to their stories to reflect this concern with accuracy. In keeping with the idea of authoring micro-histories rather than "entertainment," some participants insisted on strictly referential relationships between images and sound. For example, at one point in a story about the experience of National Service, the photograph on the screen is of a gun tripod that was only used in training, but the voice-over refers to the period following training. The participant was concerned that fellow members of the unit would think he had made a mistake in the story. He asked us to superimpose text over the image to acknowledge this fact. The nature of the participants' comments and concerns about individual stories reinforced our intuition that, in local community contexts like KGUV, the imagined audience for the participants is composed of equally knowledgeable and culturally proximate peers, not an imagined or diverse *public*. From their point of view, if not in reality, the public "out there" was literally an afterthought, despite their prior knowledge that the digital stories would eventually be viewed by a much wider audience, at the launch and on the KGUV Sharing Stories website.

## Rethinking Digital Literacy

While some of the rhetoric surrounding new media for cultural participation uses language like "enabling" and "affording," in practice this project revealed the extent to which new media initiatives like digital storytelling work not to enable creativity directly, but to *mediate* vernacular practices that are already in place. Many of our participants were already extremely active and engaged in private or community-based history practices. For some of them, the digital storytelling workshop offered the opportunity to showcase their existing work, or to draw attention to a particularly important point they wished to make out of their previous formal or informal historical research into the area. It is important to point out the extent to which this ability to amplify what the participants were already doing as vernacular historians or storytellers did not necessarily require an individual to possess direct mastery of technology on their part – the process in most cases involved a number of people with specific competencies collaborating to share skills and knowledge.

Graham, who was in his eighties at the time of the workshop, was recognized in 1992 as "Queenslander of the Year" for his dedication to community work in his local regional district. However, age and his consequent relocation prevented him from continuing to engage in community activities to the extent that he previously had. Graham was invited to participate in the KGUV Sharing Stories project and chose to make a digital story featuring personal photographs of a previously undocumented Japanese prisoner-of-war holding area. Graham's story attracted great interest from history groups and the wider community after it had featured online. Since then, Graham has co-presented walking history tours of the Kelvin Grove Urban Village site, given an address in his retirement village, and spoken to school groups around Anzac and Remembrance Days. While he did not physically use the computer to assemble his story, he had read the digital storytelling manual which was given to all participants, written the script and storyboard, and selected the images and music. When it was time to assemble all the digital elements in the video-editing application, Graham sat beside one of the trainers in front of the computer monitor, for the most part controlling and directing the process by pointing at the screen and giving verbal instructions or discussing editing choices, but without ever physically touching the mouse or keyboard.

While the project was relatively small-scale and localized, it is important to note the intensive ways in which digital stories can circulate among micro-publics, and the unintended consequences that can result. Minna, at 86 years old, was one of the most senior participants in the KGUV Sharing Stories project. She came along to the workshop with several exercise books filled with neatly handwritten histories of the Kelvin Grove Infants' School describing in great detail her experiences there as a teacher during World War II – histories that only close family members and fellow residents of her retirement home had seen before. Her story was produced with a great deal of technical assistance from the facilitators, who helped her to rework some of the information from these exercise books. The story interweaves snippets of these wartime "institutional" memories of the school with anecdotes from the nascent romance with the young man who was later to become her husband. Minna, who lives in a local retirement home, reported that the staff and other residents treated her "differently" following a screening of her story at the home. She reported receiving comments from staff and residents such as, "Make way for the movie star!" as she passed through the common areas. Most significantly, Minna remarked to us that after seeing her digital story, her children were far more interested than they previously had been in reading the detailed diaries she had kept since she was in her teens and from which the historical material for her digital story was drawn.

In a participatory public history project, the local citizens' stories are not only important sources of information; more importantly, the incorporation of ordinary "voices" can facilitate the affective communication of this history to a broader public. The representation of vernacular history through the integration of personal voices into a larger project can produce "narratives that interweave both the personal and collective" (Giunta 2004), allowing citizens' voices to become "attached to one another" (Villarreal 2004) within the organizing context of an overall project. The project attempted to "capture" vernacular history while preserving the agency of the ordinary people who are its practitioners; throughout, the stories balance personal expression with the potential to communicate with an interested, if localized, public. While we do not claim that the digital stories produced in this project represent an authoritative source of knowledge about the history of Kelvin Grove, they did prove to be very effective as a means of focusing interest and creating a public profile for the much larger range of materials – the book and living archive of oral histories, photographs, and documentation – that make up the Sharing Stories project overall, as a people's history of the Kelvin Grove area.

## Conclusion

The Sharing Stories project integrated current directions in both public history and digital storytelling practice. It was, at the time, an exceptional project, the like of which had not been previously envisaged as part of an urban redevelopment in Australia. It developed several key groundbreaking strategies for the use of "participatory public history" by community development facilitators who are keen to work from within communities. Generally speaking, the current modus operandi for public historians involves the historian collecting information, editing and compiling source material, and then presenting a finished product to the community. The public is given, at best, a limited opportunity to be involved in creating this history. This project, however, actively sought to engage participants in the process of creating historical documents. Although actively involving the community in creating this history was undoubtedly much more labor-intensive and time-consuming than a traditional approach might have been, it produced clear benefits.

In Sharing Stories, ordinary citizens became involved in making artistic decisions about the way their own accounts were quoted and represented – both in the written account of the history of Kelvin Grove, and in the production of broadcast-quality digital stories. The use of digital technologies, combined with institutional support and expert facilitation, enabled the participants to co-create the narratives that would represent their perspectives on the site's history to the public, amplifying the "ordinary voices" of popular memory. This differed from a traditional oral history approach, which focuses on archiving and collating stories and artifacts, which may be used by a historian to tell a story chosen by that researcher. The responsibilities of the public historian in this new climate can, therefore, be reimagined and extended to include translating the potential of new media into community contexts. Digital stories are not a substitute for long-form oral history, any more than oral history is a direct substitute for scholarly historical writing. However, our current research among oral history practitioners suggests that although oral histories are sometimes used by researchers, much oral history practice is focused on collection and preservation, not on public communication. Integrating a program of digital storytelling alongside these long-form oral histories might, among other things, allow oral historians to attract more public and community engagement in their work.

The participatory turn in public history occurs in tandem with the new challenges and opportunities that digital technologies and networks represent for cultural institutions (Russo et al. 2006, Miller 2005). User-led content creation and vernacular creativity are central drivers of an emerging Web-based popular culture. But despite the "participatory" turn, there is also an emerging "participation gap" (Jenkins 2006) which has supplanted the technologically focused idea of a "digital divide," presenting new challenges to the traditional role of cultural institutions as access providers. Making history "accessible" in a participatory age requires not only the provision of access to content, but also the provision of opportunities for active public participation through co-creation, and the promotion of cultural diversity and inclusiveness. But the "participatory" ethic does not necessarily require every citizen to master the technologies of production – at least, not in every case. The question, rather, is how best to articulate specific forms of professional expertise (like media production or historical research) to existing vernacular expertise (like local knowledge and oral storytelling) and communities of interest, both outside of and in connection with formal institutions.

To that end, we argue that digital storytelling is at its most effective when embedded in a well-supported context that shapes the practice of self-mediated representation toward a shared purpose – whether public service broadcasting, as in the BBC "Capture Wales" program, or the community engagement strategies of cultural institutions – see, for example, the recent and ongoing initiatives of the State Library of Queensland, where digital storytelling is increasingly integrated with public library and oral history programs (Sayer and Stumm 2008, Stumm and Sayer 2007). As the Sharing Stories project discussed here demonstrates, participatory public history projects are particularly productive "hosts" in which digital storytelling can be embedded in order to promote a sense of "shared authority" in the representation of history (Frisch 1990).

# 11

# Finding a Voice
## Participatory Development in Southeast Asia

## *Jo Tacchi*

Atanu Ray lives near a wide and beautiful stretch of the Ichamati River in West Bengal. In his digital story, in poetic Bengali, he tells us about his home. Most people here are paddy farmers: "rice is green in the fields but golden in the home." The vibrantly colorful scenes of rice fields and farmers give way to Atanu's black-and-white drawings of the impact of industry and the consequent and often devastating annual floods. One year it was so bad that Atanu and his neighbors lost all their homes and possessions and lived in a school for two months. Brick kilns and their waste are gradually making the river bed narrow and shallow, and the annual floods threaten to get worse. Atanu fears for the future of this place.

A small child called Maane, about eight or nine years old, is the focus of Sanjeela Karki's digital story. In her town of Tansen, in a hilly region of Nepal, Maane is just one of many orphaned children who resort to begging to survive. They have nowhere to live and no adults to take care of them. In this self-reflexive story Sanjeela asks herself many questions: what about Maane's future? Will he be begging all his life? Do these children have to go to sleep hungry if they do not beg? Do all orphans suffer this fate? Who is to blame? Maane's tiny, outstretched hands, cupped to receive the five rupees she gives him, his tattered clothing, and his doleful face haunt her digital story. Sanjeela reflects that if there was an orphanage in Tansen, Maane would not have to beg. He would have a place to sleep and food to eat. "We should build a fund to build an orphanage" – after all, she insists, isn't it our responsibility as social beings to do something?

Sayera Bano is a 25-year old Muslim woman from Seelampur in Delhi. Her digital story, "My Steps Forward," movingly depicts both the restrictive nature of her position as a young woman in a large family, and her efforts to

**Figure 11.1**   Article on Sayera Bano, *Mail Today* newspaper, Delhi, November 9, 2006: 8

develop a career for herself. She is one of nine children in a family that does not encourage education, in a society where most women are restricted to the local area. Sayera gained a BA degree through a correspondence course, but tells us that she "had little information about other things in this world." Her social life was restricted to rituals, weddings, and family gatherings: "I used to think that the life of a woman is confined to these things." Sayera heard about a local Information and Communication Technology (ICT) center for women and went along and saw other young women learning to use computers. She joined and learned as well. She took up photography with some flair. Her first digital story won a prize from a Delhi university and her picture appeared in Delhi newspapers. This, she tells us, gave her strength. The aim of her story is to inspire other young women from Seelampur to train for careers in areas such as the media so that they too can gain new insights into the "outer" world, and "experience new ways to earn money."

## Introduction

This chapter is about the use of digital storytelling in a research project called "Finding a Voice,"[1] a multi-sited ethnographic study of – and experiment in – local participatory content creation. The project is made up of a research network of 15 preexisting local media and ICT initiatives in India, Nepal, Sri Lanka, and Indonesia. The goal of "Finding a Voice" is to increase understanding of how ICT can be both effective and empowering in each local context and to investigate the most effective ways of articulating information and communication networks (both social and technological) to empower poor people to communicate their "voices" within and beyond marginalized communities. We are researching opportunities and constraints for local content created by and for specific local communities, for the development and communication of ideas, information, and perspectives appropriate to those communities.

We began with a broad definition of "voice" – it references inclusion and participation in social, political, and economic processes, meaning making, autonomy, and expression. With a specific focus on ICT and development at the community level we wondered about the significance of voice in terms of poverty – "voice poverty" can be understood as the inability of people to influence the decisions that affect their lives, and the right to participate in that decision making (Lister 2004). Our definition of voice has remained broad, as we see its relevance to ICT linked to issues of access to modes of expression and more generally to freedom of expression. It can be about opportunity and agency to promote self-expression and advocacy, about access and the skills to use technologies and platforms for the distribution of a range of different voices.

What better way to combine ICT and the desire to promote voice in a development context than digital storytelling? Certainly it has become a regular feature in many of the community-based ICT centers with whom we work.

In this chapter I describe and discuss the reasons for the use of digital storytelling in "Finding a Voice," and how it has been used and adapted. I discuss some specific issues around participation, and draw some conclusions about the use of digital storytelling with marginalized communities in developing countries. But first, in order to locate this project and our work, I take a little time to talk about its background and context. This is important, as it immediately acknowledges the messiness and problematic natures of both "participation" and "development," and most certainly of "participatory development," and it is in this difficult terrain that this application of digital storytelling resides.

## Background and Context

Issues of voice are receiving a great deal of attention in development communication, and development more widely – one might even consider the concern with voice to be a "development zeitgeist" (Tacchi 2008). Listening to and consulting the "voices of the poor" (Narayan, Chambers, et al. 2000, Narayan, Patel, et al. 2000, Narayan and Petesch 2002) marks a now mainstreamed or institutionalized concern for participatory approaches to understanding the lives of those experiencing poverty – the targets of development efforts. This is an approach supported and promoted, for example, by organizations like the World Bank and the Asian Development Bank (see Viswanathan and Srivastava 2007).[2] It is an approach that allows those who are living in conditions that might constitute "poverty" to tell those who are not what this experience is like, in their own words. Such an approach might challenge our "expert" conceptions of poverty itself. Taken-for-granted economic models might be seen to fall short.

Recent work on wellbeing and happiness, especially research conducted as part of the "Wellbeing in Developing Countries" project,[3] demonstrates a mismatch between incidences of poverty as measured by material indicators, and locally understood and defined subjective wellbeing and experiences of happiness (Kingdon and Knight 2006). For example, respondents in rural areas of Peru – whose poverty as measured by indicators of externally defined economic wellbeing is higher that their urban counterparts – were more satisfied with their lot than urban respondents who were unable to fulfill higher material aspirations (Copestake et al. 2007). This is reminiscent of Marshall Sahlins's (1972) depiction of hunter-gatherer societies as "the original affluent society," contrary to the popular view that sees them as the least developed form of society, and most in need of development. Copestake et al. took a eudaimonic (happiness-based) view of wellbeing. Indicators and measurements of wellbeing were determined, based on feelings of happiness and *locally* defined goals along with the ability to attain or aspire to them, rather than on global and standardized views of subjective wellbeing and measures of the same.

This strongly echoes the basis of arguments for participatory and bottom-up approaches to development, rooted in the work of Paolo Freire (1972) and actively championed for over twenty years by Robert Chambers. It is through participatory approaches that different representations of reality can be presented, and questions asked about "Whose Reality Counts?" (Chambers 1995). Such voicing may be encouraged, but nevertheless not be *heard*. Participatory approaches may themselves turn out to constitute "top-down participation," where participation constitutes "insiders" learning what "outsiders" want to hear, or simply an exercise in administrative task-sharing or the necessary rhetoric to win funding (Bailur 2007, Michener 1998, White 1996).

At the same time, in the fields of development communication and ICT for development increasing attention is being paid to the local production of content. This marks a concern with promoting a diversity of voices through media and communications. There is a discrete field called Communication for Social Change (Gray-Felder and Deane 1999), which might be considered as a point of crossover or convergence between the development agenda (here specifically concerned with "social change") and community-based, alternative, or citizens' media (Rodriguez 2001).[4] Another interesting point of convergence can be found in community multimedia centers (CMCs), largely initiated with donor funding and fitting squarely into the development agenda, and yet strongly linked to traditions of community media. UNESCO supports a global pilot project with the Swiss Agency for Development and Cooperation.[5] CMCs combine traditional media like the press, TV, and radio with new digital media like the Internet, computers, and cameras. The idea is that this convergence will provide a two-way link to global information and knowledge available through the Internet, through the "intermediary" of local traditional media (James 2004).

Most of the 15 sites in the "Finding a Voice" project can be considered CMCs.[6] The stress here is on community-produced media content and participatory approaches to its development. Participation not only in the creation of content, but also in the decision making surrounding what content should be made and what should be done with it. In this context, can digital storytelling provide a mechanism for participatory development?

## Digital Storytelling in "Finding a Voice"

Digital storytelling was used in "Finding a Voice" because it was seen as an interesting way to explore the personal voices of people who otherwise have no access to the media, and in the process teach them skills in multimedia production and a level of digital literacy. While some digital stories could be considered a form of mini- or micro-documentary, what set digital storytelling apart are the process and the purpose. The process was seen to be important, and community workshops which are community building in nature were promoted. While we anticipated that the process would be adapted to suit different contexts, we were interested in digital storytelling as it is essentially about the expression of personal voice. We wanted to explore whether personal voice could be used to effectively express social issues and promote positive social change. Another attraction of digital storytelling is that it can be distributed in a variety of formats such as DVD, video, CD, streaming or downloadable formats on the Web, television, radio (minus images), and community screenings.

Our approach had three main phases (Watkins and Tacchi 2008). The first phase was "training the trainers," where we trained members of the "Finding a Voice" sites through a series of workshops. We were initially highly influenced by a train-the-trainers workshop process taught to us by Daniel Meadows of BBC Wales, adapted from the format established by the Californian Center for Digital Storytelling (CDS), but soon found that we needed to adapt the process further to allow it to be more flexible to suit local contexts. For example, given the project's (and participants') desire to explore content that promotes social change or has some advocacy component, we combined the digital storytelling approach and its stress on story development with a journalistic technique – the five Ws: encouraging storymakers to think through *What* is happening in the story, *Who* is involved, *When* and *Where* the story takes place, and *Why* the story is being told (see Martin 2008). In addition, we encouraged thinking about the intended audience for each story, and targeting that audience.

The second phase was the local development of participatory content-creation activities in each site. Each site is different, has access to different facilities and media, and faces different local circumstances. The range of stories emerging, and varied strategies for participatory content creation employed by each center demonstrate the need to take context into account. In all sites the process of engaging people in participatory content-creation activities was challenging, for a range of reasons. Consequently a variety of strategies emerged (see Grubb and Tacchi 2008). For example, in an Indian ICT center for women located in a Delhi slum a local worker, Aseem Asha Usman, developed a vocational media course for young women.[7] Digital storytelling is one of the main components in the three-month media course, which deals with various aspects of design (including web design and multimedia production) and is tailored to fill a gap in the local employment market. This is interesting because whereas this ICT center had previously concentrated on basic computing skills (word processing, spreadsheets) and had investigated how these skills might lead to employment, Aseem found through local research that far more lucrative job opportunities were available for those with creative design skills, and indeed identified a skills shortage in this area. Digital storytelling workshops conducted in the center, such as the one Sayera Bano (see above) had attended, had already demonstrated to Aseem that the women participants had a keen interest in the *creative* and *expressive* use of technologies. Here, then, digital storytelling has become an important component in an employment-focused training program.[8]

The third phase is concerned with strategies for distribution, which depends on the message and target audience. For many of the stories produced across the sites, local screenings to small gatherings in order to generate discussion about local issues have been an effective mechanism for raising awareness, sharing perspectives, and encouraging others to make their own content and have a voice. Returning, for example, to the Indian ICT center where Aseem coordinated a range of digital storytelling activities: As well as holding local screenings to generate debate on the issues raised in the digital stories, he also used them to encourage other young women to get involved. He facilitated a group discussion with nine young women about what they might like to make a short digital story about. They came up with a whole range of ideas for stories. One young woman wanted to make a digital story about her personal feelings, her dreams, and the challenges she faces; another woman wanted to tell people about her family problems so that someone might offer her some advice. One young woman wanted to make a story about the common health problems of women in the area and prevention measures they might take. A local entrepreneur wanted to make a story in which she can show how successful she has been in developing her business, and then to show it to the government or loan agencies to sanction credits for developing her business further. In some cases, digital stories and their messages have been brought to the attention of larger audiences, such as in the case of the first digital story made by members of a rural community library in Nepal. The local researcher Sita, along with a couple of colleagues from the community library, attended a "Finding a Voice" content-creation workshop and made a story about a local woman who had learned many things from "big letter books" once she learned how to read (see Martin et al. 2007). This digital story was screened locally and at a meeting in Nepal's capital city Katmandu. The story was picked up by a national newspaper and by a local radio station. Sita realized from this experience that a local story can prove interesting and inspiring to local people as well as wider audiences, and that strategies for distribution can aid in this process but need to be tailored to each piece of local content. Across the "Finding a Voice" sites stories have been screened in local communities to generate discussion about social issues, to raise awareness, share perspectives, and to encourage others to make their own content and have a voice.

## Conclusions

The World Congress on Communication for Development, held in Rome in October 2006, produced a set of recommendations to policy makers based on an understanding that communication is a "major pillar" for development and social change.[9] The *Rome Consensus* places community participation and ownership on the part of the poor and excluded at the heart of communication for development. Among the "strategic requirements" specified in the consensus are: access to communication tools so that people can communicate among themselves and with decision makers; recognition of the need for different approaches depending on different cultures; and support to those most affected by development issues to have a say. We can interpret these requirements as the need for community-based media that is context-specific and that promotes a range of voices.

Through the "Finding a Voice" project, a range of story ideas and motivations has emerged. Some of these stories may be more "valid" than others in terms of promoting social change, for instance by advocacy on behalf of a marginalized or voiceless group, positive messages about excluded or discriminated groups, or messages that promote health-related behaviors. In fact, there is no lack of evidence in our research of people wanting to use media to highlight social issues or demonstrate how one might challenge adversity, often through the device of providing an inspirational example. But we also see other ideas, other forms of self-expression, and other kinds of engagement with media, which are as much about self-expression as social change or "development." Notions of what we term "creative engagement" are starting to appear in the practices of our sites. Interesting activities are beginning to emerge that are starting to allow different voices to be heard, demonstrating alternative perspectives and challenging our notions of the appropriate relationships between ICTs and poor communities. Various appropriations of digital storytelling have emerged across the sites, along with other types of locally created content.

Just as with technologies themselves, this project has shown that digital storytelling can contribute to development agendas, but needs to be introduced in ways that recognize local social networks and cultural contexts, and to be adapted accordingly. Our research demonstrates that digital story-telling (along with other approaches to local, participatory content creation) can form an interesting component in participatory development in contexts such as those described here.

## Notes

1 "Finding a Voice: Making Technological Change Socially Effective and Culturally Empowering" is a research project funded by an Australian Research Council Linkage Grant (LP0561848) and UNESCO and UNDP (www.findingavoice.org).
2 See go.worldbank.org/H1N8746X10
3 See www.welldev.org.uk
4 See www.communicationforsocialchange.org
5 See www.unesco.org/webworld/cmc
6 Profiles of the sites can be found at www.findingavoice.org
7 Aseem was also one of the local researchers in the "Finding a Voice" research project.
8 See Kiran (2008) for more information on this course, and the way that digital stories are used to explore difficult social issues locally, such as domestic violence.
9 See siteresources.worldbank.org/EXTDEVCOMMENG/Resources/ RomeConsensus07.pdf

# 12

# The Matrices of Digital Storytelling
## Examples from Scandinavia

## *Knut Lundby*

### The Phenomenon

This chapter adopts the type of digital storytelling that is the main focus of the present volume: the short personal story developed in a "story circle," told in people's own voices, with mostly still pictures, produced with standard software by nonprofessionals. This is digital storytelling. These stories are usually self-representations, about the person (or the group) making the story. New forms of self- representational digital storytelling have emerged in recent years, for example, in blogs, personal home pages, or on social networking sites on the Web. Much of this activity should also be regarded and studied as digital storytelling.

The time span covered by digital storytelling is short, and the uneven diffusion of digital tools and competences around the globe does not make it a full circle; geographically speaking, digital storytelling has not reached "around the world": digital divides persist. The time and space matrix of digital storytelling still has many blanks. At my northern European corner of the world, in Scandinavia, there are blanks but also fields of intense digital storytelling activity. While Denmark did not have its first digital storytelling workshop until the very end of 2007, those in Sweden and Norway came into being a few years earlier. However, by mid-2008 Denmark had a digital storytelling center in co-operation with the Centre for Digital Storytelling (CDS), as part of a European digital storytelling network.[1]

This chapter explores the global time and space matrix of digital storytelling, its wider context of institutional and economic settings, and its relations to patterns of communication, culture, and hegemony. The significance of these three matrices will be concretized with examples of digital storytelling initiatives in Sweden and Norway. The processes of "mediation" appear as the key to understanding the limited spread as well as the wide diffusion of digital storytelling.

## Time and Space: The "Digital Tsunami"

The spread of digital storytelling has been rapid, though its history covers just a short span. The digital equipment for amateur digital storytelling was not available until personal computers were reasonably cheap, handy, user-friendly and capable of multimedia tasking. The Macintosh, the first personal computer with a graphic user interface, was launched in 1984, and a year later Microsoft introduced their competing operating system, Windows 1.0. However, these machines and programs did not really have the capacity to combine text, graphics, sound, and images in ways to make digital stories. Such hardware and software were not available on the market until the early 1990s, when portable laptops were also introduced.

It is hardly surprising that the specific digital storytelling practice was born in California: most of the new digital equipment was developed, and much of the digital innovation took place in Silicon Valley, California. Joe Lambert, one of the founders of the CDS, saw the "digital tsunami" break-ing over the California coast in the early 1990s (Lambert 2006: 9). He took action to capture the wave and became an initiator of a digital storytelling movement.

CDS's first digital storytelling workshop in 1993 was held in the same year that the World Wide Web – which was to offer a new and nearly unlim-ited network for the dissemination of digital stories – was made available to early adopters through the Mosaic browser. The first workshop was held some ten years before digital cameras became commonplace: such small-scale cameras would come to enable digital photographs to be used to visualize digital stories, alongside scanned photos from drawers back home. Only with these innovations did the technological presuppositions of digital storytelling become available.

While digital storytelling depended on the technology, machines and programs in themselves do not make stories, and so the workshops and "story circles" of the digital storytelling movement became crucial. Actual stories did not appear until the storytellers had developed the competences to make use of the equipment. The initial event in Los Angeles in 1993 could take place due to the availability of early digital equipment, combined with a will to move (and share) competences from visual and audio technologies to the emerging digital realm (Lambert 2006: 8–11).

The diffusion of computers and competences for digital storytelling from its Californian cradle has been wide. It reaches out to many corners of the world. However, overviews – as in this volume – show that digital storytelling has been mainly taken up within the regions, cities, and networks of high modernity, where electricity runs smoothly, computers are available, and "ordinary people" have the competence to use them. This also applies if the phenomenon is taken as not just those examples that follow the CDS's paradigmatic principles, but "the whole range of personal stories now being told in potentially public form using digital media resources," as Couldry (2008: 374) does.

There is an emergent space of digital storytelling that occupies a distinct stage in the history of mediated communication (Couldry 2008). As a "MediaSpace" digital storytelling both creates its own space and, as a media form, is influenced by the spatial frames within which it operates (Couldry and McCarthy 2004: 2). The Internet dramatically expanded the space of digital storytelling in general, although the "story circles" of the specific digital storytelling projects may be place-bound and nurtured by the local community in which they operate.

The international research project, "Mediatized Stories: Mediation Perspectives on Digital Storytelling among Youth" that I direct[2] covers digital storytelling in six countries, from California in the USA to Georgia. The strongholds of digital storytelling are in the USA, northern Europe, and Australia; the same goes for the research on this phenomenon, as witnessed in this book. Digital storytelling takes place in digitally saturated areas.

This does not imply that the digital stories necessarily tell narratives of the rich; the stories themselves may indeed be alternative or oppositional to the affluent ways of life in these societies, not least because digital storytelling is a bottom-up media practice. The DUSTY project, "Digital Underground Storytelling for Youth," in West Oakland, California, for example, gave a voice to children and young people in an "under-served area" (Hull and James 2007). Still, the space of digital storytelling, paradoxically, is the space of media-rich societies where the media are "unlimited" and "overwhelm our lives" (Gitlin 2001).

## Tools and Competences

This matrix of tools and competences establishes itself within the time and space dimensions of digital storytelling. The extent to which these media practices have spread throughout the world within the last two decades depends on the broad availability of the digital tools as well as people's ability to use them for making digital stories. With digital technologies, "ordinary people" have the tools to make their own digital stories. The storytellers act as producers, with a wide range of the digital media's available modalities at their disposal. However, to make stories people also need the competences to use the tools.

Software for "user-generated" content creation, combined with digital cameras and the wide options of the Internet, put a whole kit of tools (Kress 2003) in the hands of the digital storyteller. A key quality of the tools for the purpose of digital storytelling is their capacity to combine text, live and still images, sound, and music into one piece of work: this is the power of digital multimodal texts in digital storytelling (Hull and Nelson 2005).

In October 2003 Joe Lambert contacted teachers at Huseby secondary school in Trondheim, Norway, pioneers in multimedia classroom expressions.[3] He invited them to the first European conference on digital storytelling to be held with BBC Wales the following month. In Wales they met the initiator of the Swedish association, "digitalbridge," which aims to expand digital storytelling in Scandinavia. This association was set up following a storytelling project for youth called "My Digital Self-Geography," which was run in cooperation with the CDS within the "Narrative" Studio of the Swedish "Interactive Institute," at Malmö University.[4] Digitalbridge launched the first Scandinavian workshop in digital storytelling in Sweden in February 2004. Flimmer Film, a company based in Bergen, launched the first workshop in Norway a month later.[5] Their initiators had been accustomed to the principles of digital storytelling through "Capture Wales" (Meadows 2003), another project inspired by the CDS. It is striking how strictly loyal these offspring have remained to the principles and core methodologies set up by the Californian CDS (Lambert 2006). It is all about the merging of storytelling competence and digital tools.

I deliberately use the concept "tools" rather than "technologies" or "media." Certainly the computers and programs put into use for story-making are digital technologies. They may also be regarded as parts of digital media. However, here the point is that digital stories are constructed – with digital tools. When it comes to storytellers' abilities to appropriate digital tools, I prefer the term "competence" to "literacy." "Media literacy" in print and broadcasting culture has referred to the reader's (or rather the viewer's or listener's) capacity to interpret the media "text." With user-generated digital media, the concept of literacy includes writing as well as reading. However, "literacy" has been incorporated into a variety of non-critical governmental uses (Livingstone 2007). The research direction on "new literacies" brings a sociocultural definition of literacy, making "sense of reading, writing and meaning-making as integral elements of social practices" (Lankshear and Knobel 2007: 2). However, for the purpose of understanding digital storytelling, I prefer "competence." This concept may enhance literacy and include the ability to handle digital tools by focusing on "narrative competence," as proposed by Stephen Dobson (2005). Literacy is "re-positioned to rest upon a competence in narratives. This competence is in turn connected with the technology and socio-cultural relations mediating the narratives" (Dobson 2005: 12). Digital storytelling encourages a specific narrative competence. When people are used to the codes and genres of film and television, and have a growing proficiency in "the language of new media" (Manovich 2001), it is a short step to build the specific competence to make one's own digital stories. Still, digital storytelling requires some specific competences, related to small-scale self-representations.

## Institutions and Economy

The matrix of tools and competences in the making of digital stories appears within a larger matrix of institutions and economy. Digital storytelling always has an institutional aspect. Although a small-scale media phenomenon, it is dependent on developments and changes in the larger economy and has to relate to contemporary cultural industries. The matrix of institutions and economy, in turn, relates to the time and space dimensions: economy and institutions change over time; even within contemporary globalization they differ throughout the world.

Digital storytelling occurs within set institutional frames: the CDS in Berkeley is an institution set up for the purpose; the "Capture Wales" project was set up by the broadcasting institution, the BBC, together with Cardiff University. The story or history of digital storytelling is developing in a similar way in Scandinavia. Initiatives are taken by committed people who may have been inspired in workshops or conferences by the pioneers of digital storytelling from the USA or Britain. In the Scandinavian welfare states, the startups find support in publicly funded research or educational institutions. Later, an institutionalization may occur. In Sweden this has taken place within a purely public institution like the Swedish educational radio corporation with the project "Rum för Berättande" (Space for Storytelling), as well as in mixed-economy institutions like "Delta Garden."[6] They cooperate closely with the CDS, hoping to become a European node of that organization. In this way the original CDS further institutionalizes.

Institutionalization of digital storytelling also happens through its inclusion in university teaching. Since 2005, Blekinge Institute of Technology in Sweden has offered a net-based course in digital storytelling with a pedagogical slant. Malmö University has a course on communicative and artistic aspects of digital storytelling. In Norway, Oslo University College runs a variety of digital storytelling training projects, aimed at the dissemination of research and the popularization of knowledge. The "Mediatized Stories" research project, based at the University of Oslo, has developed a Master's course with critical and analytical perspectives on digital storytelling.[7]

While these examples are easy to identify as projects within specific institutional frames, such frames can also apply to less structured digital storytelling: social networking sites like MySpace, Facebook, or YouTube make up new institutional settings for the creation and communication of profiles and stories. However, huge companies own these sites and despite the open access, "user-generated content" is made within specific institutional power structures.

Institutions involve patterns of power that structure the activity. Institutions that invite digital storytelling have themselves to attend to the power relations of high modern knowledge-based economies. Thus, while contemporary cultural industries might encourage creativity, they do so on tough capitalist premises (Hesmondhalgh 2007). These industries will include digital storytelling when it is regarded profitable or otherwise suitable; they make stories with their "mediation of things" in order to improve sales (Lash and Lury 2007). Even when digital storytelling appears as alternative projects, the storytellers may define themselves in relation – in opposition or appropriation – to the signs and symbols from the big cultural industries.

## Culture and Hegemony

The same year as the first digital storytelling workshop was held in Los Angeles, a path-breaking book by the Latin American scholar Jesús Martín-Barbero was made available in English (Martín-Barbero 1993). From his Latin American experience, Martín-Barbero knew how "the media" could be used by power elites as means of oppression. Oppressed people could, however, rise up through a broader understanding of media-related works. Martín-Barbero drew up matrices of communication, culture, and hegemony, which, I will argue, relate and add to the matrices of time and space, tools and competence, institution and economy.

Martín-Barbero advised a cultural perspective that observes not just the technologies or media apparatuses but rather the hegemonic stories that the institutions in power are telling. He moved the focus from the "media" to the processes of "mediations" in which they are involved. "Mediations" refer to "the articulation between communication practices and social movements and the articulation of different tempos of development with the plurality of cultural matrices" (Martín-Barbero 1993: 187). This is relevant to digital storytelling as a practice and as a movement. Couldry points out that Martín-Barbero's approach opens up connections with "the history of people's attempts at alternative 'mediation' that challenge the authority of existing media institutions" (Couldry 2000: 7).

To place the media – large- or small-scale – in the field of mediations is to place them in a process of cultural transformations, Martín-Barbero (1993: 139) holds. Communication takes place as mediations, but so does culture. Culture in itself becomes a mediating factor (Martín-Barbero 1993: 122). When powerful "media" are turned into "mediations" of hegemonic stories, they can be countered by other, counter-hegemonic, stories. This may take place in people's interpretations of the hegemonic stories in their reception processes. Martín-Barbero points to "the resistances and varied ways people appropriate media content according to manner of use" (Martín-Barbero 1993: 2). The countering of hegemonic stories, however, could also be exerted through the creation of alternative stories. Digital stories could be such stories. "neveragain.no" is a Scandinavian example, applying digital storytelling to reflect on war and human rights.[8] Martín-Barbero made his cultural or counter-cultural argument for what would today be termed user-generated content long before that term arose and before the digital tools were available.

Martín-Barbero adds to a simple time/space matrix of digital story-telling. Within the short history and limited spread of these alternative mediations, Martín-Barbero's ideas invite us to regard digital storytelling within matrices of communication, culture, and hegemony. The mediations are the key to understanding. Martín-Barbero's concept of mediation "entails looking at how culture is negotiated and becomes an object of transactions in a variety of contexts" (Schlesinger 2003: xiii). This also happens in the shaping and sharing of digital stories.

## Mediation as Key

Nancy Thumim takes up Martin-Barbero's challenge, and in her doctoral dissertation on mediating self-representations she points out the tensions surrounding "ordinary" people's participation in public-sector storytelling projects (Thumim 2007).[9] With the distinctions between textual, institutional, and cultural aspects of mediation, Thumim explains communication processes within the matrices of digital storytelling that I have laid out: institutional mediation takes place within the matrix of institutions and economy, with its opportunities and limitations; tensions of cultural mediation are played out within the matrix of culture and hegemony.[10] Thumim's category of textual mediation points to the making and display of the digital story itself. This "text" is heavily dependent upon the digital tools as well as the competence of the (prod)user.

Competence as a prerequisite for textual mediation is the ability to explore and exploit the form and technologies of digital storytelling. The processes of cultural mediation link these performative competences with the cultural-symbolic competence that a person brings to the production of a digital story. By focusing on the textual/technological as well as the wider cultural competences of the storytellers, Thumim addresses the agent or person performing the self-representation within a given institutional context. As Glynda Hull and Mira-Lisa Katz have shown, self-representational digital storytelling is about "crafting an agentive self" (Hull and Katz 2006). Thumim demonstrates how self-representations are shaped in processes of mediation.

For the concept of mediation Thumim basically builds on Roger Silverstone's work. He, again, refers to Martín-Barbero and defines "mediation" as "the fundamentally, but unevenly, dialectical process in which institutionalized media of communication are involved in the general circulation of symbols in social life" (Silverstone 2007: 109). That mediation is dialectical means it implies an ongoing exchange between the producers and the users of the media. It is uneven because "the power to work with, or against, the dominant or deeply entrenched meanings that the media provide is unevenly distributed across and within societies" (Silverstone 2007: 109). This definition of mediation refers to the big media. With small-scale media in bottom-up productions of digital stories, the power and the dialectics lean toward "ordinary people" and away from professional media work (Deuze 2007). User-generated content in general, and digital storytelling in particular, increasingly contribute to the "circulation of symbols in social life" (Silverstone 2007: 109).

## Cultural Tools

The narratives drawn upon in their stories and the digital media applied to make the stories are "cultural tools" of the digital storytellers (Erstad and Wertsch 2008). These cultural tools make it possible to take part in the general circulation of symbols in society. However, in order to grasp how this works, a link between different theories of mediation has to be made. The concept of mediation that Martín-Barbero, Silverstone, and Thumim use comes from sociologically oriented media studies, an approach that could be enriched by the sociocultural theory on mediation (Wertsch, del Río, and Alvarez 1995) inspired by the Russian social psychologist Lev Vygotsky (1896–1934). He showed that human interaction is always mediated. Indirect or mediated activity takes place with the use of "signs": in language as a means of social intercourse, and with "tools" as means or object to master or accomplish a task (Vygotsky 1978: 53–5). Mediation is a theme that runs through Vygotsky's writings. He talks of an "explicit mediation" that is intentionally and overtly introduced into the activity, where it is easy to identify the signs and tools that are employed as they appear in materiality. "Implicit mediation" may be more difficult to identify as the tools and signs typically may be hidden in spoken language (Wertsch 2007).

Digital storytellers apply both signs and tools. These "mediational means" (Wertsch 1985: 32) combine and work as "cultural tools" (Wertsch 1998). Digital media, with their capacity for multimodal "languages," make up a new kind of cultural tools. Erstad and Wertsch (2008) discuss how digital media may change the old art of storytelling, as new mediational means always transform mediated action (Wertsch 1998: 25). Narratives are themselves cultural tools that people relate to in meaning-making activities such as storytelling (Bruner 1990, 1996, Wertsch 1998). Narrative is a mode of thought and a vehicle of meaning-making. By making stories people create a version of the world in which "they can envisage a place for themselves – a personal world" (Bruner 1996: 39). There are "specific narratives" related to concrete places, characters, and events and there are "schematic narrative templates" with the tales and themes of a culture that our smaller stories may draw upon (Erstad and Wertsch 2008), where the narrative mediation may be implicit.

Erstad and Wertsch remind us that the plots in digital storytelling usually are not original and new but collected and amended from the narrative templates of our culture. However, digital technologies as new cultural tools may change the practices of storytelling. Digital storytelling in "classic" or new networking forms represents "developments in the way humans relate to each other and their surroundings. They represent new performance spaces and possibilities for mediated action. Our challenge is then," Erstad and Wertsch (2008: 37) conclude, "to grasp how these new cultural tools change the use of narratives and the act of storytelling in fundamental ways."

## Conclusion: The Matrices

Digital storytelling is to be found within sets of contextual dimensions that define the probable occurrence of this phenomenon. This applies to the now "classic" forms of digital storytelling originally developed in California from the first half of the 1990s as well as to the newer forms on social networking sites like MySpace, YouTube, or Facebook (now merging in the new video-sharing service from CDS).[11] Basically, there is the spread or diffusion in *time/space*. Digital storytelling has a certain location in recent history throughout the world; the actual spread and shape of digital storytelling is to a large extent determined by the three more substantially defined contextual dimensions discussed above:

*tools/competences*
*institutions/economy*
*culture/hegemony*

The positions and practices of digital storytelling along these dimensions define the strength of digital storytelling in time and space and represent matrices of digital storytelling. There are three meanings of the noun "matrix." There is the mathematical meaning: a rectangular array of quantities or expressions in rows and columns that is treated as a single entity. While the phenomenon of digital storytelling could not be treated in a simple statistical manner, tools and competences for digital storytelling could be understood as two dimensions in a matrix of (prod)user capacities. Similarly, institutions and economy make a matrix of operational contexts. Culture and patterns of hegemony are dimensions of the symbolic contexts of digital storytelling.

In another meaning, a matrix is a mold, a form, in which something, such as a phonograph record, is cast or shaped. In a similar way, the three said matrices – (prod)user, operational, and cultural – separately and together, as a contextual set of dimensions, mould the shaping of digital stories. Finally, the word "matrix" means an environment in which something develops: a surrounding medium or structure. Certainly, the three matrices offer environments for digital storytelling. These environments, located in time and space, mediate the shaping and sharing of digital storytelling.

All three contextual matrices of digital storytelling contain aspects of power: the matrix of culture/hegemony points to symbolic power (Bourdieu 1992); the set of dimensions related to institutions and economy may as well refer to Weber's classical forms of power, authority, and legitimacy (Weber 1978); and the matrix of tools and competences in digital storytelling invite specific studies of media power (Couldry 2000a). The "user-generated" activity of making digital stories invites agency. However, this creative participation takes place within the structural frameworks laid out by the matrices of digital storytelling. This new narrative practice, then, brings us right to the core of sociological reasoning about agency *vs.* structure (Giddens 1984). The phenomenon of digital storytelling is also to be located on the basic coordinates of time and space. While digital storytelling appears as a specific media practice, it should be approached as a significant phenomenon, to be understood from its location in relation to time and space, agency and structure.

## Notes

1   http://digitalstorytellingcenter.dk/ and http://eustorycenter.ning.com (accessed July 21, 2008).

2 "MEDIATIZED STORIES. Mediation perspectives on digital storytelling among youth," funded by the Research Council of Norway for the period 2006–10 (www.intermedia.uio.no/mediatized).

3 See www.huseby.gs.st.no/HusebySkole/InEnglish.htm (accessed December 14, 2007).

4 See www.digitalbridge.nu, www. w3.tii.se, and www.mah.se (all accessed December 14, 2007).

5 See www.digitalefortellinger.com (accessed December 14, 2007).

6 See www.ur.se/aboutUR, www.ur.se/rfb, and www.deltagarden.se (all accessed December 14, 2007).

7 See www.bth.se, www.mah.se, www.hio.no, and www.uio.no/studier/emner/ hf/imk/MEVIT4130/index.xml (all accessed December 14, 2007).

8 See forum.neveragain.no (accessed December 14, 2007).

9 I want to acknowledge the influences from Nancy Thumim's work in her yet unpublished doctoral dissertation (Thumim 2007) as well as from discussions with her within the Mediatized Stories project.

10 Processes of cultural mediation are discussed in Thumim (2008). On textual mediation, see her Chapter 14 in this volume.

11 www.storycircles.org (accessed July 21, 2008).

# 13

# Digital Storytelling in Belgium
## Power and Participation

## *Nico Carpentier*

## Introduction

Digital storytelling (DST) is part of a wide variety of formats and technologies that together construct the Web. As is often the case with (new) media, these practices are highly resistant to our "definitory" attempts. Nevertheless, a number of authors have produced fragments of definitions: Lambert (2002: xix), executive director of the Californian Center for Digital Storytelling (CDS), writes in the introduction of his hands-on book on DST: "We want to talk back, not on the terms of the governors of media empires, but on our own terms." On the CDS website, their approach is described by emphasizing "personal voice and facilitative teaching methods" (Center for Digital Storytelling n.d.). Burgess (2006a: 207) adds another piece to the puzzle, by referring to "the specific modes of production, technological apparatus and textual characteristics of the community media movement that is known explicitly as 'digital storytelling.' Digital story-telling is a workshop-based process by which 'ordinary people' create their own short autobiographical films that can be streamed on the Web or broadcast on television," while Wu (2006: 383) defines DST as "an emergent multimedia expression format, which empowers ordinary people to explore their creativity through producing a 2–5-minute film based on personal stories."

These descriptions and definitions embed DST in both the emancipatory strands of new media applications, and the community media movement. The focus on emancipation also immediately foregrounds the notion of participation, and DST offers a specific combination of micro- and

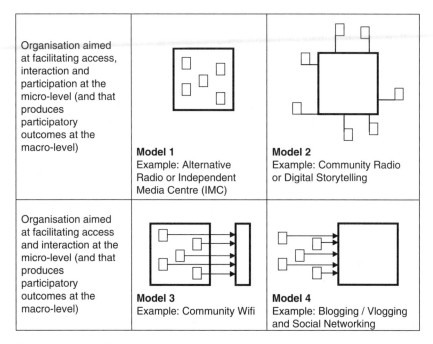

| | | |
|---|---|---|
| Organisation aimed at facilitating access, interaction and participation at the micro-level (and that produces participatory outcomes at the macro-level) | **Model 1**<br>Example: Alternative Radio or Independent Media Centre (IMC) | **Model 2**<br>Example: Community Radio or Digital Storytelling |
| Organisation aimed at facilitating access and interaction at the micro-level (and that produces participatory outcomes at the macro-level) | **Model 3**<br>Example: Community Wifi | **Model 4**<br>Example: Blogging / Vlogging and Social Networking |

**Figure 13.1** Models of (semi-)participatory organizations

macro-participation. In DST, the (macro)participation of "ordinary people" in the symbolic realm is facilitated though the publication of personalized narrations. At the micro-level of the organization, participants enter a participatory training and production process. This situation, where DST participants are not actual members of the initiating organization, renders DST different from a number of other participatory formats, like alternative radio (where participants are often members of the actual organization) or blogging and vlogging (where non-membership of participants is combined with an organizational structure that only provides access).

These two dimensions – organizational membership and participatory focus – can be used to generate a first map of the terrain of (semi-)participatory organizations. An overview of the four models is shown in Figure 13.1.

In this text, new media's and DST's acclaimed participatory nature will be analyzed by reverting to a less obvious but nevertheless highly relevant theoretical tradition, namely, anarchism. The starting point of this argument is DST's obvious intrinsic connection to the popularization of the

Internet, and its many-to-many communicative capacities. Numerous authors, spearheaded by techno-utopian authors like Howard Rheingold and Nicholas Negroponte, have pointed to the democratic-emancipatory potential of the Web. The optimism has hardly decreased with the advent of what is considered to be the next generation of Web applications (cleverly labeled Web 2.0), that will facilitate social interaction and networking, (virtual) community building, file sharing, and co-creation even more.

Arguably this change in the communicative landscape is rather considerable, at least if we take into account the number of people using these technologies. For instance, in mid-September 2007, Technorati.com reported tracking 103.7 million blogs and over 250 million pieces of tagged social media. In many cases, these new Web applications are geared toward individual media participation and self-expression – some would even say narcissism (Carr 2006). At the same time, a multitude of small, decentralized, and autonomous (self-)organizations are providing the "backbone" of this cultural phenomenon.

This specific combination between individuality and community is very reminiscent of anarchist theory, at least if we follow Alan Ritter's (1980) claim that anarchism exceeds the mere search for individualistic freedom and combines a focus on individuality with a search for a "real community." In order to show this connection between the Internet's democratic-emancipatory potential and anarchist theory, and to illustrate (the strength of) this connection through the analysis of two DST projects, we need to go back to some of the basic principles of anarchist theory. Before doing so, two points need to be made: one on anarchism as a cultural force, and one on the diversity of anarchist theory.

## Anarchist (New Media) Theory

As Jennings (1999: 145) rightly argues, there is little left of anarchism as a political force: "if we were asked to assess the constructive achievements of anarchism in the twentieth century we would have to acknowledge that they have been slight." Of course there are a number of exceptions, for instance in the case of the May 1968 student revolt, the more recent alter-globalization movement, and the variety of smaller organizations that practice direct action, but as a mass movement it has disappeared. Nevertheless, a number of authors have argued that anarchism has played a crucial role at the cultural level. David Weir (1997: 5) made this point for the role of anarchism in the arts, arguing that "anarchism succeeded cultur- ally when it failed politically." A less dichotomizing variation is Graeber's (2004: 76) reference to the role of anarchy in contemporary everyday lived culture: "The moment we stop insisting on viewing all forms only by their function in reproducing larger, total, forms of inequality of power, we will be able to see that anarchist social relations and non-alienated forms of action are all around us."

Anarchist theory is characterized by a diversity of strands. Bookchin (1996 [1984]: 19) mentions but a few: anarcho-syndicalism, anarcho- individualism, anarcho-collectivism, and anarcho-communism. Many other variations, such as platformism, primitivism, and mutualism, can also be distinguished.[2] These variations bring different epistemologies and ontolo- gies, but also different practices and utopias. Especially when it comes to the revolutionary future, both in strategy and in objectives, the variations in anarchist theory tend to diverge tremendously. For instance, the status of violence ranges from Tolstoy's preference for disobedience and pacifist resistance to Bakunin's calls for violent revolution. Despite these differ- ences, the different strands in anarchist theory share a number of commu- nalities, which are rendered below in the overview of the basic principles of anarchist theory.

## Anarchism's basic principles

Arguably the dominant feature of anarchist theory is the distrust of govern- ment, which is seen as a threat to the autonomy and freedom of individuals and communities. Given the primacy attributed to individual freedom, the constraints and coercions generated by the machinery of government are rejected. Although often intimately connected, the rejection of government (or better, of being governed) does not necessarily imply the total rejection of the state. Crowder (1991: 64), for instance, claims that anarchist theory accepts the state, as long as it only performs purely administrative func- tions. May (1994: 47) captures this difference by pointing out that anarchist theory consists of the rejection of representation, and that "the state is the object of critique because it is the ultimate form of political representation, not because it is founding for it."

The distrust of government and the rejection of (political) representation are fed by a discourse of anti-authoritarianism, which resists the establishment of societal hierarchies and systems of domination and privilege (Bookchin 1996 [1984]: 29). Illustrative for this is Bakunin's (1970 [1882]: 31) statement: "It is the characteristic of privilege and of every privileged position to kill the mind and heart of men." The problematization of privilege not only concerns the political sphere, but also the economic realm, where classic anarchist theory was "critical of private property to the extent that it was a source of hierarchy and privilege" (Jennings 1999: 136). Even Proudhon's famous dictum – property is theft – only relates to situations where the power balance is disturbed through so-called windfall earnings as interest on loans and income from rents, which move structurally beyond the legitimate ownership of what is needed in everyday life. In contrast to domination, privilege, and struggle, anarchist theory legitimizes itself by (often implicitly) reverting to what May calls a "humanist naturalism" (May 1994: 65), foregrounding harmony, solidarity, and a belief in a "benign human essence" (May 1994: 63). A case in point is Kropotkin's (1902) engagement with Darwinism in mutual aid, where he tries to "scientifically establish" an evolutionary model that is built on the survival of the altruistic, and not on the survival of the fittest.

These discourses of anti-authoritarianism and solidarity are combined with the rejection of (political) representation, which leads to the third feature of anarchist theory: a strong emphasis on participation and decentralization as principles of decision-making. As Jennings (1999: 138) formulates it, there is a "generalised preference for decentralisation, autonomy and mass participation in the decision-making process." Through the free and equal participation of all, government as such becomes unnecessary and an equal power balance in these decision-making processes can be achieved, maximizing individual autonomy. Similarly, within the economic realm, the principle of capitalist struggle is replaced by a decentralized gift economy.

The fourth and last feature of anarchist theory is the voluntary association as organizational principle. As mentioned before, anarchist theory attempts not to lapse into individualism and atomism but strives for a balance between the individual and the community. The privileged organizational structure to achieve this balance has received many names in the course of anarchism's intellectual history: Proudhon's natural group, Kropotkin's voluntary association, Godwin's parishes, Bookchin's affinity groups, etc. Despite the differences, these small-scale structures are seen as tools to again protect individual freedom and autonomy, as Kropotkin (1972 [1892]: 145) formulates it: "And with our eyes shut we pass by thousands and thousands of human groupings which form themselves freely ... and attain results infinitely superior to those achieved under government tutelage." But the scale of these organizational structures is not always that small, and approximates civil society; for instance, Kropotkin refers to the "countless societies, clubs, and alliances, for the enjoyment of life, for study and research, for education" (1902). More contemporary authors – like Graeber (2004: 40) – have broadened the scope further when describing anarchist forms of organization that "would involve an endless variety of communities, associations, networks, projects, on every conceivable scale ... Some would be quite local, others global."

*Beyond government critique: anarchist theory and media studies*

The focus has not necessarily to be placed on the state as such, however, this has been one of the main focal points of anarchist theory. As May (1994: 60) remarks, there is ambivalence in anarchist theory whether the state or government should be seen as the only sites of the exercise of power. As mentioned above, the economic realm is relatively often incorporated, as the critiques on the equality distorting role of capitalism are easily reconciled with the critiques on political decision-making structures. A number of authors have pleaded to incorporate more societal spheres, claiming that there is "no final struggle, only a series of partisan struggles on a variety of fronts" (Ward 1973: 26). Poststructuralist anarchist theory has enabled a more complex analytics of power of a variety of societal spheres. This allows us to focus on

> a politics that is more local and diffuse than the large-scale politics that is better suited to grand narratives. It struggles not only on the economic or state levels, but on the epistemological, psychological, linguistic, sexual, religious, psychoanalytic, ethical, in formational (etc.) levels as well. It struggles on these levels not because multiple struggles will create a society without the centralization of power, but because power is not centralized, because across the surface of those levels are the sites at which power arises. (May 1994: 94–5)

Through this broadening of the scope, combined with the necessary de-essentialization of anarchist theory, the media system has become one of the many possible sites of analysis. Support for this repositioning of anarchist theory can first be found in the importance generally attributed to contemporary (mainstream) media systems, their symbolic power and their perceived potential as new governing bodies that (re)produce hegemonies, which renders them necessary targets for anarchist critique. On a more positive note: these media systems' potential to stimulate a more participatory culture and to enhance a semiotic democracy also legitimizes attention from an anarchist perspective.

The Chomskian strand of anarchist theory has incorporated the vitriolic critique of the mainstream media system, although even alternative media sometimes share in these critiques, as Bradford's (1996 [1980]: 263) analysis of pirate radio suggests. Apart from the traditional problems with the remnants of essentialism, these media analyses are often characterized by a fundamental distrust of technology, which is seen to reinforce "class and hierarchical rule by adding powerful instrumentalities of control and destruction to institutional forces of domination" (Bookchin 1996 [1984]: 26).

Some authors have managed to incorporate anarchist theory in a more balanced way. Downing, in *Radical Media* (Downing et al. 2001: 67 ff.), distinguishes two models for the classification of radical media organizations: the Leninist model and the self-management model. Downing (2001: 69) explicitly relates the latter model – where "neither party, nor labor union, nor church, nor state, nor owner is in charge, but where the newspaper or radio station runs itself" – to what he calls a "socialist anarchist angle of vision." Although Downing mainly points to the problems caused by this "angle of vision" (see below), his theoretical reflections and case-study analyses clearly link self-managed media to the anarchist tradition. Further, Hakim Bey (1985) – Peter Lamborn Wilson's pseudonym – reflects on the upsurge (and disappearance) of temporary anarchist freespaces. He distinguishes between the "Net" and the "Web," where the Net is seen as the "totality of all information and communication transfer" (Bey 1985: 106), while the Web is the counter-Net that is situated within the Net. In the Web, media technology plays an important (although not all-determining) role: "The present forms of the unofficial Web are, one must suppose, still rather primitive: the marginal zine network, the BBS networks, pirated software, hacking, phone-phreaking, some influence in print and radio, almost none in the other big media" (Bey 1985: 107).

Interestingly, both Downing and Bey use the island metaphor, but in an inverse way. Downing (Downing et al. 2001: 72) critiques anarchist theory for being satisfied with creating "little islands of prefigurative politics with no empirical attention to how these might ever be expanded into the rest of society." Bey, on the contrary, celebrates (the temporality of) the islands in the Net, replacing the permanent revolution by the temporal uprising, legitimized by the argument that "our own particular historical situation is not propitious for such a vast undertaking" (Bey 1985: 98).

## Participation and Power

If anarchist theory can indeed be broadened and de-essentialized in order to be applied for media analyses, one important additional step needs to be taken. This necessary step is the clarification of the concept of participation and its link with power. As Downing argues (Downing et al. 2001: 71), the assumption of anarchist theory that "its" voluntary organizations are per definition participatory and democratic is highly problematic. Downing refers to Freeman (1971–3), who shows the workings of hierarchy in feminist discussion groups that reject hierarchy, to make the point that equal participation cannot be taken for granted.

Part of the problem is that participation is an ideologically loaded and highly contested notion (e.g., Pateman 1970). Different strategies have been developed to cope with this "significatory" diversity, most of which construct categorization systems. Although many exist (see Carpentier 2007), one of the most important categorizations is Pateman's (1970) introduction of the difference between full and partial participation. Partial participation is "a process in which two or more parties *influence* each other in the making of decisions but the final *power* to decide rests with one party only" (Pateman 1970: 70, emphasis added), while full participation is "a process where each individual member of a decision-making body has equal *power* to determine the outcome of decisions" (Pateman 1970: 71, emphasis added).

As power plays a crucial role in these definitions, it becomes unavoidable to further clarify the notion of power, staying in line with May's development of poststructuralist anarchism. Foucault (1978) stresses that power relations are mobile and multidirectional, without excluding the existence of domination or non-egalitarian distributions of power within existing structures. From a different perspective this implies that the level of participation, the degree to which decision-making power is equally distributed, and access to the resources of a certain system are constantly (re-) negotiated. Foucault (1978: 95) also states that power relations are intentional and based upon a diversity of strategies, thus granting subjects their agencies. But at the same time he emphasizes that power relations are also "non-subjective." Power becomes anonymous. Foucault argues that "people know what they do; they frequently know why they do what they do; but what they don't know is what they do does" (quoted by Dreyfus and Rabinow 1983: 187). Through what Giddens (1979: 91) calls the dialectics of control, different strategies of different actors produce specific (temporally) stable outcomes, which can be seen as the end result or overall effect of the negation between those strategies and actors. The emphasis on the overall effect that supersedes individual strategies (and agencies) allows Foucault to foreground the productive aspects of power and to claim that power is inherently neither positive nor negative (Hollway 1984: 237). As generative/positive and restrictive/negative aspects of power both imply the production of knowledge, discourse, and subjects, productivity should be considered the third component of power. Finally, resistance to power is considered by Foucault to be an integral part of the exercise of power (Kendall and Wickham 1999: 50). Thus, as Hunt and Wickham (1994: 83) argue: "Power and resistance are together the governance machine of society, but only in the sense that together they contribute to the truism that 'things never quite work,' not in the conspiratorial sense that resistance serves to make power work perfectly."

In the model shown in Figure 13.2, the elements are brought together into one visual representation. The dialectics of control is composed from generative and restrictive power aspects, which are combined with resistance. The outcome of this power play impacts (through the workings of productive power) on both structural and agency-related elements of the social, which in turn influence the dialectics of control.

## Two Case Studies: Narrating Dordrecht and Brussels

A number of cities have initiated DST projects that allow inhabitants to narrate their relationships with urban geographies. Some of these projects are already well established: the two selected projects – *Verhalen van Dordrecht* (VvD) and *Bruxelles nous appartient/Brussels behoort ons toe* (BNA–BBOT)[3] – had already featured in a 2003 inventory which mapped 44 different DST projects and was used to select both case studies.[4]

Both DST projects have long histories and can hardly be considered *temporary* autonomous zones: VvD started as a 1999 arts project initiated by

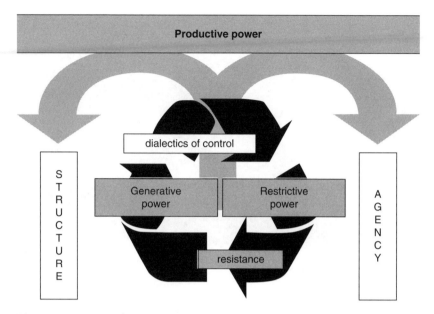

**Figure 13.2** Foucault on power

the Rotterdam artist Wapke Feenstra and subsidized by the Centrum Beeldende Kunst Dordrecht (CBK).[5] While originally focused on the city centre of the Dutch city of Dordrecht, from 2003 onward, when the hundredth story was published, the project also started to include stories from the outer districts of Dordrecht, focusing each year on one district. From 2005 Feenstra and the project team appointed a leading artist, responsible for organizing promenades in the selected district and for generating new stories. In August 2007 the total number of stories was around 200, all mapped on the central interface, about half of them written by people living in the centre of Dordrecht, and between 20 to 30 stories originating from the Krispijn, Reeland, and Staart districts. Anne Pillen, the leading artist in 2007, toured the Wielwijk–Crabbehof–Zuidhoven district with what she called a "story organ" (see Figure 13.4), which can best be described as a recording studio designed to resemble a barrel organ.

VvD's approach to DST is specific in two ways: they use a freelance editorial team which actively seeks writers (in corporation with the curators), interviews potential participants, and/or edits the stories in order to increase their narrative quality. This freelance editorial team consists mainly of

**Figure 13.3**   VvD's 2007 story organ

"ordinary" people living in various districts of Dordrecht. Secondly, VvD is (at least partially) inspired by an artistic approach, aimed at what Feenstra calls the creation of a fragile cultural space (interview and feedback, 2007). Talking more generally during the 2003 interview, Feenstra describes the tension this creates: "I want to capture their experience, the way they experience the territory, how they move through that territory. That's something I really want to know. But translating that to a visual representation, [that is a profession]." She later adds: "I make it, and watch how it blossoms or collapses, and then I fix it or leave it as it is and make something else" (feedback, 2007).

BNA-BBOT, the second DST project which started in 1999, uses a slightly different approach but has similar objectives: to give a voice to the inhabitants of Brussels. The BNA-BBOT website claims: "The conversations generate artistic excrescences of all sorts, a new kind of creation that leads to a new imaginary Brussels. It's the intention that everybody speaks, that everybody comes to listen to the other one's story, that everybody can collaborate to create a new representation of Brussels that is close to the inhabitants." BNA-BBOT's nerve center – a so-called "story shop" – is located in the centre of Brussels, and houses an editing studio. Here, inhabitants are invited to enter, borrow the necessary recording equipment, record their stories, add metadata to them, and, upon their return, have them uploaded into the database. If necessary, inhabitants are assisted by one of the three staff members.

**Figure 13.4** The BNA-BBOT story bike

Apart from archiving and webcasting the sound collection, which has more than 1,100 stories with an average length of 50 minutes each, BNA-BBOT is active in organizing workshops, and participates in festivals and projects. One of the similarities with VvD is BNA-BBOT's focus on socio-artistic projects. In the case of BNA-BBOT, individual artists are invited to make use of the database, to use their window display, or to organize workshops. BNA-BBOT has also collaborated more structurally with cultural organizations. A second similarity with VvD is that BNA-BBOT organizes outreach activities, which bring the stories out into the public spaces (e.g., by using a fake UFO that can be used to listen to stories on site, or by installing a "Bed d'Amour" on one of Brussels' city squares), and which allows new stories to be recorded (e.g., by using their "story bike" – see Figure 13.4).

BNA-BBOT also has a number of specificities. The first is its bilingualism: the combined and intertwined use of Dutch and French symbolizes the mixture of languages spoken in daily life, and the way the inhabitants of Brussels have managed to find their own *modus vivendi* which contradicts Belgium's sometimes antagonistic language politics that often divides the country into disconnected language groups. Not surprisingly, BNA-BBOT is subsidized by a variety of different regional and local administrations, from both north and south Belgium (however, this situation may increase BNA-BBOT's financial instability). A second particularity is BNA-BBOT's connection to the alternative radio scene. Radio Campus, one of the few Belgian university-based alternative radio stations, hosts a weekly show based on BNA-BBOT's sound collection. This further strengthens BNA-BBOT's embeddedness in the civil society of Brussels, which is already reasonably strong owing to the project's material presence in the city. Finally, and most importantly, BNA-BBOT uses a model of minimal intervention. There is in principle no editing, and a tendency to keep the material as intact as possible: "Sometimes they ask us: can you help me to delete this or that part? And then we say, oh, but let's first listen to it. Are you sure you want to delete this? We then try to convince not to delete it. But of course if they really want to, then we'll delete it' (interview with Van Wichelen, 2007). Although there are clear format- and content-related preferences, BNA-BBOT does not often block access to its database.

## The Two DST Projects, Anarchist Theory, and Power

Both DST projects have quite a lot in common. As participatory organizations they approximate the second model described in Figure 13.1. They facilitate the participation of storytellers by providing access to a database where their work is published, by supporting these participants, and by allowing them to publish their stories (in written or in oral form). At the same time, the central position of the expert groups (the staff members and artists) and of the technology (the database and the interface) allows us to question the intensity of the participatory process. For that purpose, we can use the main characteristics of anarchist theory as sensitizing concepts – à la Blumer (1969) – for analyses. Not surprisingly, we can find some traces of all four characteristics.

As both DST projects are embedded in a civil society structure (in the Gramscian sense – see Gramsci 1999 [1932]: 306), they can almost automatically be classified as forms of voluntary association which generates the much sought-after balance between individuality and communality (Ritter 1980). They have both created a careful distance with the political system, government, and authority, by focusing on the lived experience of inhabitants, who are articulated as experience experts (interview with Feenstra, 2007).

Although politicians and government/city officials are not excluded from participating, if they do so, they are disarticulated from their political activity. For instance, there is a story by the mayor of Dordrecht on the VvD website, but in this story he writes about his new house.⁶ A second component that protects the civil-society identity of these organizations is the emphasis on their independence. VvD is part of an independent cultural centre and the BNA-BBOT project is supported by two NGOs. Finally, and most importantly, their discourses have a strong focus on participation and decentralization. VvD and BNA-BBOT are structural tools to allow the voices of the inhabitants to be heard. As was asked rhetorically in a VvD press communiqué in March 2007: "What is nicer than becoming part of the personal stories on your city and district?" BNA-BBOT, especially, with its particularly bottom-up strategy, uses a participatory discourse: "Talking about daily events has a political dimension, allows questioning the economic order, and uncovers inequalities and unequal opportunities. Participating in BNA-BBOT shows that that you are an active person and no passive consumer of the city" (BNA-BBOT brochure, 2006).

But this application of anarchist theory also shows the weaknesses of these DST projects, as they provide us with a toned-down version of each of the four characteristics. First, both projects maintain a critical distance toward the government, but simultaneously receive direct and/or indirect government funding for their activities. In the case of BNA-BBOT especially, the list of funding agencies is rather impressive, but at the same time the fairly large scale of this organization necessitates a permanent search for resources, and threatens to turn the organization into a(n involuntary) temporary participatory zone. This paradox is quite common in the Netherlands and Belgium, where a substantial number of independent civil society organizations receive government grants to support their activities. In a number of cases even radical organizations benefit from this grant system, without becoming (practically or discursively) incorporated by these government agencies. Secondly, VvD and BNA-BBOT do not use a blatant anti-authoritarian discourse. They implicitly position themselves as third-sector (between market and state), but do not take an active antagonistic stance. However, they do position themselves as non-state and non-market, and gently construct barriers between themselves, politics, and the market by focusing on the subject position of the inhabitant. Thirdly, as civil society they can be defined as voluntary organizations, but the differentiation between staff members and inhabitants, and the organization of outreach activities, do raise questions about the status of the voluntary engagement. In the case of non-membership participatory organizations (see model 2 of Figure 13.1), the volunteers-participants interact with them only for a limited time and with a limited intensity. Moreover, these volunteers-participants can hardly be seen as owners of the process or the organization.

Finally, the focus on participation and decentralization: if we revert to the poststructuralist strand of anarchist theory and the Foucauldian model of power discussed earlier, we can compare the generative aspects of the power relationship on the one hand, and the restrictive aspects on the other. In both projects, the participants are granted the opportunity to generate stories and are supported in this activity by a group of experts and by the necessary technological infrastructure that facilitate the process of writing or recording. At the same time both the experts and the technology un-avoidably impose restrictions. But here the differences between VvD and BNA-BBOT are substantial, as VvD uses a more top-down model (although Feenstra prefers the term "connected model"), while BNA-BBOT applies a more bottom-up model. The end result is a difference in the intensity of the participatory process. In the case of VvD, restrictions apply at the level of participant selection; the genre and format used, which embed narrations of the self within a socio-artistic discourse; and the required quality (as much literary-narrative as technical). As Feenstra (interview, 2007) remarks, their editing team has the final say (and the ownership of the project), although the participants still have to approve the final version of a text.

> It's quite ambiguous. The editing team is also dependent on the authors, so they need maintain a friendly relationship. And they always need to look for new authors, so for them it is like a hunt. Ultimately, they have the final say, but it's more of a negotiation where the editors are the hunters, and the authors are the game, which also empowers them.

The above quote also shows that this process – with its uneven power rela-tions – is still a negotiation between editorial team and participants, and that the participants still have a power base and the possibility of resistance, given the dependency of the editorial team on the stories produced by the participants. Moreover, the project team still has a caring attitude toward the participatory process, as Feenstra (feedback, 2007) describes it: "In my work there is less [artistic] drive and more care." In the case of BNA-BBOT, the balance between generative and restrictive power relations is more even, due to the strong participatory attitude of the staff members. This does not imply that there are no restrictions, as the technology, BNA-BBOT's procedures, and the specific nature of the projects (through which they finance their operation) all impact on the participatory process.

## Conclusion

DST remains one of the important forms that allow for the organization of participation. One of its main distinguishing characteristics – the difference between the expert group of facilitators and the participants – is both its strength and its weakness. One of the many witticisms from the world of participatory media is that participation and efficiency are each other's opposites. In the case of DST, the long existence of VvD and BNA-BBOT is evidence of the importance of an organizational embeddedness and of the efficient attribution of resources, which allows for high-quality support and outcomes. These choices come with a price, as the strong presence of an expert group impacts on the depth of participatory processes, especially when the organizational culture is oriented more toward the facilitation of micro-participation than macro-participation, as is the case with VvD.

If we use the main characteristics of anarchist theory as sensitizing concepts, it remains somewhat remarkable that the two projects can be analyzed from this perspective. Not only does this show that anarchist theory, and more broadly speaking anarchism as a cultural phenomenon, is leading a subterranean existence with considerable impact (see Weir 1997), but also that participatory media projects like VvD and BNA-BBOT are still influenced by many of its core principles. Interestingly, the radicalness of these anarchist concepts has been lost, and each of the core principles has been rearticulated to comply with present-day cultures and conjunctures. This also applies for the participatory component of these projects, which has been variously affected and translated through the processes of expert guidance and the embeddedness in socio-artistic cultures and organizational practices.

Arguably the notion of full participation as an anarchist-democratic imaginary (or utopia) still remains important. In social practice we remain confronted with persistent power imbalances, but the anarcho-social imaginary of full participation can be applied to legitimate (and understand) a plea for the maximization of generative and the minimization of restrictive power mechanisms, in a diversity of participatory processes. The two digital storytelling projects, and especially BNA-BBOT, show that it remains feasible to approximate this imaginary. Although these projects can only be considered – to use Downing's (2001) and Bey's (1985) metaphor – little islands of high-intensity participation in a hegemonic context of one-way communication, combined with forms of low-intensity participation (or interaction) – as materializations of the anarchist-democratic imaginary they are nevertheless treasure islands.

## Notes

1   In these four models, the potential processes of participant co-creation (linking the individuals) are not visualized.

2   A number of authors, following Murray Rothbard (1989 [1973]), have even argued in favor of what they termed anarcho-capitalism, although they were more covering a 1970s New Right ultra-liberal agenda than developing a strand of anarchist theory.

3   The Dutch name of the DST project, "Verhalen van Dordrecht," can be translated as "Stories from Dordrecht" (see www.verhalenvandordrecht.nl). The Belgian DST project "Bruxelles nous appartient/Brussels behoort ons toe" has a bilingual Dutch–French title, which means "Brussels belongs to us" (see www.bna-bbot.be).

4   This original inventory was made possible by the support of the Cultural Policy Research Center "Steunpunt Re-Creatief Vlaanderen" and the Flemish Community of Belgium (Program for Policy Research Centers). On January 15, 2003, as part of this inventory project, Wapke Feenstra of VvD was interviewed. She was interviewed again on September 11, 2007. Anne Van Wichelen (BNA-BBOT) was interviewed on September 18, 2007. Feedback from Wapke Feenstra and Anne Van Wichelen on the relevant segments of a draft version of this chapter was received by email on September 19, 20, and 21, 2007.

5   "Centrum Beeldende Kunst Dordrecht" means "Center for the Visual Arts Dordrecht" (www.cbkdordrecht.nl).

6   See www.verhalenvandordrecht.nl/verhaal.php?nummer=297

# 14

# Exploring Self-representations in Wales and London
## Tension in the Text

## *Nancy Thumim*

### Introduction

Representations must always be mediated by how they are made; what tools they are made with; and where, when, and how they are displayed. Of course processes of mediation begin before, and continue after, the actual production and display of "texts" (Silverstone 1999, Couldry 2006, Martín-Barbero 1993). In this chapter I limit the field of enquiry to one dimension of the mediation process, the "processes of textual mediation,"[1] and to one kind of representation, self-representation. Self-representation has been explored from a range of perspectives.[2] Here the term highlights the fact that in the projects discussed members of the public are *invited* to represent *themselves* on the platforms of publicly funded media and cultural institutions, and that this invitation to self-representation is presented as an intervention into standard practices whereby the public are represented *by* professionals, implying that established power relations are challenged when people represent themselves.

The term "digital storytelling" is used here to describe an activity that takes place in two projects. The first, "Capture Wales" (CW) (also discussed by Meadows and Kidd in Chapter 5 of the present volume), follows the Berkeley-based Center for Digital Storytelling (CDS) model. The second project, "London's Voices" (LV), has no connection to the CDS. LV was a three-year oral history project at the Museum of London, funded by the UK's Heritage Lottery Fund. CW and LV are examples of digital storytelling in a broad sense: both involve the digitization of the self-representations of "ordinary people" through their display on the websites of two publicly funded cultural institutions. In what follows, textual analysis of selected self-representations displayed on the LV and CW websites is used to show how processes of textual mediation are constituted through tensions in four areas: the construction of "ordinary people," the construction of "community," the purposes of publicly funded self-representations, and defining and achieving "quality." In the following discussion, "tension" is understood to be both challenging and productive, but above all tension is revealing of where power lies and how it works in processes of mediation.

## Tension Surrounding Purposes of Self-representation

In CW sophisticated, digital technologies are employed. However, Creative Director, Daniel Meadows, suggests that digital storytelling delivers a "scrapbook aesthetic" (Meadows 2003). The aim is to teach people to use professional tools in order to make their voices most effective. Self-representations are framed as different from other kinds of representations produced and displayed by these institutions. The CW stories are marked as material produced by non-professionals, thereby alerting the audience that they might be read differently. This particular framing undermines the ability of these self-representations to have the same authority as those produced by expert media producers. Here, then, there is a tension between, on the one hand, the political intention to intervene in how members of the public are represented in the media, by facilitating them in representing themselves (experts on their own experience) and, on the other hand, the fixing of the members of the public in their place, as one where they do not (cannot) speak with the same authority as professional media producers.

*Mr Transitional* is the title of a poem by "Harry," a participant in a South London Library Services Afro-Caribbean Reading Group, who took part in the LV project, *London 16–19*. Here is a teenager representing himself and the product displayed by the Museum of London, underlining the supposed validity and importance of his voice. At the same time, however, this self-representation is framed by a title and Web page. That this framing is considered necessary implies an assumption that self-representation must be explained as such to the audience. The explanation that accompanies the self-representation functions to identify it as different from more familiar representations of members of the public on view in media or in museums. The explanation alerts the audience that this is a particular kind of content, implying it is to be read in a particular kind of way. If self-representation is a generic form, then the museum's framing alerts the audience to the kind of genre on view – representation of personal experience by non-media professional members of the public.

The poem appears as typed text on a white background, as if a typed poem has been scanned. It is written in the third person. The first line introduces the characters of the piece: "boy," "parents," "lover." This poem fits the stereotype that working-class Afro-Caribbean teenagers become parents at a young age. But, at the same time, the stereotype is powerfully dispelled, because the situation is shown from the boy's point of view, with his "Heart beating like a boxer pounding a punch bag." This is not any "Mr Transitional"; rather, it is a particular person's experience. Nevertheless, the title "Mr Transitional" encourages an understanding of the poem as yet another example (like the other poems titled "Mr" and "Miss" "Transitional") of a universal experience of passing from teenager to adult. Thus, despite the detail of Harry's particular experience, the framing encourages us to consider what teenagers have in common with each other, across their evident differences.

The particularity of the detail in "Harry's" poem is thus in tension with the framing. There is the poem: "Harry" uses writing to make his self-representation, but this writing is scanned and fitted into a designed website that presents the collected self-representations by young people. The opening page of *London 16–19* states:

> The Museum of London collaborated with six groups of young people to represent their lives in London today. The young people involved shared their stories and opinions and reflected their lives through photography, poetry, fashion, music and oral history. Based on their own experiences and addressing issues that are important to young people in the city today, *London 16–19* highlights the talent, diversity and creativity of those who took part. (June 29, 2005, www.museumoflondon.org.uk)

This frames the self-representations, suggesting that they can be understood as a relatively homogenous group. However, it seems equally true that the self-representations are distinctive, precisely because they look different (and are made differently) to representations *of* the public, *by* professionals.

"Harry's" poem, *Mr Transitional*, is written in the third person; are we, in this distancing from the first person, invited to imagine that this might be fiction? Does it matter? The same question is played with on the CW website, where speaking in the first person is a prerequisite of self-representation, the producers state:

> Are all the stories true?
> We publish these stories in all good faith but, as Alys Lewis hints in her History or Mystery? story, it's sometimes difficult to tell where the border between fact and fiction lies. (June 29, 2005, www.bbc.co.uk/wales/capturewales/about)

In CW, self-representation takes place within the strict construct of what constitutes digital storytelling for the project's producers. And yet, as the above quotation signals, there is no certainty that what we hear is in fact truth, recalling debate about truth in documentary (see, e.g., Bruzzi 2000, Dovey 2000, Nichols 1991). In CW and LV, while the notion that we are hearing the truth is central, the existence of the texts and their content makes clear that whether or not this really is the truth cannot in fact be determined. Projects that facilitate self-representation draw attention to the necessary shortcomings of any one historical account. Yet these self-representations are justified as having a place on the platforms provided by these institutions, precisely because they are intended to give the audience access to a true(r) representation of "ordinary lives."

## Tension Surrounding the Construct "Ordinary People"

The paradox whereby the extraordinary is central to the ordinary (Highmore 2002) is highlighted by the websites produced by LV and CW, in both cases the very thing being constructed, the "ordinary person," is, at the same time, necessarily undermined as a possibility. The digital stories on the CW website are reached by various routes, for example, geographical area or theme:

> Challenge
> Community
> Family
> Memory
> Passion
> (July 25, 2005, www.bbc.co.uk/wales/capturewales)

If the user clicks on the hypertext theme "Family," she goes to thumbnail stills of all digital stories that are categorized as such by the producers. Each image is accompanied by the participant's name and a quote from their story. The trailer for Dai Evans's story, for example, shows a photograph of two faces looking at each other; one is a man and the other is the green head of a female shop mannequin. The accompanying text reads: "I have two families. One in the house and one in the garage" (July 25, 2005, www.bbc. co.uk/wales/capturewales/tg/family.shtml).

This beginning calls on audience knowledge of family – family is "ordinary." But the sentence, "One in the house and one in the garage," immediately undercuts the "ordinary" family tale we may have thought we were going to hear. Clicking on the thumbnail image of the man and the mannequin takes us to information concerning place, date, title, and author. Hypertext links offer opportunities to "view the movie" and "read the transcript," and alongside the image a column of text introduces Evans and functions to frame the story:

Model artist?
Dai Evans is a photographer and his story reflects his love for his family that lives in the house, and his second (rather odd) family.

This text indicates that the story's domain is family life, though with a twist. Thus the story is located within the generic conventions of self-representation: a story about "ordinary" experience, but, at the same time, with "oddness" at the centre, a combination that destabilizes the "ordinary."

What's your background, Dai?
I was a miner when I was 14 years old, and a coal-lorry driver before I retired in 1989. I am married with two children. I have a lot of interests, such as photography, gardening and enjoying being a grandfather. I am a member of "Amman Valley Camera Club" and I'm also an active member of "Swansea Camera Club." (July 25, 2005, www.bbc.co.uk/wales/capturewales/back ground/dai-evans.shtml)

Evans is located in his daily life; we are shown working background, family life, and creative hobbies. This information tells the Web user who takes part in CW: "Ordinary person" is not mentioned, but is evoked by this contextual information.

Below the interview is a place for feedback from Web users, which becomes part of the text and also functions to locate the digital story's author as an "ordinary" member of the audience:

> I was intrigued by the title, but at first I thought it was going to be another (rather boring) family memoir; but Dai was full of surprises and his warm, wry, mischievous sense of humour came across very effectively in the voice-over. Great pictures, too! (Nick Passmore, Llandrindod Wells, Wales, February 2003, www.bbc.co.uk/wales/capturewales/background/dai-evans.shtml, accessed July 4, 2005)

This comment suggests that there is a recognizable genre – "ordinary people" speaking about family life, at the same time making clear that the construction of the "ordinary person" cannot hold and, moreover, is not what is interesting about people.

For the first part of Evans's story we pan across family photographs as we are introduced to his personal history. The tone thus far is matter of fact, as if to say, "I'm telling you what you would expect to hear, a typical tale of a man like me" – the stuff of "ordinary" (everyday) experience. Following this introduction we cut to a more intriguing kind of photograph – a close-up of the man looking guiltily, or sneakily, to the left, out of frame, at something we, the viewers, can't see. The voice-over comes in again: "I have an unusual second family," the tone of voice becomes more playful and continues, "that help me out," and we pan out to see that the man in the photograph is looking at a dark green female shop mannequin. Suddenly we are in out-of-the-ordinary territory. The voice-over continues, to an accompaniment of increasingly bizarre photographs of mannequins in various scenarios, at the end of which Evans's explanatory tone returns: "Time with my models and photography I feel creative and refreshed. When people laugh at my pictures it's a real bonus. Go out there and create, anything, get off the couch and live a life."

These final remarks invoke the passive, TV-viewing "couch potato," suggesting that this "couch potato" is "ordinary" in the everyday sense. But Evans's self-representation, and the responses to it, highlight the fact that no one wants to be that mythical "ordinary person," and imply that examination of self-representations reveals that, in fact, no one is. At the same time, the story constructs the "ordinary" because the first half dwells on common experience, and the ending suggests that everyone – that is, every "ordinary person" – can make and produce, rather than only receive media representations.

In CW and LV the grouping together of many stories by "ordinary people" and their framing in the institutions' websites creates tension over the idea of the "ordinary person." The broad framing is contradicted by the varied, detailed, unique content of the self-representations. There is tension because of the contradictions, which the very evocation of the "ordinary person" must bring to light, and this tension is unavoidably at the heart of what these self-representations are. Paradoxically, what takes place in LV and CW is simultaneous exposure and containment of these contradictions.

## Tension Surrounding the Construct "Community"

The Web page for LV lists the sub-projects that made up the overall program. Above the title and synopsis of each of these projects, a short paragraph summarizing LV as a whole is accompanied by a graphic rectangle made up of eight faces of different ages and racial origins. These images suggest that London is made up of a diverse range of people, a fact celebrated on this website, by this project. The juxtaposition of faces combined with text repeatedly referencing "Londoners" invokes a community of Londoners: "*London's Voices* explores, reflects and celebrates London's great diversity through the voices, memories and opinions of Londoners. It opens up the Museum of London's rich oral history collection" (July 5, 2003, www. museumoflondon.org.uk/MOLsite/londonsvoices)

At the same time as this diverse London-wide community is invoked, the idea that the city consists of a range of separate (overlapping) communities is also suggested, both through the juxtaposition of summaries of projects working with different groups and sometimes through explicit statements. The summary for "Voices Online," for example, reads: "Access full oral history interviews and explore the connections that we have within our families, our communities, the city and the world (July 5, 2003, www. museumoflondon.org.uk/MOLsite/londonsvoices)

That communities exist is a given in the texts of the LV website, specifically in this macro text, framing the individual self-representations. But at the same time a project that encourages community awareness and community building suggests that "community" is considered to be lost and is something we want back, recalling Silverstone's observation that "Ideas of community hover between experience and desire" (1999: 97).

On the LV homepage, community is presented as something that we all know. Community in London is plural; in London, it seems to suggest, we inhabit a range of communities. At the same time, the existence of the LV project seeks to bring Londoners together, through emphasizing their shared experience; so that there is a wider and less explicit notion of London community hovering here, nearer perhaps to "desire" than to "experience." Building community appears to be an intended outcome of LV, delivering another paradox: something is being built, something that, it is assumed, we all know already exists.

"Questioning London" was another LV sub-project, which invited visitors to the museum to complete questionnaires described as the "Voices Alternative Census." A total of 2,600 questionnaires were completed and the results presented on a website. The "Questioning London" website emphasizes individual experience and point of view. However, summaries are presented as statistics in the form of statements such as: "X number of respondents said if they could change something about London it would be the transport," and exemplary quotes such as:

> We asked … how would you label yourself?
> "A rebellious, ponderous, socialist."
> "They are labeling me: 'illegal immigrant.'"
> "Afro-centric and eclectic."
> "East London and common as muck."

This presentation collectivizes the experiences of the individuals, bringing together the separate experiences of London's inhabitants. Here, those individuals are shown to each other and this has the effect of creating an impression that a civic community does exist. Thus, in the website, community is built *by* the LV producers out of individual responses to the questionnaire. Concurrently, the showcasing of the responses equally exposes the fact that, when we look into the individual texts, the idea of the London community seems to come apart. The community presented here is clearly constructed from individual experiences that are not necessarily experienced as communal. The producer's explanation on the top of the *London 16–19* website reads:

> The Museum of London collaborated with six groups of young people to represent their lives in London today. The young people involved shared their stories and opinions and reflected their lives through photography, poetry,

fashion, music and oral history. Based on their own experiences and addressing issues that are important to young people in the city today, *London 16–19* highlights the talent, diversity and creativity of those who took part. (July 5, 2005, www.museumoflondon.org.uk/frames.asp?http%3A//www. museumoflondon.org.uk/MOLsite/londonsvoices/web/mainmenu.asp)

Photographs taken by the participants are displayed in thumbnails that the user can click to enlarge. In one photograph, by "Kimberley," a young woman scowls at the camera. Her light brown hair is scraped back in a tight ponytail; she wears a red hooded top, studded belt, and black jeans; and her long-nailed hands are on her hips. In the background a scaffold-covered building blocks out most of the sky. Big trees add to the darkness, while in the background more houses contribute to a hemmed-in atmosphere. This is a striking and yet "ordinary" photograph, combining the girl's defiant glare with the inner-city background. "This is where I live, this is who I am," or, "this is where we live, this is who we are," the photograph seems to say, in response to the text above which tells us how to understand these images – as young people's own representation of their lives in London today.

The photograph invokes the kinds of photographs you might see on hip-hop record covers, of the "hard" inner-city girl. Her portrait tells us a lot about what identity the girl in red, and her photographer friend, want to present. The tight ponytail and long American-styled nails locate her in a particular style group, that of "street style," a style signifying "cool" that is adopted by young, white working-class people, but drawn from the black working class (Diawara, in Skeggs 2004). At the same time, the girl in the photograph looks vulnerable; the defiant look might be sad, or maybe she is retrained by an overbearing background. Above the thumbnail photographs the following text is dominant on the page: "Growing up around ✳✳✳✳✳✳✳ estate in ✳✳✳✳✳✳✳, this group of young people have captured local life through photography to show what it's like to be a teenager in a tough urban community."

The framing phrase, "what it's like to be a teenager in a tough urban community," is somehow at odds with the power, humor, and complexity of the photographs. The explanatory text tells the Web user what this material is: these are self-representations about X. And yet the notion of community is strange here, in the context of the phrase "tough urban community," because "community" mostly carries positive connotations (Bauman 2001, Silverstone 1999).

Both knowingness and humor figure in the photographs presented in *London 16–19:* a photograph of a pet dog through bars; a photograph of lads posing in front of scooters and graffiti and next to bin bags of garbage; a photograph of an old man sitting on his bed, holding a black-and-white photo of himself as a young boxer; a photograph of a high-rise ("this is where we are"); a photograph of kids play-fighting; a photograph of kids against the railings of a concrete sports field. Again, in the tension between the micro-texts (the self-representations) and the macro-texts (the LV websites on which they appear), the LV project both builds and destabilizes this notion of "community." What is the community that these very different photographs, selected and displayed together, present? Is it really there?

## Tensions over How to Define and Achieve Quality

The photograph of the girl in red was selected by the young people to contribute to those displayed on the *London 16–19* website, but the curator selected it *from* that selection. These self-representations are framed by the clean, white background of the Museum of London website. There is a sharp contrast between what we see in the photographs and the look of the website on which they are displayed. This background imposes an order on the self-representations – they are branded by the museum and by the particular aesthetic of the museum platform.

In LV and CW quality is signaled in the macro-texts of the websites and television programs framing the self-representations. Here, quality is about the authority of the institutions and this is indicated by a serious, "tasteful" institutional aesthetic. But, at the same time, LV and CW give space to images taken by participants who were learning skills – in photography, in Photoshop, in computer editing, in writing. There is a strong sense, therefore, in which quality is about enabling members of the public to learn, in order to make their voices effective. Information about these processes through which the self-representations get made is delivered in the macro texts of the websites, becoming part of how we understand the self-representations themselves and part of the processes of textual mediation.

The CW digital stories are recognizable as digital stories that have been produced by that project. They are of a uniform length (between two and three minutes), all use first-person voice-over and focus on personal view or experience. These self-representations are purposefully and clearly marked as constructed from the family albums of "ordinary people." But they are crafted, as if to give weight and value to those family albums, and to the memories that are spoken in voice-overs.

Val Bethell's story begins with the word "Hiraeth" in green curly letters and her name beneath in white. The background is a photograph of a tree in silhouette against a stormy sky. We cut from the title page to a black-and-white photograph of a smiling group in front of a rural house. Bethell's voice-over begins: "I know the meaning of the Welsh word, Hiraeth; it has called to me all my life." An anonymous family photograph now gains meaning – we can guess that Bethell is a child in this photograph. As the sentence "all my life" finishes, we cut to a landscape with sun setting over a valley and the voice-over continues: "I would happily travel west, but north, south or east were *so* difficult." The voice-over is slow, carefully enunciated, and clear; it is a storyteller's voice.

The digital stories displayed on the CW website are defined as "broadcast quality."[3] This might suggest that digital stories look or sound the same as other (professionally produced) programs on television, whereas digital stories are visually marked as self-representations by members of the public. Indeed, quality in LV and CW is located in the proclaiming of an "amateur aesthetic" (Atton 2002).

## Conclusions

The validity/usefulness of textual analysis to understanding media has long been called into question (see, e.g., Couldry 2000a). The process of looking at these texts was discomfiting, and I want to conclude by addressing this. It seems to me that the very oddness encountered in producing these textual analyses is actually revealing about the four areas of tensions that, I have argued, constitute the processes of textual mediation shaping the self-representation in LV and CW: the question of what these self-representations are intended to achieve, the construct of the "ordinary person," the construct of the "community," and tension over how to define and achieve quality.

First, my unease highlights the pervasiveness of the division which situates these self-representations as "amateur" – thus by definition not professional – content. Further highlighted is the fact that this division is hierarchical – professional content being deserving of critical attention, while the purpose of amateur content is something else and, therefore, not supposed to be read in the same way. Yet, analysis suggests that tension over purpose is part of the processes of mediation shaping what self-representations in LV and CW are. Second, the idea of the ordinary is highlighted by the discomfort encountered in textual analysis. If these self-representations are by, and of, "ordinary people," then the implication is that they must be interchangeable, and it does not matter which are looked at in detail; yet a sustained analysis highlights how these self-representations are each unique and so troubles the categorization "ordinary." At the same time, however, the framing of the self-representations by the institutions defines them as representations of "ordinary people" – of whom there are by definition many more.

Third, the idea of community is raised: should these individual self-representations be plucked from their framing as part of a community? Do they make sense on their own, removed from that context? The discomfort encountered in producing these textual analyses suggests that some of the sense of what these self-representations are is lost when they are taken out of the communal context in which they are always displayed. And yet the analysis of the individual self-representations, the websites framing them, and the relationship between these two, shows that tensions about the idea of community are present in the processes of mediation shaping the self-representations.

Fourth, how can the fact that these individual self-representations are moving, which is why they work, be conveyed and understood, without a detailed exploration of what they consist of in terms of form, content, and narrative? And here the question is about quality – look at too many of these self-representations at once and you could be overwhelmed; they may feel sentimental and even repetitive, but viewed individually, they can feel powerful. How the self-representations are made, how they seem to work, and how the issue of quality is implicated in these questions, suggests that tension over quality is a key factor in the processes of textual mediation shaping these self-representations.

I have tried to show how tensions over the purposes of self-representations, the construction of "ordinary people," the construction of "community," and defining and achieving "quality" are key to the processes of textual mediation shaping the self-representations produced and displayed by two publicly funded projects, CW and LV. This co-production between institutions and members of the public does useful work in bringing these tensions to the surface. Finally, it is likely that tensions, such as those discussed here and no doubt others, must shape self-representations across other mediated settings where the role (and power) of producers, and producing institutions, may be less explicit – for example in the websites described by the term Web 2.0.

## Notes

1  This chapter draws on research in which three dimensions of mediation process are conceptualized: processes of institutional, textual, and cultural mediation. How these areas of tension operate in the views of participants is discussed in terms of "processes of cultural mediation" in Thumim (in preparation).
2  Namely, talk shows (see, e.g., Livingstone and Lunt 1994), documentary and reality TV (see, e.g., Corner 1994, Hill 2000), mass observation (see, e.g., Highmore 2002), museum practice (see, e.g., Bennett 1995, Hooper-Greenhill 1997, Message and Healy 2004), the Internet (see, e.g., Cheung 2000, Dovey 2000, Pariser 2000, Hermes 2006), and alternative media (see, e.g., Atton 2002, Rodriguez 2001).
3  Daniel Meadows, Creative Director, "Capture Wales," interview with the Nancy Thumim.

# Part IV

# Emergent Practices

# Digital Storytelling as Play
## The *Tale of Tales*

## *Maria Chatzichristodoulou [aka Maria X]*

*I find myself anticipating a new kind of storyteller, one who is half hacker, half bard.*

Janet Murray (1997: 9)

## Introduction

This chapter explores the Tale of Tales multiplayer online game *The Endless Forest* as a digital narrative.[1] It approaches this multifaceted piece as a cyber-drama, a story, and a game, asking questions about the ontology of narrative in digital storytelling. The chapter suggests that *The Endless Forest* and multiplayer online games as a genre provide a model for the development of digital narratives that are experiential, multiple, and relational – thus making for rich, engaging narrative systems.

Log on to *The Endless Forest* tale-of-tales.com/TheEndlessForest

## Your Life As a Deer

You are a fawn, a baby deer (Figure 15.1), which will grow up to become a stag – a beautiful male deer (Figure 15.2). You live deep within an idyllic, peaceful forest. You spend your time roaming around the forest with other deer. There are a lot of things to do in the forest: everyday things like eating, sleeping under the shadow of the trees, drinking fresh water from the pond,

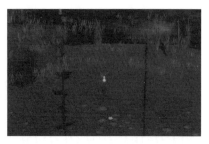

**Figure 15.1**   A fawn in The Endless Forest. *Screenshot from ToT's website*

**Figure 15.2**   A stag in The Endless Forest, at The Pond. *Screenshot from ToT's website*

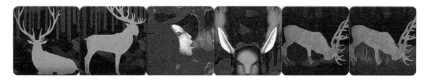

**Figure 15.3**   Different actions a deer can perform. *Screenshot from ToT's website*

resting by the ancient ruin, picking up flowers, or rubbing against a tree (Figure 15.3). There are also things you cannot do in the forest: you cannot speak, for example. Language is replaced by body language, actions, and sounds. But this is not just any forest. It is *The Endless Forest* (*TEF*), a place where magical things can happen: animals can fly, all the flowers can bloom at once, stones can fall from the sky, the rain can be made of gold – nobody ever knows what the Twin Gods will come up with to entertain themselves.[2] Deer can also perform magic and cast spells on other deer. While in *TEF*, there are no goals to achieve or rules to follow. Being there, together, is what the experience is about.

Being together is an important aspect of the *TEF* experience. *TEF* is an online virtual world, where people meet and interact through their deer-avatars. As there is no language, you cannot speak with other deer, but there are other ways to communicate and express your feelings: you can express sadness, confusion, anger, merriment, respect, or amazement. You can also express yourself through actions such as hopping, standing on your back legs, shaking your head, dancing, or being affectionate to another deer. In that sense, *TEF* is not unlike other social networking sites or virtual worlds such as *Second Life* (*SL*), where people can meet and socialize (and more) through their avatars. Unlike *SL*, though, *TEF* is an authored environment:

whereas *SL* duplicates elements of *Real Life* (*RL*) within a virtual context, *TEF* is a fairytale world that places its users straight within a specific narrative (Chatzichristodoulou 2007). Although *TEF* does not have a plot as such, it is a narrative environment that transports interactors from their everyday lives into a fairytale world of narrative possibilities; a context which is open-ended (no outcomes specified), (a)live (interactions with other deer take place in real time), and relational (the forest is a public space, and while you are there you relate to others).

## Tale of Tales

*The Endless Forest* (2005–)[3] is a hybrid work-in-progress created by the Belgium-based games development studio Tale of Tales. The studio was founded in 2002 by web designers and artists Auriea Harvey and Michaël Samyn (see Figure 15.4).[4] Tale of Tales' aim is to design and develop "immersive web sites and multimedia environments with a strong emphasis on narration, play, emotion and sensuality" (Tale of Tales 2005a). The target audience is "people who are not enchanted by most contemporary computer games, or who wouldn't mind more variety in their gameplay experiences" (Tale of Tales 2007). In order to achieve this, they produce works that

**Figure 15.4**    Auriea Harvey and Michaël Samyn, founders of Tale of Tales

"feature innovative forms of interaction, engaging poetic narratives and simple controls" (Tale of Tales 2007). *TEF* is ToT's second project, but their first fully developed title. The first one was a single-player PC game called 8, which was put on hold owing to lack of funding. *TEF* is a hybrid, complex piece that resists easy categorization: it is a screensaver, an online multi-player game, a live performance environment, a virtual world, a social space, and a collective fairytale. *TEF* is a work-in-progress, with new features being added over time. The artists have their own plans for its evolution, but players can also discuss these and make suggestions through the Forum.

## The Endless Forest as Cyberdrama

Janet H. Murray, in her germinal book *Hamlet on the Holodeck*, argued that early experiments in digital storytelling, such as websites and shooting games, have aroused appetites "for participatory stories that offer more complete immersion, more satisfying agency, and a more sustained involvement with a kaleidoscopic world" (Murray 1997: 251). She coined the term "cyberdrama" to describe such stories: "emphasizing the enactment of the story in the particular fictional space of the computer" (Murray 2004: 4). I suggest that several important elements stand out in Murray's discourse:

- first, she talks about *participatory* stories and agency, which implies that the storyteller (if there is one) is no longer the single author of the story;
- second, she calls for a more *sustained involvement* with the story-world, which would require that interactors have (the possibility of developing) a durational rather than a one-off experience;
- third, she places the story within a *kaleidoscopic world*, which suggests that the story-world is not one but multiple, constantly changing, or seen through multiple perspectives;
- fourth, she approaches the story as enacted – and thus dramatic – as opposed to narrated, situating the interactors at the very heart of the story (*immersion*), as its protagonists.

Is *TEF* a cyberdrama? I believe it fulfills the above criteria: It is participatory, as the forest can only come to life through the presence of interactors-deer; interactors have a certain degree of agency, too, as they can change other deer's appearance by casting magic spells, decide how to spend their time in the forest, and suggest further features. *TEF* is always accessible online, thus allowing for the interactors' sustained involvement with the story-world. Indeed, providing this possibility has been a major concern for the artists and one of the reasons that led them to develop *TEF* (Chatzichristodoulou 2007). Furthermore, each deer, even if present in the forest with other deer, has a specific view of the world depending on where it chooses to be and how it decides to spend its time. The world itself is not static but in constant evolution, as new features are being added and unexpected events take place whenever the Twin Gods decide to make use of their godly powers. Finally, *TEF* is an enacted story, as the interactors become the deer. However, we should raise another issue here: *TEF* qualifies as a cyberdrama, but is it a story to start with?

## The Endless Forest As Story

ToT have always considered themselves as storytellers. They insist that, through *TEF*, they are telling a story – it might not be a linear story with plot and characters, but it is a fairytale world their audiences can inhabit (Chatzichristodoulou 2007). While I am writing this, I am in the forest myself. It is evening and it's snowing. The forest is dark and looks slightly sinister, but I am sleeping under the moonlight, next to a bed of purple flowers. Before I went to sleep, while lying in a sunny spot enjoying the warmth, I suddenly found myself surrounded by three massive mushrooms. I tried nibbling on one of them, but it wasn't edible; the mushrooms disappeared within a few minutes. I also made a new friend; a black deer with red flowers on its antlers. I woke up at 6 P.M. UK time on October 6, 2007, to find out that the Twin Gods had gone wild: I could hear loud operatic music and, running towards the Gods (they appear in the forest as two white statues; see Figure 15.5), I found myself at a spectacular deer festival. There was bunting on the trees, colorful lights, massive light-reflecting bubbles, and disco balls hanging from the sky. I saw a deer being turned into a pigeon, and I had spells cast on me that turned me white. A bunch of deer were hopping around, dancing, casting spells on each other and showing their respect to the Gods.

This is the micro-narrative of my life as a deer on October 6, 2007, which I created for myself through my presence within and interaction with the virtual world created by ToT. As Murray points out: "In a procedural world,

**Figure 15.5**   The Twin Gods. *Screenshot from ToT's website*

the interactor is scripted by the environment as well as acting upon it"
(Murray 2004: 6). My micro-narrative is very much defined by the narrative
context created by ToT (a forest with deer), the degree of agency they have
allowed their interactors (for example, you can act but cannot speak; only
named deer can cast spells), and the interventions they made to the virtual
world on that specific date (deer-festival, which was a live Abiogenesis performance; see Figure 15.6). Nevertheless, my own choices and actions created my unique, personal narrative for the day. Can this be approached as
storytelling despite the fact that no concrete story is being narrated or
enacted? Life as a deer opens up a number of narrative possibilities – but
can we call them *stories*?

## The Endless Forest as a Game

*TEF* is described by ToT as different things (social screensaver, virtual
world) but, first and foremost, it is described as a multiplayer online game
(Tale of Tales 2005b). A number of debates have been unfolding regarding
the definition and function of narrative in games.[5] I will concentrate on the

**Figure 15.6** An Abiogenesis performance. *Screenshot from ToT's website*

discourse of Celia Pearce, who has called for a "play-centric" approach to gaming narratives, that is, one that concentrates on *play* and the *player experience* as opposed to *telling a story*. Pearce argues that "the function of narrative in games is to engender compelling, interesting play" (2004: 144). She has identified "the emergent narrative that develops out of ... the game ... as experienced by the players themselves," as the one narrative "operator" that is a component of all games (145). According to Pearce, the one fundamental characteristic of all games, when it comes to the development of their narrative, is the fact that this emerges experientially, through the interactor's active engagement with the game and their specific inter/actions. If we accept Pearce's proposition we also accept the emergent aspect of any gaming narrative as one that is constantly in the process of becoming. Since each interactor generates their own narrative through their own unique personal experience, any gaming narrative is always personalized and subjective. In that sense, we do not talk about one "grand" narrative, but a number of micro-narratives which are as many as the interactors of any single game.

Murray has used the term "multiform story" to describe "a written or dramatic narrative that presents a single situation or plotline in multiple versions, versions that would be mutually exclusive in our ordinary experience" (1997: 30). I would argue that, in order to discuss narrative contexts such as multiplayer online games, we need to revisit the expectation that the narrative itself presents a single situation in multiple versions. What *TEF* and other social games do is to create the (shared) conditions that provide interactors with a sufficient degree of agency for them to each enact one (or, often, more) of these versions. The important difference is that each and all of these versions are – to refer back to Pearce's discourse – emergent and unexpected, rather than predetermined paths of action and, thus, narrative possibilities. In that sense, a game like *TEF* provides a single narrative platform for the emergence of multiple micro-narratives that converge to generate a multi-narrative system: a system where the stories narrated are at least as many as the stories enacted at any single time.

I discussed the fact that micro-narratives are subjective, unique, and personal. How, though, are these generated? What would my day as a deer have been like had I been alone in a private endless forest? I would have still been able to enact a personal micro-narrative through my interaction with the virtual world, but my story would have been very different and, I think, considerably less exciting. I could still have had a degree of agency to do with my interaction with the world itself, and the world could still be changing as a result of commands built within the system. Nevertheless, I believe that a private forest would not have been able to sustain my long-term engagement. I could have gone back a few times to look for new developments and would have probably interacted differently with the system each time, but the narratives generated by these visits would had been more predictable and less emotionally engaging. What made my micro-narrative rich, surprising, enjoyable, and emotionally engaging (to me, at least), were the others: deer and gods crossed my path several times, and I never knew what to expect. My personal narrative was shaped by these of other interactors, and vice versa. Living in *TEF* is a private but relational experience.

## Digital Storytelling

I asked: "Life as a deer opens up a number of narrative possibilities – but can we call these *stories*?" Now I can answer: "We can, and indeed we must." I suggest that multiplayer online games as a genre, and *TEF* in particular, provide a useful model for the development of future experimentations in digital narratives. Specifically, they provide a model for creating narrative contexts that can allow for the emergence of multiple micro-narratives which are generated by the interactors themselves (rather than provided by a "grand" multiform narrative) through their continuous involvement with the story/world and their relations with each other. Thus, audiences become not only co-authors but co-actors of the story, through the experience of enacting each their personal narrative. *TEF* goes even further in providing a model of digital storytelling that is free of language. As Pearce argues, every single gaming narrative is experiential (Pearce 2004: 145). *TEF* is not only experiential, but it is also a story about a live, relational experience. What would life be like if you were a deer, in a forest, together with other deer? This is *TEF*'s "grand narrative." What ToT did is to build the forest, provide the avatars of deer, and make this available for you to experience. You can now answer for yourself. The question now is: how do you live your life as a deer in *The Endless Forest*?

I suggest that *The Endless Forest* points toward the future of digital narrative as an open, (a)live, relational, and collective Endeavour. Tell us your story.

## Notes

1   See www.tale-of-tales.com (accessed August 2006).
2   The Twin Gods are the artists themselves, Auriea and Michaël who, through a system called Abiogenesis, are able to "play God" and make changes to the virtual forest-world any time they please, or as a planned online performance.
3   *TEF* is free for people to download from the Tale of Tales website.
4   They are also known as Entropy8Zuper! See www.entropy8zuper.org (accessed August 2006).
5   For more in-depth discussions on these issues refer to the work of Henry Jenkins, Janet Murray, and Eric Zimmerman, among other theorists.

# 16

# Commercialization and Digital Storytelling in China

## *Wu Qiongli*

"Digital storytelling" (DST) has a general meaning, referring to new forms of digital narrative such as hypertext, interactive stories, and narrative computer games. However, the DST discussed here focuses on the Californian/Welsh model used throughout this book. That approach consists of a personally narrated (voice-over) story, personal pictures or videos, and a musical soundtrack, edited into a 2–5-minute film. The uniqueness of this form is that it "presents itself as a tractable, engaging and seemingly popular form for the average person to use" (Salpeter 2005). It bridges the gap between professional media broadcast and grassroots creativity by empowering people to showcase their creativity without trepidation (Burgess 2005b). DST "takes the ancient art of oral storytelling and engages a palette of technical tools to weave personal tales using images, graphics, music, and sound mixed together with the author's own story voice" (Bernajean Porter, in Salpeter 2005).

The main features which distinguish DST from other storytelling forms are summarized below.

- **Story-oriented**. The spirit of the DST is the story, and not the technology. DST returns the creator's attention to the personal story, such as family tales and community narratives which, owing to their "ordinary" and "personal" nature, are different from mainstream tech-focused digital arts. The priority of DST is the stories first, the digitalization second.
- **Disciplined**. The Center for Digital Storytelling (CDS) in California recognized that giving a map or outlining a framework is an efficient approach to help people to understand and adopt the concept (Center

for Digital Storytelling 2004). DST is a well-disciplined approach: that is, it has a practical framework, which illuminates the possibilities and at the same time controls the form, quality, and efficiency of the process. DST is therefore not only simply implemented, but it is also easy to migrate from one environment to another (although interoperability and IP problems remain).

- **Authentic**. DST uses the teller's original voice to narrate their personal stories, using the first person. Most of the pictures show real persons in real settings. The emotions brought by the stories come directly from people's hearts. From this perspective, it is even more authentic than the documentary format or reality TV shows.

- **Multimedia**. Compelling stories are revealed through the interweaving of narratives, images, video, music, and voices. DST is integrated multimedia. All existing media forms (such as animation, artwork, and letters) can be merged into DST.

- **Simple technology**. The basic equipment for DST is a personal computer with a microphone. A scanner and a digital still/video camera are also useful. Nonlinear editing software packages have many options: the most popular are Premiere and Apple iMovie. As technological knowledge requirements are simple, and the CDS model provides its own complete skills manual, people without computer skills can quickly learn DST.

- **Found materials**. By way of contrast to many professional digital creations, DST largely exploits preexisting visual archives – such as family albums, home videos, and hand-drawn illustrations (Center for Digital Storytelling 2004). CDS prefers this approach, since it "puts the participant in the editing chair, with a minimal amount of preparation" (Wikibooks 2005). This feature enables "people participation" and has the added advantage of rapid outcomes.

- **Collaborative creativity**. Currently, most digital stories are produced in intensive workshops. Joe Lambert, one of the founders of CDS, believes that "storytelling is meant to be a collaborative art" (Wikibooks 2005). Jean Burgess (2005a) also points out that beyond communicative creativity, DST actually privileges "collaborative creativity." For this reason, even though information about DST is available online and people can easily grasp it through self-learning, workshops are still the preferred choice for production. The notions of sharing and inspiring are everpresent throughout the whole creation process. This makes the shared experience shared fun.

These features differentiate DST from the various digitized forms of expression otherwise available; and they enable DST to be taken up in a wide variety of contexts – across nations and across disciplines. There are excellent examples from the professional news media, such as *USA Today's* "Tale of two holidays" (Thomassie et al. 2004) and *The New York Times'* "Freeing Sex Slaves" (Kristof 2005);[1] most current practices focus on education and community building: for instance, the Teacher Institute program at the US National Gallery of Art (Springer, Kajder, and Brazas 2004).

There is, however, little commercial practice of digital storytelling. One case I found was the Converse Gallery, a promotional program for the sports brand Converse.[2] It asked consumers to make a 24-second film embodying the values and spirit of Converse from their personal stories (conversegallery.com, 2005; since taken down). Most of the films were shown on the website and a few were aired on television. The Converse Gallery clearly stated that what it wanted were not professional commercials but the customer's authenticity, originality, and creativity. On one hand this approach helps Converse develop customer relationships; on the other hand it exploits consumers' creativity to co-promote and co-brand Converse.

Apart from the co-branding application, DST has commercial potential that is yet to be fully explored in terms of its embedded features. For example, it has great potential in cultural tourism. Travel and adventure stories are often the subject of digital stories, but the form is yet to be used in any significant way by cultural tourism operators. Personal perspective and grassroots creativity can assist tourists to find the sense of authenticity they pursue; a multimedia form enables better cross-cultural understanding; and personal archives of travel pictures and videos are a great resource for DST. Furthermore, in terms of allowing intercommunication within tourism activities, stories about a city, a restaurant, or cultural events and places not only enhance locals' community belonging, but also give outsiders insights about the values and connections within the local community (Lambert 2003). A good example is the DST program at the Australian Centre for the Moving Image (ACMI 2005), which is highlighted as a contemporary arts site in most Australian tourism manuals and maps.[3]

Traveling is about mobility and the desire to share stories. Experiences often occur spontaneously. This also provides a big opportunity for the commercial application of digital storytelling – mobile digital storytelling. HP Labs are experimenting with a multimedia storytelling service called StoryCast, which allows people to easily capture, create, and instantly share stories using their camera phones or other mobile devices (HP 2005). After trying this service, Lee Bruno, a senior editor with *RedHerring* magazine, described it as "photoblog on the fly" (Beckett 2005). Services like StoryCast can be used by media professionals as a medium for reporting, and also can be used by nonprofessionals (that is, "ordinary" people) to keep an audiovisual journal, to create a virtual tour of a museum or event (Beckett 2005).

## Business Opportunities in the Chinese Context

The advantages and opportunities for DST are now beginning to appear in international practice. Can China provide the same opportunities? How is it possible to introduce the DST concept into China? Trendwatching.com (2005b), an independent and opinionated trend agency, has identified a global "Generation C" phenomenon. In their view, the "C" stands for "content." It captures the huge amount of user-created content on the Web, from weblogs, reviews, and comments to photography, drawing, design, music, and video clips. From these outputs, the meaning of the "C" has extended the "content" to a "creative" level, since most of those participations and contributions are the outcome of Generation C's creativity.

This concept can be related to the notions of the "netizen" and the "prosumer." Netizen is a term coined by Michael Hauben in 1992 (Wikipedia 2005), a combination of "Internet" and "citizen." Netizens are those who actively engage in online communities through participation, contribution, or creation. According to Wikipedia, this "term has been used most frequently recently in Korea and China where there are vigorous netizen movements." The word "prosumer," coined by the futurologist Alvin Toffler (1981), refers to new consumers who also are producers (see Bruns 2005, Bruns and Jacobs 2006). The idea of the prosumer recognizes that consumers are not – or are no longer – passive, but active, interactive, and even productive. It reveals the blurred lines between producer and consumer, amateur (hobbyists) and professional, and also redefines the relation of producer/provider and consumer/receiver as a conversational, co-productive partnership.

The relations between Generation C, netizens, and the prosumers can be understood in an intimate way (see Figure 16.1). Some prosumers create off-line (e.g., home improvement), and a section of netizens do not create at all. Generation C is found at the intersection of netizens and prosumers.

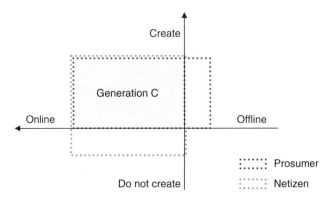

**Figure 16.1**   Relations of netizen, prosumer, and Generation C

As the arrows show, the population of Generation C is increasing, with more prosumers going online and more netizens engaging in creative contribution. The global Generation C phenomenon has been quickly taken up by the commercial world, for instance, where customers' homemade short films are used in commercial advertising, or personal photographs appear on the labels of soft drinks (Trendwatching.com 2005a).

In China, the prosumer transformation can be seen largely in the "do-it-yourself" (DIY) phenomenon (Hartley 1999). DIY enthusiasm has become a new consumption philosophy, covering areas such as home furnishing, computer, craft, and independent tourism (eastday.com 2003). In the virtual world, Chinese netizens form a vast pool of grassroots creativity. Flourishing online communities and the boom in online original content show that Chinese Generation C desire to build their self-esteem and derive fulfillment through contributing and creating. Beyond online surfing, e-commercials, online-learning, and online entertainment, Chinese Generation C engage in all kinds of creative activities, such as virtual community building, online literature creation, multimedia blogging, online game design, Flash animation, digital video creation, and writing and performing original music. If we take Generation C as the main target market of digital storytelling, the market demand is quite clear, and is based on their desire to stretch and showcase personal creativity, to develop self-talent, and to have fun.

Cultural tourism is "the movement of persons to cultural attractions away from their normal place of residence with the intention to gather new information and experiences to satisfy their cultural needs" (Bonet

1998:187). With the rapid development of transportation and communication, tourism no longer simply focuses on the transportation, accommodation, and destinations, but places increased emphasis on the understanding of local cultures and the experiences of authentic local lifestyles. There is evidence that more marketing efforts are designed to promote the cultural amenities specific to certain place-related destinations (Carpenter 2004).

China has huge advantages in its cultural tourism. It has a long history, ancient cultural heritage, various ethnicities, and rich traditions. However, tourism development has until now focused mostly on the improvement of facilities, the promotion of destinations, and the protection and exploitation of historical heritage, elements that lack people-focus. The challenges as well as opportunities for China's cultural tourism are to add experiential dimensions to place-related destinations, to offer the experience of local art and culture, to bring about communication between visitors and local communities (Carpenter 2004). In 2004 the China National Tourism Administration created an international promotion motto, "Catch the Lifestyle-China 2004," to introduce the unique lifestyle of Chinese people to overseas tourists (He 2001, CUHK 2004). Questions arise: How to transmit an intangible lifestyle and culture effectively and efficiently? What other approaches might work, apart from the existing ones?

From another perspective, one of the problems with tourism information systems is that experiences gained during a trip are not efficiently shared (Watson et al. 2004). Industries have not paid enough attention to *reminiscing*, the third tourist experience after *planning* and *touring*. Nevertheless, the evolving Chinese online tourism service is to some extent endeavoring to fill this gap through an emergent bottom-up business model. They draw on consumers' creativity and intelligence, utilizing post-travel experiences (e.g., destination reviews, photographs, and digital-video sharing) and tourists' feedback and reflections to guide or reshape tourism industry development. The natural follow-up question is how to offer a more comprehensive *reminiscing service* through new technology and new models.

The opportunities for DST here are obvious. DST enhances the connections between places and people, bridges the past and the present, and transmits cultural experiences through local memories and daily life stories. DST can also offer a multimedia form of expression for the post-travel experience and can evoke communication among multiple cultures by encouraging tourists from different origins to share their experience of a given destination.

The international exploration of the *nomadic access to tourist services* has been conducted for some time. The European IST project, "Creation of User-friendly Mobile Services Personalized for Tourism" (CRUMPET), has suggested some recommendations on future services, such as personalized and location-sensed tourist attractions, interactive maps, and multimedia information about tourist attractions (Schmidt-Belz and Poslad 2003). Beyond theoretical explorations, industry practitioners are creating new ways to generate revenue through wireless value-added services. For instance, the Zagat Survey allows customers to download restaurant reviews for up to 67 cities to their handhelds (Stellin 2005). Vindigo, a New York City company, introduced a mobile city guide, including local listings for restaurants, museums, stores, bars, movie theaters, and even nearby ATMs and bathrooms (Stellin 2005).

In China, which has the world's largest mobile telecom market, the top early growth engines of wireless content were colorful ring-tones, interactive voice response, multimedia message (MMS), wireless application protocol (WAP), and Java downloads (*China Business Weekly* 2005). But as technologies like 3 G improve and expand, there is a demand for more media-rich content. In addition to licensing traditional media content such as TV programs, the grassroots creations in MMS, digital pictures, and videos would appear to have a big role to play. The challenges are what will be the next popular wireless content format and how to further the engagement of the mobile users through wireless value-added services.

## The Digital Storytelling Solution

For DST, the opportunities are to offer a user-friendly and disciplined mobile content creation format, to employ mobile users' creativity, and to fulfill the demand of multimedia content in a 3 G environment. The digital storytelling solution proposed here is to provide a DST commercialization framework (see Figure 16.2).

In this framework, a platform is established to promote and diffuse the concept and skills of DST, and to showcase and cultivate Generation C's digital storytelling creativity. This operation is conducted with a commercial approach, using a new business model. Outcomes will not only be economic but also socially beneficial, such as community building, citizen participation, digital arts education, and so on. The following discussion will focus on the commercial operation and new business model evaluation.

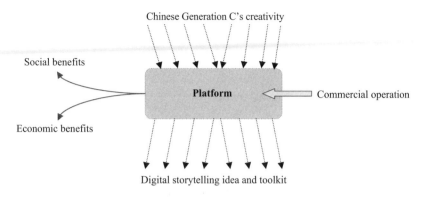

**Figure 16.2**  The framework of the digital storytelling solution

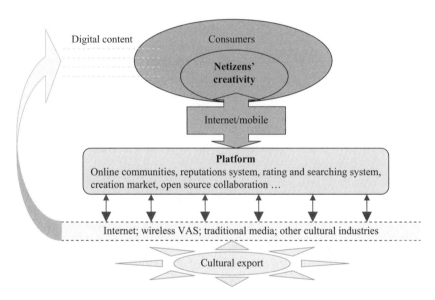

**Figure 16.3**  The new business model of commercializing netizens' creativity

A new business model in China's Internet industry is emerging (see Figure 16.3), where netizens' grassroots creativity is commercialized via mainstream content industries. Websites (online communities) provide a multifunctional interactive platform, where netizens are helped to develop, showcase, and add value to their creativity, and the mainstream content industries are assisted to find "market-guaranteed" resources through the reputation system. For instance, in the online music sector, netizens'

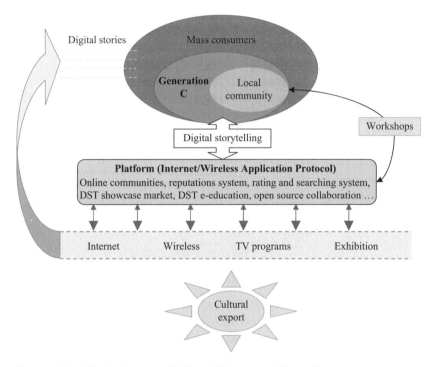

**Figure 16.4**   The business model for a digital storytelling solution

outstanding original music creations and performances are filtered out through the online reputation system, adopted by the traditional record company, and eventually distributed to mass consumers. One essential fact of this model is that netizens create as well as consume, which to some extent guarantees the core profitability of this model. The application of this model to digital storytelling case is illustrated in Figure 16.4.

The platform focuses on DST e-education and assistance, DST works showcasing online community building, and reputation system building. Generation C can access this platform via the Internet or a mobile phone. They learn DST skills through the DST e-education system and thus create and showcase their own stories following the guidelines. The works are viewed and reviewed in the online community. High-quality and appealing works are automatically sorted out through the online reputation system (such as rating system and hit parade). Then the websites will modify and repackage these popular digital stories and distribute to other media such as an Internet portal, wireless value-added services, TV programs, and exhibitions at tourist attractions. Meanwhile, another off-line approach can adopt the international mature workshop model to reach out to non-netizens in the local community. Digital stories created in the workshop are also showcased and reviewed on the platform.

This proposed business model adopts a hybrid revenue model, which combines subscription (e.g., membership fee); fee-for-service (e.g., download or MMS); production (e.g., film package, CD, and DVD); copyright management (e.g., licensing the digital stories to other entities); and online advertising. The commercial strategy is a combination of the B2C model (e.g., online shops for digital stories), C2B model (e.g., netizens sell their copyright to publishers), and C2C/P2P model (e.g., sharing content through email, instant messaging, and mobile phones).

## Key Issues in Product and Services Development

### Possibilities

The potential of this model can be demonstrated from several angles. From the perspective of Generation C, their active participation and digital creation capability are largely shown in the online photo gallery, Flash animation, and multimedia weblogs. From the perspective of technology environments, broadband use in China, sales of digital cameras, and digital cable television are all growing fast. Millions of Chinese are empowered by digital instruments and are inspired by the rich information environment to express, share, and interact in new ways. From the perspective of the DST model, there is already a mature model with experience from international practice. The only thing which needs to be considered here is how to tailor it for the local context in China. From the perspective of the revenue model, it is based on the existing practice of China's Internet industry, such as online literature and music. From the perspective of cost, R&D investment is not prohibitive. The main investment areas are human resources, Internet servers, and computer hardware and software.

### Quality control strategies

One big concern about the commercialization of DST is whether the quality of the grassroots creation is good enough to be commercially valued and marketed. However, there is no doubt that outstanding creativity is coming from the grassroots; moreover, Generation C's creativity and capability in the practice itself can be built upon and improved. One main goal of this solution is to control and improve the quality of the grassroots creation. To achieve this goal, the following strategies can be adopted:

- set up quality-oriented social norms in the online community, where certain rules of quality control are built into community participation;
- use the reputation system to filter the creations through their quality, such as ratings, reviews, and a Top 10 chart;
- set different levels for the participants to submit their works, such as professionals, students, enthusiasts, and amateurs, which can maintain quality between levels and encourage the growth of individuals;
- set up expert review systems, inviting industry experts to evaluate the works and give suggestions.

### Multiple distribution channels

This solution targets three different markets:

1   Generation C (offering DST toolkits, showcasing space, and other services);
2   mass DST consumers (offering them value-added DST works); and
3   mainstream digital content industries (offering them broadcast-quality DST products).

Apart from the platform itself, other distribution channels are as follows:

- **Television**: Since DST works can be outputted into a film format, they can be easily broadcast on television. Suitable programs include a large range of genres, especially those about cultural tourism, people and cities, and people's daily lives. This has been successfully demonstrated by the BBC's exploitation of DST on a television platform (e.g., "Capture Wales").
- **The Internet**: DST can be repackaged around certain topics and distributed through other websites. For instance, a series of digital stories about the sporting activities of the people of Beijing can be linked to Beijing Olympic websites as part of a citizen participation movement. Stories about unique tourist attractions could enrich local tourism websites.

- **Exhibitions**: Another distribution channel is exhibitions at museums, arts galleries, and tourism sites. For instance, nostalgic stories of old Beijing city can be shown at heritage exhibition sites.
- **Wireless value-added services**: As the HP Labs' StoryCast example demonstrates, the technology of mobile digital storytelling is already possible. It will not be too long before DST is created directly onto mobile phones, even in China. Both China Unicom and China Mobile have launched services to provide TV programs for mobile phone subscribers (Xinhua 2005). DST has the advantage over larger formats, because of its feasible size (2–5 minutes) and complete content (a whole story). Future DST wireless distribution might largely lie in P2P sharing, where users share their own or their favorite digital stories with family and friends. Another potential development is place-sensed services. DST offers content enrichment linked with the e-map: when people are searching certain tourist attractions, they can view relevant digital stories to extend the experience and understanding.

### Multilingual and cultural export

Cultural export is another challenge for DST in the cultural tourism sector, promoting Chinese culture all over the world. In this solution, online collaborative creativity is fully utilized to provide multilingual versions of DST. Multilingual DST can be achieved by adding alternative language subtitles or translation voice-overs. Multilingual digital stories are encouraged through online guideline and community norms. Cooperation among participants is supported through dedicated online social markets, where people can ask for translation help or even bid for the best translation. Furthermore, the platform can be built bilingually in the first instance, in Chinese and English, and be open to international participants as well. International participation is encouraged so that visitors can express their impressions and experiences of Beijing or other places in China through DST.

### Competitive position

This DST solution fully utilizes DST's easy-uptake feature to explore ordinary people's creativity, therefore enhancing cultural expression and

**Table 16.1**    The benefits raised by DST services in China

| Key stakeholders | Benefits |
| --- | --- |
| Generation C | New ways to explore and showcase creativity |
| | New ways to express and communicate |
| | Empowered to be creator and director |
| | Self-fulfillment through digital arts education |
| | Entertainment and enjoyment |
| | Economic benefits |
| Local community | Develop local community wellbeing |
| | Improve the fulfillment of regional objectives |
| | Strengthen communication and cultural exchange |
| | Strengthen belongingness and local identity |
| | Narrow the digital divide |
| | Improve cross-generational understanding |
| Tourism industry | Enrich tourist destinations and attractions |
| | Preserve and explore local culture |
| | Extend the authentic experience of cultural tourism |
| | Develop cross-cultural understanding |
| Digital content industries | New form of digital content |
| (e.g., Internet-related SPs, | Low cost of content product development |
| TV, digital content | Market-guaranteed product |
| publishers) | Constant and rich suppliers |
| | A large contribution by prosumers |
| Electronics information | Encourage the adoption of personal electronic |
| industry | information products, such as digital still/video |
| | camera, scanner, camera mobile |
| | Promote the creative consumption of electronic |
| | products |

community communication. Its unique position is based on the benefits it offers to all stakeholders and the advantages over its competitors. The benefits raised by DST services are shown in Table 16.1.

## Copyright

China has a poor track record in the protection and preservation of intellectual property rights (IPR). However, IPR enforcement is just one side of the story. The free availability of knowledge, information, and creativity is still vital for future creation and innovation. It is crucial to keep the right balance in a copyright system between total control and total freedom in order to sustain creativity. Creative Commons is an experiment that offers a layer of reasonable, flexible copyright, to protect creative works while encouraging certain uses of them.[4] For instance, the BBC's Creative Archive allows people to download, keep, manipulate, and share BBC factual programs for noncommercial use (BBC 2004). This DST solution will build a digital materials library through cooperation with content resources organizations and adopt a flexible copyright system for such resources.

At the same time, the next concern is how to protect the works generated by this DST solution from infringement. First, a comprehensive contract should be signed and implemented between the website and the participants. Second, technological protection can be built into the platform. Third, distribution through mobile phones will be a relative easy area in which to provide protection, since mobile phone content distribution is within the control of the mobile operator: "the contracts between mobile operators and service providers usually state that mobile operators can terminate the relationship without warning if the service provider is caught infringing other parties' intellectual property rights" (Boltz and Comey 2005).

## Conclusion

DST has proved its commercial value through authentic and multimedia creativity, productive outcomes, ease of adoption, and a feasible operation framework. Its commercial value is further confirmed by the great market demand expressed by Generation C and the opportunities arising from cultural tourism, one-off events such as the Olympic Games, and value-added services for mobile and other subscriber devices. These three areas can be integrated through a DST solution, in which an interactive platform is built to promote the DST concept, generate DST content, and filter out high-quality and popular digital stories for further distribution. In terms of benefits across all three perspectives, DST utilizes local communities' memories and daily life stories to breathe life into historical heritage and tourism attractions. It brings a bottom-up perspective to the promotion of, for example, the Beijing Olympics and generates creative communication and cultural sharing in the use of mobile phones.

This proposed DST solution is advanced from a strategic perspective and is based on theoretical research. In its application, it will require more modifications based on market research. With DST becoming more widespread internationally, China's Generation C will mature and their creativity will begin to have commercial value. So, the moment for introducing DST into China's market is approaching. The Beijing Olympics and its associated promotion, encouragement of citizen participation, and increasing tourism market all indicate a bright future for DST in China. The future vision of the DST solution is now encapsulated into one statement: "Experience authentic Chinese culture through the locals' storytelling at any time and any place."

## Notes

1   Tale of Two Holidays: www.usatoday.com/news/graphics/snsflyover/flash.htm; Freeing Sex Slaves: www.nytimes.com/packages/khtml/2005/01/19/opinion/20040119_CAMBODIA_FEATURE.html
2   See www.conversegallery.com
3   See www.acmi.net.au/digitalstorytelling.jsp
4   See http://creativecommons.org (accessed November 18, 2008).

# 17

# Digital Storytelling with Youth
## Whose Agenda Is It?

## *Lora Taub-Pervizpour*

An important locus of activity within the digital storytelling movement is the widespread focus on engaging marginalized youth as producers of the stories that matter to them most. In this chapter, I take stock of some of the moral and psychological tensions (Coles 1997) that are likely to confront those of us who organize digital storytelling programs for community youth. Since 2001, as a faculty member in a department of media and communication at a small liberal arts college in Allentown, Pennsylvania, USA, I have collaborated with other faculty and community partners to provide meaningful technology-based afterschool activities for local youth. Like other digital storytelling initiatives with marginalized youth, I believe our efforts help local youth raise their public voices and contribute to the development of their "agentive selves" (Hull 2003). Digital storytelling, and other forms of community media practices, do provide powerful opportunities for youth to experience themselves as producers (rather than consumers) of mediated messages. Equally compelling is the fact that when their stories are brought to public view, community members have the opportunity to see young people as allies in addressing problems within the community, rather than as "problems" themselves, as they are so commonly positioned across a range of institutions and discourses.

At the same time, doing digital storytelling with youth in my community has also immersed me (and students in my courses who assist in the workshops) in some profoundly contradictory and conflicted situations that have forced me to do business with my own social identity and to take stock of my location within the very structures of power that youth often name – and critique – in their digital stories. In this chapter I pose several questions that come directly from my digital storytelling experiences with local youth, questions about objectivity and subjectivity, questions about methods: how do we organize digital storytelling for marginalized youth? How do we engage youth in the digital storytelling process? What and whose interests shape our programs and practices? The questions posed here are intended to provoke reflection on our role as organizers of digital storytelling activities, how we position ourselves in relation to the stories that emerge in our workshops and programs, and how who we are informs which stories get told, by whom, and for whom.

For many compelling reasons, most reflections on young people's digital stories are celebratory. Sometimes their stories speak compellingly from a youth perspective on social issues; sometimes their stories make us feel good about the potential of youth as advocates for community change; sometimes they make us cry, and have the power to evoke our moral outrage over the suffering and injustice that youth in our communities too often bear. At the same time, explicit stories about class, race, power, and culture frame our digital storytelling collaborations with marginalized youth. For those coming to this work from locations within institutions of higher education, ours is a position of privilege, while our youth participants are most often positioned, as Warschauer (2003) has aptly noted, on the "wrong side of the digital divide." And while we aim to mobilize the various resources of our institutions (in terms of space and technology, as well as the human resources of students who often serve as mentors and assistants in digital storytelling programs) in the service of community youth so that they might tell their stories, there is also the matter of our stories, stories about where we stand in relation to the community where we do this work, in relation to its young people, its institutions, its histories, and inequities.

My focus here is on the social interactions between adults and young people that structure and inform digital storytelling production. What are our responsibilities to youth as we become witness to the experiences, hopes, and hardships that they document in their stories? What are our moral obligations to them as they put their stories – their identities – on the line for others to see and hear? To be sure, we do more than witness stories produced by community youth. To varying degrees we become co-producers of their stories. In what ways do we intervene in young people's digital storytelling production? How do we conceptualize our role in the production process? How do we reconcile our hopes and goals with those of our young collaborators? How do we navigate between multiple agendas which may be at odds with each other and which almost inevitably at moments collide: the agendas of the institutions that support and fund our work, the agendas of community partners, young people, not to mention our own agendas? And when the workshops end and the stories are told, how do those stories continue to live with us, and how are we to live with the knowledge they have taught us? What are we to do about the oppressions, struggles, and hopes that are given voice and vision in these stories?

A common flashpoint for tension and contradiction between young people and the adults who organize their digital storytelling activities is consumer popular culture. As others have documented (Hull 2003, Seiter 2004, Dyson 1997), young people regularly invoke the images and symbols of popular culture in their original media productions, and they do so to complex and mixed responses by participating adults. I should not have been surprised when these tensions surfaced early on in an afterschool digital authoring program, "In Our Eyes," that I co-organized with the director of a local church-based community action organization for young people from an Allentown neighborhood known as the "weed and seed" district. The name comes from the federal grant strategy designed to "weed out" drugs, violence, and other criminal activity and to "seed" the designated area with programs designed to meet the community's social and economic needs. As one effort in the broader initiative to engage youth as active participants in this revitalization, we sought to leverage documentary and digital storytelling tools to foster young people's evolving identity as agents of neighborhood change. Youth spent the first weeks of the program learning fundamental and more advanced techniques of photography, walking their neighborhood streets with the task of documenting things they wanted to change and other aspects of their social world they looked upon with pride. Their images documented some of the community's most pernicious problems: poverty and urban blight (pictures of dilapidated buildings); safety (pictures of signs indicating "children at play"); gangs (pictures of graffiti the children recognized as gang-related); drugs (pictures of shoes hanging over a telephone wire that the children understood to mark the location of a crack house); and alcohol abuse (pictures of corner liquor-store windows plastered with alcohol advertising). Pictures of police cars doubled as symbols of crime and representations of racism as youth spoke about police unfairly treating them as would-be criminals. Their photos also documented signs of community strength and revitalization: stoops lined with pots of blooming chrysanthemums, prospering local storefronts, a mural illustrating diversity and unity, families gathered on porches, an inviting, freshly painted playground.

On a weekday afternoon, center-city children sat in pairs around 16 computers in the classroom where my students are usually 18–20-year-old undergraduates. Ready to get their hands on the digital photo-editing software, they were asked to select one of their "problem" photos and digitally "fix" the issue represented. Many turned to popular culture for quick fixes. A scene of downtown's once thriving commercial street, now marked by empty storefronts with "FOR LEASE" signs, was revitalized by locating SpongeBob SquarePants on a central corner. Two teenage girls enlivened a street devoid of any people by copying and pasting a traffic-stopping image of J. Lo. To be sure, these photos in part represent the children's efforts to negotiate space in the adult-designed program for their own interests in surfing the Web for their favorite pop stars. But more than this, their photos also suggest their awareness of how much consumer media culture has co-opted public life. My community partner was excited by their agility with the digital-imaging software (how facile they were with the tedious outlining tool), but unimpressed with their focus on pop stars. She worried aloud that her peers and the community decision-makers, who were an important audience for these works, would see an image of a cartoon character and too easily dismiss the program designed to empower youth as agents of community change. While this "play" was fine for learning the software, the following week she began our session by reminding the youth that they were involved in the "serious" work of digitally illustrating "realistic" solutions to the real-world problems they photographed. While a few students protested that their favorite celebrities could help the community, the possibilities of this conversation were left hanging. I wanted to hear more of this perspective, but I also wanted to be respectful of the goals as they were defined by my community partner. While it seemed we had not done justice to the young participants' ideas about the role of popular culture in community life, I had responsibilities to uphold – and limited time in which to do it. But I wondered about my ethical responsibilities to the young storytellers throughout this process, and worried too that we might not be fully hearing their voices or fully seeing their visions of community life. As Anne Haas Dyson asserts: "Children have agency – not unlimited unstructured agency but agency nonetheless … they appropriate popular culture to participate in and explore their worlds … they find in the media powerful and compelling images" (1997: 181). If we are trying to help young people render their stories, in their own voices, in their own terms, then we will have to reconcile our own complicated relationships with and our assumptions about young people's investments in popular culture, and the terms we establish regarding the inclusion (or more likely, the exclusion) of popular culture in their digital storytelling work. Prohibiting popular culture references may seem arbitrary and even unjust to the young collaborators who so generously share their stories with us.

Building upon this afterschool work, we proposed and secured funding for a two-week summer workshop called the Kids Access Media Project, or KAMP. Similar to the first project, KAMP was designed to serve the community organization's interest in developing young people's skills as advocates for community change. Most days a cadre of church volunteers transported 12 young people 16 city blocks west from their church to the college campus, where we spent half-days working with digital media technology in the otherwise quiet summer space of my department's classroom and labs. Early in the first week, we spent two days conducting "field work" for their projects in their neighborhood, equipped with disposable and digital cameras ready to record sites and scenes they considered beautiful and sources of pride in the neighborhood as well as the things that were not working and that they wanted to change. The young documentarians found pride in a neighborhood mural, a downtown fountain (inviting on that particularly hot summer morning), a well-equipped and clean park. At the same time, there was no shortage of evidence calling out for neighborhood improvement, documented in photos of heaps of trash on the sidewalk, litter, a park slide tagged with graffiti, cars driving dangerously fast down alleys where children play, and other scenes marking the presence of crime recognized and documented by these discerning eyes.

Printing their photos back on campus late in the evening, my colleague, inspired by their attention to detail, to human actuality, created an exhibit of prints to greet the KAMPers when they returned to the air-conditioned classroom the following morning. Between the time we left in the evening and 8 A.M. the next day, those photos themselves became the targets of disturbing racist and denigrating graffiti. Because the building was locked overnight, we were at a loss to figure out who might have been responsible for this injustice, and we wrestled with our own responsibilities to the young people, our worry that unwittingly we had made them available for such attack. Five girls, of diverse racial and ethnic locations, were photographed together, posed in front of a prominent downtown building. Scrawled above the head of the black girl was the phrase, "Whatchew talkin bout Willis?" Other photos, shot inside the classroom during media literacy sessions taught by a faculty colleague, were tagged with remarks that imposed upon the children pictured a lack of intelligence and inability to speak ("my wist hurt" is graffitied over the head of a girl raising her hand in response to the professor's question). These photos, the very products of youth engagement and critical awareness, are transformed by graffiti that attributes to them stereotypes of urban youth as lazy, disengaged, and disrespectful (in a photo where the white female professor is gesturing with her arm up, words scrawled above a Latino boy's head read "put yo arm down wench").

The original images shot by the children for their digital stories are a direct challenge to those who would dismiss urban youth. While documenting their community, they are also documenting themselves in the process of becoming agents of community change. Their photos and digital stories give powerful voice and vision to their aspirations to remake their social world. That morning, the graffiti across their beautiful photos stopped my colleague and me in our tracks. We held in our hands yet further evidence of the very issue of racism that underpinned several of the community stories that were emerging in the workshop. We agreed that the vandalism to their creative work itself demanded documenting. There was our own dismay (but not surprise) that the representations of urban youth as thoughtful, active community members would be so threatening (and the nagging question of who was responsible). But we wondered especially about our moral obligations in this instance to our young workshop participants. There was surely a "teachable moment" to be had with those photos. But at what cost? Such a conversation, we worried, might risk reinforcing the real boundaries that separate their neighborhood (the place they were documenting) and the college (the place where they were producing their documentary stories). In stark contrast to the "Welcome!" signs we had posted around the building, the vandalized photos sent the message: "You are not really welcome here." With no more than minutes to decide prior to the children's arrival, we chose to take down the vandalized photos and keep them from their view. The children encountered the remaining photos with delight and obvious pride in seeing their original work displayed and valued. Our instincts had been to shield them from those who had devalued and defaced their work, but we had to live with the fact that their ongoing work was taking place within a context not entirely within our control, a space that was proving to be not entirely friendly to urban minority youth. We reported the incident to the campus police later that day, but there was no follow-up until a week later when the workshop was completed and the children were no longer on campus. Again we questioned whether we had been responsible enough. We were prepared to be supportive allies to these youth as they took stock of injustices in their local environments. But we had been stopped in our tracks when confronted with injustice within our own environment.

I have not said much here about the courageous stories by young producers that I have been privileged to know here in Allentown. I doubt that I could do justice to their particularity in the short space of this chapter. But I can call attention to the conditions we make possible (and impossible) for the production of young people's digital stories. On his website, Daniel Meadows has written that a digital storytelling workshop "gives its participants courage, for making a digital story isn't easy." A critical method for facilitating digital storytelling, I argue, calls upon the facilitators to be courageous as well, to ask difficult questions about the roles we play in this process, and about the theories and methods that we bring to these encounters. What are our responsibilities to the community youth we engage in digital storytelling, to their stories, and to the calls for action their stories invoke? Anyone who does digital storytelling with youth has surely witnessed the struggles of young storytellers as they work with voice and image, and confront their own stories of oppressions, suffering, injustice, and resistance. As the custodians of this process, how can we be more mindful of our role in the construction of new cultural practices and the meaning-making that emerges through these practices? Digital stories by community youth often have the power to awaken a community's awareness of social injustices – so many of which are born on the backs of poor and minority young people. While much of what we do focuses on helping these youth tell their stories, we must also begin to consider what happens to us as we listen to our young collaborators' stories. Listen deeply, the Center for Digital Storytelling website commands. And then, once we have listened deeply, what are we to do? What actions do young people's stories of injustice demand of us? What is required is a critical engagement with youth as they struggle to render their stories, but that engagement should not end with the stories. We need a critical engagement that requires us to do business with our responsibilities to these young people now that their voices have been raised.

# 18

# Digital Storytelling in Education
## An Emerging Institutional Technology?

## *Patrick Lowenthal*

Education is susceptible to fads (Maddux and Cummings 2003). Technological innovations have brought about a number of fads in education that have failed to meet expectations (Oppenheimer 1997). Despite storytelling's recent renaissance, storytelling is not a fad; it has been used throughout history for teaching and learning (Abrahamson 1998). Stories help make meaning out of experience (Bruner 1996, Schank 1990). Experience, and the stories created to make sense of that experience, is key to learning (Schank 1990, Zull 2002). Stories also help build connections with prior knowledge and improve memory (Schank 1990). As a result, good stories "are remembered longer by students than lessons that lack them" (Rex et al. 2002: 787). Given storytelling's central role in living and learning and the technological explosion since the late 1980s, it is not surprising to find digital story-telling entering the academic mainstream (Ohler 2005/6). However, despite the growing popularity of digital storytelling, its place in the classroom is still unclear.

### Digital Storytelling and Education

Digital storytelling is used to describe a variety of different things. However, when educators talk about it, they are typically talking about the Center for Digital Storytelling (CDS) tradition of digital storytelling. Thus, related trends using digital moviemaking (e.g., Sweeder 2007), video case studies (e.g., Harris, Pinnegar, and Teemant 2005), and telling stories online (e.g., Mellon 1999) are beyond the scope of this chapter. Instead, I focus on how the CDS tradition of digital storytelling is being used (and trans-formed) for educational purposes.

A digital story, in the CDS tradition, is a 2–3-minute personal story told with the use of graphics, audio, and video. It includes many, if not all, of the following seven elements:

1. Point (of View)
2. Dramatic Question
3. Emotional Content
4. The Gift of Your Voice
5. The Power of the Soundtrack
6. Economy
7. Pacing (Lambert 2002)

These elements, coupled with the short duration, are what differentiate a CDS digital story from other types of digital stories or other media (e.g., film/TV/YouTube/blog). Digital storytelling is quickly capturing the hearts and imaginations of educators because it combines traditional storytelling with modern-day pop culture and technology. Educators have identified a list of educational benefits of digital storytelling; I list the most cited ones below.

### Increase student engagement

Students are motivated, engaged, and interested in digital storytelling (Davis 2004, Hofer and Swan 2006). This is because digital storytelling, unlike traditional instructional strategies, engages students in the "language of their generation" (Hofer and Swan 2006: 679). Whether it is the Internet, television, film, or video games, students are interested in multimedia (Kajder 2004). As a result, digital storytelling offers educators a new and exciting way to captivate students' interests like never before.

### Give access to a global audience

Another benefit is the fact that digital stories can be shown online. Students are motivated by the possibility of showing their story to a global audience

(Roland 2006, Salpeter 2005). In fact, Standley (2003) has claimed that this alone makes digital storytelling more powerful than other forms of storytelling. Putting digital stories online serves other educational purposes. The value of storytelling lies both in the telling and the retelling (Brown and Duguid 2002). Digital storytelling enables a student a chance to tell their story time and time again.

## Amplify students' voice

Perhaps one of the greatest benefits is digital storytelling's ability to reach the many "unheard and unseen students" in our classrooms (Bull and Kajder 2004). Storytelling gives students voice (Burk 2000). However, digital storytelling can give students voice "in ways that are not possible without the technology" (Hofer and Swan 2006: 680) because it can amplify a student's voice (Kajder, Bull, and Albaugh 2005). Further, it can help give voice to struggling readers and writers (Bull and Kajder 2004) and students with special needs (Salpeter 2005), as well as students who do not fit the typical academic model (Ohler 2005/6).

## Leverage multiple literacies

Literacy is no longer viewed simply as reading and writing. To be effective communicators in the twenty-first century, students need to be able to employ a number of different literacies (Porter 2006). Digital storytelling helps reach students' existing multiliteracies (Kajder, Bull, and Albaugh 2005). Further, multimodal texts, like digital stories, "increase the meaning-making potential of a text" (Hull and Nelson 2005: 225), thereby giving students a different kind of meaning-making and a different way of knowing.

## Student emotion

Emotion has been shown to be central to teaching and learning. One of the benefits of digital storytelling is its unique way of giving voice to, space for, and validation of student emotion. Digital storytelling has been shown "to provide closure to deeply emotional issues in … [students] lives" (Robin and Pierson 2005: 713).

## Agency

Perhaps the most complicated and least understood benefit is digital story-telling's ability to create agentive senses of self (Hull and Katz 2006). The stories we tell about ourselves influence our sense of self (i.e., who we see ourselves as and who others see us as) (Bruner 2002, Schank and Abelson 1995). Hull and Katz (2006) and Davis (2004) have shown how digital sto-rytelling can serve as a tool for self authoring and agency (and hopefully change).

Some other commonly identified benefits range from increasing student reflection (Barrett 2004), engendering student creativity (Hofer and Swan 2006), increasing students' technology skills (Robin 2006), developing com-munication skills (Porter 2006), appealing to diverse learning styles (University of Houston n.d.), creating critical thinkers (Ohler 2005/6) and critical viewers of media (Howell and Howell 2003), improving research skills (University of Houston n.d.), and, finally, building learning commu-nities (Standley and Ormiston 2003).

## Trends

Digital storytelling is being used for educational purposes in elementary and secondary classrooms, computer courses, after-school programs, and college classes, as well as in professional development settings. Below, I address some of the ways it is being used.

### Digital storytelling contests

One method of integrating digital storytelling into schools, districts, and communities has been through the use of digital storytelling contests. Notable here are the iDidaMovie and Island Movie. Contests like these have been successful with uniting people and building learning communities (Standley 2003). In these contests students and teachers develop and share digital stories (Standley and Ormiston 2003).[1]

## After-school clubs

Another commonly used method is to integrate digital storytelling into after-school clubs. DUSTY in Oakland, California (Hull and Nelson 2005) and the Cyber Cougar Club in Denver, Colorado (Davis 2004) are two examples from the USA. These types of programs often develop partnerships with colleges and universities to serve socially and economically marginalized children; some are also part of the fifth-dimension network of after-school programs. Some of the best empirical studies on digital storytelling have been done in these types of programs (e.g., Davis 2004, Hull and Katz 2006, Hull and Nelson 2005). However, it is important to highlight that these programs often involve faculty, graduate students, and volunteers who work individually with students to help co-construct their digital story.

## Classroom integration

Perhaps the fastest growing method involves integrating digital storytelling projects into elementary, secondary, and post-secondary classrooms. Educators have had students create their own digital stories in language art classrooms (Banaszewski 2002, Kajder 2004), undergraduate and graduate IT courses (Hofer and Swan 2006, Robin and Pierson 2005), and in teacher preparation courses (Lathem, Reyes, and Qi 2006) to name a few (see Rudnicki et al. 2006 for other cross-discipline examples). Educators have also created their own digital stories to enhance lessons (Robin 2006) as well as to introduce themselves to students when teaching online (Lowenthal and Dunlap 2007).

# Issues

Despite its growing popularity, there are a number of technological and pedagogical challenges with using digital storytelling for educational purposes (Hofer and Swan 2006). The following are just a few issues that educators need to consider.

## Time

Creating digital stories takes time (Hofer and Swan 2006, Kajder 2004). The CDS takes 3–4 full days in their workshops to create a digital story; others have spent 4–6 months on digital storytelling projects (Banaszewski 2002, Davis 2004). In addition, today's standardized curricula leave little time to spend days or weeks creating digital stories (Kajder, Bull, and Albaugh 2005). Therefore, educators need to be prepared for the time commitment a student-centered digital storytelling project may require.

## Training

Creating digital stories is not easy (Meadows 2003). In fact, the average educator does not have the technical skills to facilitate a digital storytelling project. While Ohler (2005/6) encourages educators not to be intimidated, I suggest that proper training in both technology and pedagogy is a vital component of a successful digital storytelling project. The CDS offers workshops on how to create a digital story. While students often possess the skills needed for a digital storytelling project, they often still need guidance.

## Curriculum

Digital storytelling is not a panacea; it is the pedagogy and not the technology that makes the difference. Educators need to identify what their students need to know and be able to do and then decide how digital storytelling can accomplish this; Ohler claims that "if digital stories are going to survive in education, they need to be tied to the curriculum" (2005/6: 46). In other words, student-centered digital storytelling projects must be aligned with appropriate standards and support student learning (Hofer and Swan 2006).

## Structure

The success of a digital storytelling project depends on its structure. Without adequate structure, students begin adding images and music rather than focusing on their story (Standley 2003). The story should always be in the foreground (Banaszewski 2002, Bull and Kajder 2004). By emphasizing a story-centric approach, educators can help prevent students from creating a techno-centric, special effects-driven product. Educators also need to be clear about their expectations; their expectations can often "help determine the quality, focus and direction of student products" (Hofer and Swan 2006: 681).

*Emotion and trust*

Some students are not comfortable with the depth of emotion that is some-times involved in creating a digital story. Educators need to create a safe and trusting environment if they hope to tap into student emotion. In fact, Banaszewski (2002) recommends that educators create their own digital story to demonstrate their willingness to take the risk of sharing.

*Access*

Perhaps the most important issue is access. While some are optimistic that all educators need "is a digital video or still camera; a scanner; a networked, multimedia computer; video-editing software" (Roland 2006: 26), others point out that educators rarely have easy access to what they need (Kajder, Bull, and Albaugh 2005). Educators should not assume that students have access either; thus, educators should think twice before expecting students to complete digital storytelling projects at home. However, this is also one of the reasons to provide students – especially marginalized students who are being digitally excluded – an opportunity to become media producers rather than consumers (Tucker 2006).

*Assessment*

One last issue that educators must consider is assessment. Assessment of student learning is an important component of any digital storytelling project and must be carefully planned for (Hofer and Swan 2006). Barrett (2006) provides some rubrics that can be used as a starting point; Ohler (2007) also has written an entire chapter on assessing digital stories. However, educators need to be aware of the complexities of assessing student work that might be very emotional and that they themselves might have helped coauthor. After-school programs and digital story contests often avoid this dilemma by not formally assessing or separating develop-ment and assessment.

   There are, of course, other challenges and issues (e.g., copyright) that educators need to consider, but with proper planning and forethought, these issues can be addressed.

# Conclusion

Despite the lack of research, educators appear to be having great success using digital storytelling for educational purposes. As digital storytelling grows in popularity, it continues to change and take on a local flavor (Salpeter 2005). However, many questions arise as educators continue to experiment with this emerging instructional technology. For instance, are certain elements of a digital story more important than others? What happens if a digital story is lacking a first-person "point of view?" Does a digital story have to have "emotional content" to be effective or to even be considered a digital story in the CDS tradition? While Bernard Robin (2006) argues that there are different types of digital stories, I often find that the further educators get from the CDS model, the weaker the digital stories become. Perhaps the power of digital storytelling is not in the CDS method but rather in providing students with an opportunity to have a voice and to create something that is meaningful to them and relevant to their life.

# Note

1   For more information on the rules of a contest like this, visit www.aste.org

# 19

# Digital Storytelling in Organizations
## Syntax and Skills

*Lisa Dush*

Organizations are highly coordinated, structured, and stable. They have a job – to educate children, to manufacture lug nuts, to elect political candidates – and their structures, processes, and people are all arranged so that this job gets done. Because organizations are so focused, most of their business happens within predictable structures. We might say every organization has its syntax, a fairly rigid set of norms and practices that coordinates its daily business. The people within organizations, on the other hand, are not so orderly. They get bored, disillusioned, antsy, ambitious. They want more money, more glory, more fun. They see the behemoth they work for slowly churning along and think: we could do better. They go to training workshops, they start initiatives, they occasionally try to break the syntax and feel that their work is fresh again.

Digital storytelling, for many people within organizations, promises a break from syntax. Representatives of schools, nonprofits, and community organizations imagine uses for digital storytelling and they seek out training, most often in the form of three- or four-day "train-the-trainer" workshops. My research has been focused on what happens *after* these workshops. Train-the-trainer workshops are predicated on two assumptions: first, that digital storytelling has positive value to organizations, and second, that novices can be taught to help others produce digital stories. To investigate these assumptions, I followed up a number of organizations whose representatives attended workshops run by a digital storytelling training business on the east coast of the USA called Stories for Change (hereafter SFC – a pseudonym), and I spent 15 months doing a detailed study of digital storytelling implementation at one newly trained organization, a college and career bridge program called Tech Year (also a pseudonym).

This chapter explores some of the difficulties that organizations face when they try to start or sustain digital storytelling projects. Digital storytelling is deceptively complicated. Although it involves user-friendly tools and draws on "vernacular" literacies (Burgess 2006a), the attention and orchestration required to produce and use digital stories is intense. As one participant at an SFC workshop said, "I've done a lot of training over the years, with all different kinds of ages, but this is a lot. It's different than doing a technical training[; it's not] like 'this is how you use Photoshop.'" Complicating matters for these new trainees is that nothing is ever done in isolation in organizations, and multifaceted new projects like digital storytelling can rub against many aspects of organizational practice, often in ways that cause discomfort or discord. Even those trainees who have or develop the technical and pedagogical skills necessary to deploy digital storytelling in their organization may find that the organization's syntax – its established structures and norms – gets in their way.

As Kevin Tharp and Liz Hills (2004) note, the potential of any new media is not intrinsic to that media, but rather realized in context. In other words, digital storytelling will not change the world because it is a media form that revives storytelling or repositions media consumers as producers. It will, rather, change the world because social groups and organizations figure out meaningful ways to use the practice and the stories. To have real effect, then, digital storytelling requires implementation: this chapter offers some guidance on how to accomplish that.

## The Digital Storytelling Skill Set

Although digital storytelling is often aligned with forms of participatory media such as blogs and fan fiction, these online genres are much leaner and more fully supported by existing technologies, primarily the Internet. Trained facilitators make digital storytelling workshops work; as Jean Burgess (2006a: 209) says, digital storytelling is an "institutionally supported" form of composition as of now. That institutional support can be formidable. Daniel Meadows (2003: 190), for example, described his team for the "Capture Wales" project as having the following members: a project manager, a script expert, a video editor, IT support, and a creative director. Meadows's team also included Welsh-speaking experts to negotiate language and cultural differences. This large and professional team was surely key to the success of the "Capture Wales" project.

Organizational members who have just finished a digital storytelling train-the-trainer workshop will not have at their disposal a team like Meadows's. If they are lucky, they will have an enthusiastic and supportive supervisor, a small budget, and a little staffing support or release time. If the new trainee seeks out published information to help her plan a workshop, she will likely find "how-to" articles, which tend to distil digital storytelling practice into a set of composition-based steps. Kajder, Bull, and Albaugh's (2005) list of steps is representative, and includes the following: write an initial script; plan an accompanying storyboard; discuss and revise the script; sequence the images in the video editor; add the narrative track; add special effects and transitions; and add a musical soundtrack. Table 19.1, which distils observations I made in my research study at Tech Year as well as comments from follow-up interviews with other SFC workshop attendees, suggests how these steps parse out into component skills. For the sake of comparison, column C shows how an expert team, like Meadows's support team for "Capture Wales," likely divides and manages the many skills required to produce digital stories in a group workshop.

My interviews with participants who had learned digital storytelling at SFC workshops and returned to their home organizations, eager to implement digital storytelling, raise several points about the process illustrated in Table 19.1. First, many organizations who trained with SFC were stymied very early in the digital storytelling process, in the "Planning and setup" stage at the top of column A. I've noted that stage, along with the eighth stage, "Post-production and distribution," in italics, as these are not on Kadjer et al.'s (2005) list of steps and are seldom mentioned in how-to articles. Few trainees have much experience with the logistical and technical setup required to organize their own digital storytelling workshop. Laura, a professor at a school of public health who had sent two graduate students to the SFC workshop, along with a representative from a community health organization with which the school had a partnership, described the early-stage difficulties she encountered:

> It's been frustrating for me, just the logistics. Every single logistic. From the getting people trained – and that's a frustration, you know you train people but they leave. [… and] you can't expect that the person who got trained is going to be so proficient that they can pass on the skills easily. So the training/ retraining, the technical issues of do we have the right computer, do we have

**Table 19.1** The steps, skills, and support team involved in the DST workshop process

| A: Kajder et al.'s steps | B: Component skills | C: Meadows's CW team |
|---|---|---|
| *0. Planning and setup* | Buy equipment<br>Install software<br>Recruit storytellers<br>Find lab space with adequate computers<br>Reconfigure 3-day workshop schedule in a way that fits organization's/storytellers'schedules | pro project manager |
| 1. Write an initial script | Teach story generation<br>Teach story structure<br>Find model stories to show<br>Teach personal writing<br>Help low-literacy writers write<br>Negotiate cultural and language differences | script expert<br><br><br><br>cultural liaison |
| 2. Plan an accompanying storyboard | Understand and teach multimodal composition<br>Understand copyright law and find copyright-free resources<br>Understand file formats<br>Teach image editing software<br>Understand file transfer and storage | creative director<br><br><br><br>video editor,IT support |
| 3. Discuss and revise script | Create a comfortable writing workshop<br>Give group and individual writing feedback<br>Negotiate difficult personal issues | script editor, creative director |
| 4. Sequence the images in video-editing software<br>5. Add the narrative track<br>6. Add special effects<br>7. Add music | Teach video-editing software<br>Troubleshoot video-editing software<br>Record audio<br>Edit audio<br>Enforce deadlines | video editor, IT support |
| *8. Post-production and distribution* | Post-produce video<br>Compress files<br>Prepare CDs and DVDs<br>Distribute stories via the Web | Secure permissions and consent<br>Determine how to use stories in concert with existing organizational materials |

the right software – I'm not that interested in learning that, I just need to know what we need. And then just also the community aspect, which I'm obviously much more familiar with, because this is no different than any other community work we do. But it's difficult. It's time-consuming.

Laura isolates a number of common difficulties faced by SFC trainees. First, many new trainees simply did not know the story-making process well enough to teach it to others. Second, the technical and logistical steps necessary to plan a workshop are both complicated and for many people, uninteresting. Third – and this is a problem I saw often, which occurred primarily in either the planning and setup or scriptwriting stages – is what Laura calls the "community aspect." Many organizations that are drawn to digital storytelling are so drawn because they work with little-heard, disenfranchised communities. This was the case with Laura and her team, who wanted to help members of the Cambodian community make digital stories about depression. While representatives of under-represented communities have compelling and valuable stories to tell, they also often have difficult and hectic lives, which do not pair well with the time-intensive nature of digital storytelling. As one of the graduate students working on Laura's project said of the Cambodian women she was working with, "their lives are complicated." Issues like low literacy, cultural and language differences, and even lives of exile, in which personal photos have been lost or left behind, were common difficulties that the SFC trainees faced as they worked on community-based digital story-telling initiatives.

When new trainees successfully navigated the digital storytelling planning process, still other hitches arose. Some trainees were uncomfortable with being a teacher, a stance required of a digital storytelling facilitator. Carmen, who had led other technical training in the past, said that the intricacy of digital storytelling made it particularly key to do one of her least favorite things, "be the bad guy," and keep people on task during steps 1–7 in Table 19.1. Others were challenged by the particular tact and grace required by step 3, discussing and revising the script. Ray, an after-school educator, said: "I think [the SFC train-the-trainer workshop] worked because of the [story] circles. That was something I couldn't duplicate."

The last step of the digital storytelling workshop which, as I said, is given scant attention in articles about digital storytelling, is post-production and distribution. To have an impact, digital stories need to get off of computers and into distribution channels – either the Web or media like CDs or DVDs – and this is perhaps the most technically complicated part of the digital storytelling process. SFC trainees had a host of problems with post-production and distribution, ranging from minor problems, like an inaudible showing because no one thought to bring external speakers, to major ones, like being unable to turn video software files into *any* distributable format.

An elaborated list of skills, like those in Table 19.1, can be helpful for new digital storytellers as they plan the organizational deployment of the practice. If an organization is unaware of all of these steps or unwilling or unable to delegate people to do them – either from their own staff or outside consultants – then it is unlikely they will be able to run on-site digital storytelling workshops.

## The Syntax of Organizations: A Genre Model for Digital Storytelling Implementation

Organizational use of digital storytelling, however, can be even more complicated than this extensive list of skills suggests. Deeper difficulties arise, particularly when organizations wish to sustain the practice rather than run a one-shot production workshop. One or many of digital storytelling's component parts may also require that organizational members step outside of the familiar syntax within which they do their daily work. Stepping outside of these norms can cause stress, discord, or breakdowns in work processes.

Getting a grasp on the nature of an organization's syntax, the complex and interdependent structures that coordinate organizational work, is difficult. Much of the analysis of my case-study site, Tech Year, involved testing what I saw happening during their implementation efforts against various theories of how order is maintained and processes are changed in organizations. Tech Year is a multi-site, one-year intensive education and technical skills training program, with its headquarters in Boston, Massachusetts. Its aim is to get recent high-school graduates on a successful life track through classes and a paid corporate apprenticeship. After attending SFC's train-the-trainer workshop, Tech Year's head writing teacher, Madeline Davis, returned to Tech Year hoping to integrate digital storytelling into the program's Business Writing curriculum.

Ultimately, it was North American genre theory that I found most helpful in illuminating those implementation difficulties at Tech Year that could not be explained from a skills perspective. For over twenty years, genre theorists have been investigating how standardized text forms, known as organizational genres, mediate and reinforce social practice in organizations.

Genre theory is based on the idea that recurrent patterns of text use both reflect and constitute social action within organizations (Miller 1984). In other words, the way that organizations do their work is in large degree reflected in and determined by the texts they use. For example, the work order in an engineering firm, a document engineering firms use to trace the progress of projects, affects how power is distributed between engineers and technicians, and establishes the rhythm of their work (Winsor 2003). The intake form that a social worker fills out to process a new client regulates how the client is positioned and limits the range of possible dynamics between client and social worker (Paré 2002). Both of these examples suggest how generic texts *constitute* organizational practice. But the structure of generic texts also *reflects* organizational practice. The engineering work order, for example, developed and persists because it regulates action important to engineering firms, project-based engineer-technician cooperation.

An organization's texts and textual practices – its genres – are then in a tight, interdependent relationship with local context. This context can be broken down into six dimensions, as shown in Figure 19.1. Digital storytelling, as a new textual practice learned *outside* of the organization, may not be closely aligned with all of these dimensions. It may, in fact, contradict or conflict with some aspects of an organization's context. It is these misalignments and "dis-coordinations" that cause many of the problems new digital storytellers face as they try to deploy the practice in their organizations.

Moving around Figure 19.1, the genre–context graphic, we can clarify how genres work by looking at one genre that Tech Year hoped to supplement or replace with digital storytelling – the five-paragraph essay that was used as an assignment in the business writing classroom. The five-paragraph essay, with its standard structure (the first paragraph introduces the thesis, the next three paragraphs each address a single point pertaining to that thesis, and the fifth and final paragraph summarizes the discussion and restates the thesis), is ubiquitous in writing classrooms. But at Tech Year, the five-paragraph essay genre also fit fairly well with the organization's syntax. First, the assignment was aligned with the core functions of the writing course, the *organizational actions* that the writing class was designed to achieve: to prepare students for corporate apprenticeships and to prepare them for college. Second, the assignment allowed for a typical range of *personal action* from both students and teachers. Students, for example, could write the essay for a grade; teachers could give grades and feedback.

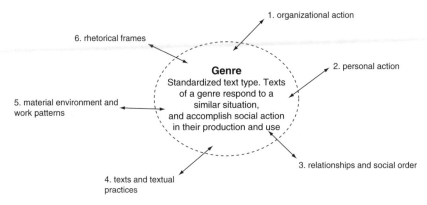

**Figure 19.1**    The genre–context graphic. This shows the relationship between a genre and six dimensions of organizational context. Genres and their context are in a reciprocal, or dialogic relationship, as indicated by the double arrows: genres reflect their context and help constitute that context

Third, the five-paragraph essay encouraged students and teachers to relate in familiar *relationships and social orders*, positioning the teachers as expert coaches and evaluators, knowledgeable about the essay's form. Fourth, the five-paragraph essay assignment was deployed with a familiar set of *texts and textual processes*, including already-written handouts and familiar ways of drafting and revising. Fifth, the genre fit with the typical *material environment and work patterns* at Tech Year, where students in writing classes sat at desks, as opposed to in a computer lab or a story circle. Sixth, and finally, the existing genre of the five-paragraph essay made sense within naturalized *rhetorical frames*, the familiar mental frameworks that individuals at Tech Year applied when they envisioned the purpose of the business writing class.

Madeline Davis, the writing director at Tech Year, was excited about digital storytelling because she recognized its potential – were it to replace assignments like the five-paragraph essay – to shake up many of Tech Year's familiar ways of being. And in fact, during Tech Year's pilot efforts with digital storytelling, many of the dimensions of organizational context at Tech Year did change, at least temporarily. Students had access to a new range of personal action through their classroom work: they posted their stories on YouTube and forwarded them to professional mentors, the later a proactive move not typically motivated by classroom work. Teachers, plunged into the new world of multimedia composition, were positioned as learners alongside their students. Student voices took on new importance and played a part in carving out a space for new organizational action, like the staff-wide discussions of individual students that were occurring after the staff viewed students' digital stories. New texts arose, such as a Web portal where class assignments were posted. But alongside these new potentials were new difficulties. Some students were resistant to the new social roles they were being asked to inhabit in the classroom, such as that of confessional storyteller or Tech Year spokesperson. A number of Tech Year staffers objected to digital storytelling because it did not fit within the rhetorical frames they used to account for the business of the business-writing classroom, which they understood to be rehearsing forms of professional communication and improving grammar and mechanical correctness.

For those organizations like Tech Year that strive for a sustainable, long-term implementation of digital storytelling, the concepts of genre theory clarify the challenge they face: how to make digital storytelling – a foreign practice learned outside of the organization – into a genre that fits with these six dimensions of their organizational context.

## Last Words

A break in syntax can help people see their world afresh. But without a map or an expert to guide us though these changes, times of syntactic variation can feel disorienting and unproductive. Genre theory and the genre–context graphic can provide such a map. Organizations can use the graphic as a heuristic at the beginning of an implementation, to ensure careful planning. When problems arise during implementation, a close look at a range of contextual factors may clarify their source. For new digital storytellers, it takes both skills training and a clear sense of the challenges ahead to get digital storytelling out of expert-led trainings and into their organizations, where its real potential lies.

# 20

# Beyond Individual Expression
## Working with Cultural Institutions

## *Jerry Watkins and Angelina Russo*

## Introduction

The digital storytelling genre originated by the Center for Digital Storytelling (CDS) trains citizens to create their own story, in their own voice, without interference from media professionals. We suggest that the genre is a reactive – rather than interactive – medium whose strength lies in its prescriptive format. This format provides a method and tools to support the individual creative process. However, this emphasis on individual expression may limit the sustainability of the genre. Using examples of community co-creation and distribution projects, we argue that a strategic team-based approach to participatory content creation may provide a more sustainable approach for communities and organizations engaged in this kind of collaboration.

## Interactive or Reactive?

The application of communication technology to provide an interactive media space created and populated by citizens is an ongoing process. Amateur radio, citizens' band, community media, citizen journalism, and social media are just some of many examples of participatory communication and content creation. Should digital stories sit within this genealogy?

The term "digital storytelling" can be applied to many narrative forms including hypertext, interactive stories, and computer games (Wu 2006). This chapter uses the term to describe the format popularized by the CDS.

Using the CDS definition, a digital story might fit the description of a homemade video more closely than that of an interactive medium. It is a three-minute mini-movie made by non-professionals which uses images and a narrated voice-over. It is a personal story, conceived, written, edited, and narrated by the storyteller – apparently free from any interference from media professionals. It is a work of individual creativity; a one-way communication destined for viewing by a limited audience of the storyteller's family and friends. At least, this seems to be the case for the substantial digital storytelling programs at the CDS and the Australian Centre for the Moving Image (ACMI). To date, very few of the stories made by workshop participants at these centers are available on the respective organizations' websites. A wider audience can usually only watch these stories if the creator chooses to upload them to YouTube or similar. So far, the distinguishing features of a digital story could be applied to a wedding video. But there's at least one big difference in terms of production: we don't need a video camera to make a digital story. Our family photo albums provide more than enough memories and materials to create this unique form of "scrapbook TV." That is, as long as we have access to a scanner, personal computer, and photo manipulation and video-editing applications – and someone to teach us how to use them.

Fortunately there exist some online digital story collections, which may lead us toward a definition of digital storytelling as an interactive medium. The BBC's "Capture Wales" project features a substantial collection of digital stories created in workshops by community participants and accessible by an online audience via the project website. Perhaps this portal constitutes an interactive medium? The visitor to the site can browse, point, and click; and also has the facility to "have a say" by typing a comment into a text box, on condition that "The BBC reserves the right to select and edit comments."[1] Yet this level of interaction with the digital collection is relatively poor in comparison with the complex many-to-many interactivity afforded by social utility and networking sites such as Facebook and Flickr. If an interaction system is one "in which both actor and reactor are engaged in a mutually affecting experience" (Shedroff 2001), then we can echo Kidd's view (2005) to suggest that the "Capture Wales" portal is another example of "reactive" rather than "interactive" technology (Williams 1974).

If the stories themselves are one-way communications – and if examples of online collections do seem to behave rather more reactively than interactively – then perhaps digital storytelling is interactive at the interface between the storyteller and the cultural sphere during the creative process?

Is the very act of creating one's own digital story, free from censorship or interference, an interaction with the cultural or even political sphere? Arguably not. Workshops guide participants to originate a personal story from personal memories, rather than respond to an ongoing debate. They are not meant as a direct contribution to a conversation; neither do they invite an immediate response or dialogue: "In this sense the workshops represent one-off interactions that can have no real lasting impact upon the 'media' as we know it. They do not leave a more democratic media system in their wake" (Kidd 2005).

Interactivity is an evolving concept. In the days when the World Wide Web was little more than a twinkle in the eye of Tim Berners-Lee, some first-time PC users were very unfamiliar with the idea of a PC application "interacting" with a user in the form of simple instructions or requests via monologue and dialogue boxes. Some decades later, an online PC is not considered interactive unless it simultaneously offers user-generated content, bitstreamed video, live social networking, and automated external defibrillation (for the more extreme immersive games). If we widen our consideration of interactivity beyond the interface to include participatory content creation, even a brief visit to YouTube demonstrates the diversity of user-generated content – when it is produced outside of a prescriptive storytelling format. YouTube also shows that an amateur wedding video featuring Michael Jackson's *Thriller* soundtrack has amassed over three million hits at time of writing.[2] In comparison to this level of interactivity, digital storytelling may perhaps fall short. We propose that one of its great strengths comes from the very fact that it is a prescriptive, even a restrictive co-creative format.

## Creative Tools and Systems

Digital stories are individual expressions which largely rest in post-production isolation. By perusing the impressive collection on the "Capture Wales" site, we may detect that these stories are not made free from interference. There is little to no profanity, nudity, violence; these stories have been made within creative restrictions and preset themes, with varying degrees of input from workshop trainers. Perhaps the effectiveness of digital storytelling – and those genres evolving from it – derives from the restrictions it places on the co-creative process. A short script and an emphasis on using still images rather than video makes both the writing and editing processes more achievable. Copyright restrictions inhibit the addition of commercial music as a soundtrack, simplifying the audio mix. Limited workshop duration applies the time pressure that provides momentum to complete a creative product: "What can be considered a hindrance, for example time pressure, can be considered by others to be a facilitator (the ironically positive effects of an impending deadline)" (Nakakoji, Tanaka, and Fallman 2006).

The consideration of creativity is increasingly important in interaction design circles, within which it has been acknowledged for some years that "one of the most important skills for almost everyone to have in the next decade and beyond will be those that allow us to create valuable, compelling, and empowering information and experiences for others. To do this, we must learn existing ways of organizing and presenting data and information and develop new ones" (Shedroff 1999). Traditional approaches to the study of interaction design emphasize the role of the individual user in overall system design and performance. However, the ongoing move to Web 2.0 products and systems challenges interaction designers and content creators to consider the needs and behaviors of *communities* of users. If we agree that "the new computing is about supporting human relationships" and "participating in knowledge communities" (Shneiderman 2002), then it is not difficult to imagine how digital storytelling can play a role in the new paradigm by providing a creative process for cultural participation by communities. As Julie Springer, Sara Kajder, and Julia Borst Brazas (2004) argue: "Stories put us in touch with ourselves, others, and our surroundings. Using innovations in multimedia technology, students and adult audiences can make personal connections ... through new ways of storytelling."

The digital storytelling workshop provides a toolkit with which participants can use digital media to achieve creative outcomes. This kit provides:

- tools to train people to develop creativity, or skills of creative thinking;
- tools to support people's creative process while engaging in a creation task;
- tools to enable people to have new kinds of experiences that they would not be able to have without using these tools ... [to] allow people to engage in completely new experiences of producing expressions. (Nakakoji 2005)

During this consideration of the importance of user communities, we may also wish to reflect upon the limitations of a workshop structure that emphasizes individual creativity. If we are trying to achieve sustainable community creative processes, then we can observe that ongoing creative practice is achieved by teams rather than individuals: composer and lyricist; director and cinematographer; art director and copywriter. Digital storytelling initiatives have also been criticized for emphasizing the tools of individual creativity at the expense of systematic considerations, particularly content distribution: "issues such as the distribution of content in a participatory environment, as well as media skills dissemination and narrative structure, are yet to be fully thought-out" (Rennie 2004). This discussion now turns to other initiatives which incorporate systematic considerations such as distribution and program sustainability as part of wider content-based community co-creation initiatives. These initiatives have moved beyond the traditional individual expression of digital storytelling to focus instead on the team-based co-creation of microdocumentaries.

## Digital Clubhouse

The Digital Clubhouse network was founded in 1996 as a place where people of all ages and backgrounds could share life experiences and/or technological expertise. An intergenerational storytelling program uses microdocumentary production to encourage community members to capture and share dreams, memories, thoughts, and histories in a collaborative environment. Since 1998 the program has focused on "Stories of Service," an initiative in which young people work with seniors to tell veterans' stories of serving their country. The storytelling aspect of the program is based on the CDS model, whereby participants attend creative workshops to train in writing and multimedia production. But the workshop's emphasis is on creative teamwork rather than individual expression. Veterans and young people working together to produce a microdocumentary based on a veteran's personal experience, rather than an individual artistic expression. Through "Stories of Service" and its other community storytelling programs, Digital Clubhouse has achieved a comprehensive and sustainable strategy that encompasses:

- a sustained digital literacy and networking program for underrepresented youth;
- project management, writing, interviewing, and research skills for young people;

- an avenue for veteran communities to share personal stories;
- a platform for sustained intergenerational storytelling.

Participants are sought from public schools within the borough of New York, with emphasis on Spanish, African American, and Asian communities. Through workshops, these participants have access to high-end computers (rarely seen within their own communities) and are trained to create microdocumentaries while receiving skills, credit, recognition, and mentoring while focusing on preserving community stories. The training curriculum is mapped to national US school standards. The creative outputs of the program are shared with the community, and/or become part of participants' college applications. This ability to distribute creative output is of great importance to program participants. To that end, Digital Clubhouse works with a number of distribution outlets:

- local communities, through screenings and dedicated events, i.e., Veterans' Day;
- online (both within Digital Clubhouse's bespoke online theater and on other sites);
- cable television: History Channel and a website;
- local terrestrial television and affiliates;
- various museum organizations.

Through the "Stories of Service" program, veterans share their memories and histories with other members of the community in a very personal way. By working with them creatively, young people are encouraged to develop a sense of civic engagement and responsibility, alongside digital literacy skills. Program leaders are proactive in providing opportunities through which various components of the community come together, either in the production of the stories or the presentation of the stories at community events. These events have attracted civic leaders, businesses, civic groups, veterans' groups, schools, and museums; thereby providing valuable social networking opportunities for participants and community alike. This coherent strategy demonstrates the potential for microdocumentary production to operate as a key element within a wider system for community engagement and interaction via content co-creation and distribution. This essential strategic consideration is also evident in Wu's (2005) proposal for a commercial digital storytelling derivative for use in cultural tourism, which emphasizes the importance of content distribution (see also Wu's chapter 16 in the present volume).

## Community Co-creation

Such innovative creative engagement between an organization and the community has been described using the term "co-creativity." Co-creative technologies are described as those that offer assistance in the creation process: "People are naturally creative and are almost always more interested in experiences that allow them to create instead of merely participate" (Shedroff 1999). Although there may be some question as to just how many people are "naturally creative," this basic position is key to the concept of everyday creative participation.

Much of our own work has focused on the design of co-creative systems for enhanced interaction between cultural institutions and communities of interest. Digital media are becoming more prevalent in major libraries, galleries, and museums. It has even been suggested by humanities commentators that information and communication technology (ICT) is now so deeply embedded in our daily lives – at home, work, and school – that in many places it is shaping a "new landscape of communication" and "new learning environments" (Nixon 2003). Putting aside the observation that the latest communication technologies have been shaping such a landscape and environment since the invention of the printing press, questions remain as to whether cultural institutions are using this technology to better represent the needs of the community they serve; or to simply solidify existing top-down curatorial practice. The digital storytelling experiments by both ACMI and the BBC are good examples of a community-focused co-creation program. In Australia, the State Library of Queensland's Mobile Multimedia Laboratory (MML) project is designed to widen and deepen the sharing of cultural knowledge by creating a platform for content creation by communities of interest. The MML is a fully portable digital toolkit which allows Library trainers to travel within the enormous state of Queensland in order to train communities in digital literacy skills. These regional sessions include community training in the use of the Internet, and skills-upgrade workshops for regional library staff. The Library provides the MML and support staff to communities who have particular events or histories to record, as part of its "Queensland Stories" project. Community participants learn to prepare a short multimedia narrative based on the three-minute digital storytelling format (although not necessarily recounting a personal revelation). The finished stories are published on the Library's website for viewing by an online audience (Watkins and Russo 2005a).

The Australian Museum is one of a number of cultural institutions exploring innovative forms of community co-creation as part of the "New Literacy, New Audiences" research project.[3] The Museum is involved in informal learning programs. Its own studies suggest that communication with communities of interest requires more than just efficient information-transfer mechanisms (Groundwater-Smith 2006), and that learning messages can be enhanced through the use of narrative, storytelling, and the human face, as opposed to the anonymous graphics panel so prevalent in museum exhibitions. Therefore the Museum decided to experiment with narrative-based co-creative production. It was recognized at the start of the pilot that a successful and sustainable implementation of co-creative social media could not be purchased and plugged in, but rather would require organizational buy-in and change, both top-down and bottom-up. Thus a strategic decision was made to train staff teams from across the Museum in microdocumentary production, derived from the digital storytelling format. This decision was based partly upon the significant adoption of new communication technologies by museums in recent years. It is believed that such technologies will enable audiences and communities of interest to interact more directly with the museum, its knowledge bases and collections, and the information and issues which surround them (Watkins and Russo 2007). Experiments with media tools such as blogs, podcasts, and microdocumentaries within the cultural sector demonstrate that such tools can allow individualized meaning-making, leading to nuanced interpretation of cultural content – enhanced and/or encouraged by networked conversations (Fisher and Twiss-Garrity 2007). A rising number of museums, galleries, and libraries worldwide are experimenting with digital content-creation activities not only as a route to increased visitation rates, but also as a means by which to strengthen community relationships on the basis that "cultural products or activities create audiences as people engage with them" (Gillard 2002). The content-creation program developed for the Australian Museum trains a three-person team of writer, producer, and editor to produce an original microdocumentary. A close creative collaboration is essential to devise and deliver the finished item within an accelerated two-day schedule. Although off-the-shelf creative applications are a feature of the workshop, its focus is firmly on team-based digital content-creation techniques, rather than individual expression. Partly due to this focus, the Museum has established a core team of content creators after only two training workshops. This team has already successfully completed a number of microdocumentary co-creation projects with external communities. The Museum will expand its participatory content-creation strategy in line with the implementation of a redesigned website with Web 2.0 functionality.

It should be noted that community content creation is not a new field of study. Since the 1960s, cultural institutions in the USA and the UK have broadened their public programs to include community interaction with content through education (Vergo 1993). In 1994, Schuler argued that communities were distinguished by lively interaction and engagement on issues of mutual concern and that their well-being contributes to the well-being of the state as a whole (1994). He proposed that ICT could play a role in community life by improving communication, economic opportunity, civic participation, and education. His position extended to community-oriented electronic communication where community networks have a local focus. However, while communities are beginning to interact with cultural institutions, the artifacts they create are not usually collected, registered, and archived within an institution's collection. Therefore community interaction has been restricted to entertaining ways of "making meaning" from existing content, without providing an avenue for the collection and distribution of artifacts created through this interaction. This limits the long-term value of community interaction with content. But the relationship between institution and community has a far greater potential than the one-way provision of access and facilities. The digitally literate community not only has the tools to consume digital culture; it can also work with the institution to create its own digital artifacts. This relationship underpins the process of community co-creation. When community co-creation programs – like those run by the State Library of Queensland or the Australian Museum – include preservation and distribution strategies for traditional forms such as community narratives, they present an opportunity for communities of interest to preserve their stories and distribute cultural knowledge to a wider audience. In framing the development of projects and strategies, it will be important to consider the changes which digital media bring to modes of content production, consumption, and interaction. This holds implications for the different types of cultural artifacts for display and preservation as well as the new skills required by professionals to enable community interaction (Watkins and Russo 2005b).

# Conclusion

Digital storytelling is a prescriptive method that privileges individual expression. The genre "has its roots in community arts and oral history; it stretches from pre-literacy cultural traditions" (Meadows 2003). Perhaps this community arts heritage prevents digital storytelling practitioners from realizing the potential for distribution and genuine interaction offered by Web 2.0 platforms and co-creative philosophies. Those organizations which integrate key elements of the digital storytelling format within a wider participatory content-creation system may well achieve a more sustainable and widespread interaction with their target communities.

Initiatives by Digital Clubhouse, the State Library of Queensland, and the Australian Museum have replaced the personal stories of traditional digital storytelling with a team-based microdocumentary approach. These initiatives mark an important new phase in online interaction between cultural institutions and communities of interest (Russo and Watkins 2007). It may be argued by adherents of the traditional form that a "real" digital story is a revelatory narrative about the storyteller. However, this prescriptive view may contradict the ambition of digital storytelling to equip the creator to tell a story of their own choosing. We look forward to the ongoing and sustainable evolution of the microdocumentary form at the hands of communities of interest worldwide.

## Notes

1   See  www.bbc.co.uk/wales/audiovideo/sites/galleries/pages/capturewales.shtml (accessed September 6, 2007).
2   See www.youtube.com/watch?v=OPmYbP0F4Zw
3   See nlablog.wordpress.com/; and the Acknowledgments in the present volume.

# References

Abrahamson, Craig Eilert (1998) "Storytelling as a pedagogical tool in higher education." *Education*, 118(3), 440–51.

ACMI (2005) Digital storytelling program at ACMI. www.acmi.net.au/digitalstory telling.jsp (accessed June 7, 2005).

Albernaz, Ami (2002) "The Internet in Brazil: From digital divide to democracy?" www.aaplac.org/library/AlbernazAmi03.pdf (accessed October 1, 2007).

Allday, D. Helen (1981) *Insurrection in Wales: The Rebellion of the Welsh Led by Owen Glyn Dwr*, Appendix IV. Lavenham, Suffolk: Terence Dalton.

Atchley, Dana (1990–2000) Next Exit. www.nextexit.com/drivein/driveinframeset. html (accessed March 2, 2006).

Atchley, Dana, Joe Lambert, and Nina Mullen (1994) Center for Digital Storytelling. Core Methodology. www.storycenter.org/coremethod.html (accessed March 1, 2006).

Atton, Chris (2002). *Alternative Media*. London: Sage.

Bailur, Savita (2007) "The complexities of community participation in ICT for development projects: The case of 'Our Voices'." In *Proceedings of the 9th International Conference on Social Implications of Computers in Developing Countries*, São Paulo, Brazil, May.

Bakunin, Michael (1882/1970) *God and the State*. New York: Dover.

Balot, Ryan K. (2001) *Greed and Injustice in Classical Athens*. Princeton, NJ: Princeton University Press.

Banaszewski, Tom (2002). "Digital storytelling finds its place in the classroom." *Multimedia Schools*, 9, 32–5.

Barrett, Helen (2004). Electronic portfolios as digital stories of deep learning. www. electronicportfolios.com/digistory/epstory.html (accessed May 1, 2007).

Barrett, Helen (2006) Researching and evaluating digital storytelling as a deep learning tool. www.electronicportfolios.com/portfolios/SITEStorytelling2006. pdf (accessed May 1, 2007).

Baulch, Emma (2007) *Making Scenes: Reggae, Punk, and Death Metal in 1990s Bali.* Durham, NC: Duke University Press.

Bauman, Zygmunt (2001). *Community: Seeking Safety in an Insecure World.* Cambridge: Policy Press.

BBC (2002) Culture Vulture by Nicky Delgado. www.bbc.co.uk/wales/capturewales/transcripts/nicky-delgado.shtml.

BBC (2004). BBC Creative Archive pioneers new approach to public access rights in digital age. *BBC*, May 26. www.bbc.co.uk/pressoffice/pressreleases/stories/2004/05_may/26/creative_archive.shtml (accessed March 2, 2005).

BBC (2005a) Aftaag Family by Said Dualeh. www.bbc.co.uk/wales/capturewales/transcripts/said-dualeh.shtml (accessed February 20, 2006).

BBC (2005b) A Centenary Celebration. www.bbc.co.uk/wales/capturewales/background/said-dualeh.shtml (accessed February 20, 2006).

BBC (2006a) Capture Wales Digital Storytelling. www.bbc.co.uk/wales/capturewales (accessed February 20, 2006.

BBC (2006b) Capture Wales Digital Storytelling: About Capture Wales. www.bbc.co.uk/wales/capturewales/about/ (accessed December 21, 2006).

BBC Wales (2006/7). *Annual Review.* London: BBC.

Beckett, Jamie (2005) Red Herring reporters to test experimental storytelling technology. hpl.hp.com/news/2005/apr-jun/redherring.html (accessed June 7, 2005).

Bennett, Tony (1995). *The Birth of the Museum: History, Theory, Politics.* London: Routledge.

Bey, Hakim (1985) *The Temporary Autonomous Zone, Ontological Anarchy, Poetic Terrorism.* New York: Autonomedia.

Bhabha, Homi (1995) "Signs taken for wonders: Questions of ambivalence and authority under a tree outside Delhi, May 1817." In Homi Bhabha (ed.), *The Location of Culture*, London: Routledge, pp. 102–22.

Blumer, Herbert (1969) *Symbolic Interactionism: Perspective and Method.* Englewood Cliffs, NJ: Prentice Hall.

BNA-BBOT (2006) BNA-BBOT brochure. Brussels: BNA-BBOT.

Boltz, Paul and Charles Comey (2005) "Spread your content far and wide." *China Business Review*, 32(2), 28.

Bonet, Lluís (1998) "Cultural tourism." In Ruth Towse (ed.), *A Handbook of Cultural Economics*. Cheltenham: Edward Elgar.

Bookchin, Murray (1984/1996) "Anarchism: Past and present." In Howard J. Ehrlich (ed.), *Reinventing Anarchy, Again*. Edinburgh: AK Press, pp. 19–30.

Bowman, Shane and Chris Willis (2004) *We Media: How Audiences Are Shaping the Future of News and Information.* Paper of the American Press Institute, hypergene.net/wemedia/weblog.php

Bradford, George (1980/1996) "Media – capital's global village." In Howard J. Ehrlich (ed.), *Reinventing Anarchy, Again*. Edinburgh: AK Press, pp. 258–71.

Brown, John Seely, and Paul Duguid (2002) *The Social Life of Information*. Boston: Harvard Business School Press.

Bruner, Jerome (1990) *Acts of Meaning*. Cambridge, MA: Harvard University Press.

Bruner, Jerome (1996) *The Culture of Education*. Cambridge, MA: Harvard University Press.

Bruner, Jerome (2002) *Making Stories: Law, Literature, Life*. Cambridge, MA: Harvard University Press.

Bruns, Axel (2005) *Gatewatching: Collaborative Online News Production*. New York: Peter Lang.

Bruns, Axel and Joanne Jacobs (eds.) (2006) *Uses of Blogs*. New York: Peter Lang.

Bourdieu, Pierre (1992) *Language and Symbolic Power*. Cambridge: Polity Press.

Bruzzi, Stella (2000) *New Documentary: A Critical Introduction*. London: Routledge.

Bucy, Erik and John Newhagen (eds.) (2003) *Media Access: Social and Psychological Dimensions of New Technology Use*. Mahwah, NJ: Lawrence Erlbaum.

Bull, Glen and Sara Kajder (2004) "Digital storytelling in the language arts classroom." *Learning and Leading with Technology*, 32(4), pp. 46–9. cs2.cust.educ.ubc.ca/csed/400/csed_readings/display%2024.pdf

Burgess, Jean (2005a) Creativity, play and communication. February 10. Blog entry. hypertext.rmit.edu.au/~burgess/2005/02/10/creativity-play-and-communication/ (accessed June 6, 2005).

Burgess, Jean (2005b) The Work of Stories. April 12. Blog entry. hypertext.rmit.edu.au/~burgess/2005/04/12/the-work-of-stories/ (accessed June 6, 2005).

Burgess, Jean (2006a) "Hearing ordinary voices: Cultural studies, vernacular creativity and digital storytelling." *Continuum: Journal of Media & Cultural Studies*, 2, 201–14.

Burgess, Jean (2006b) "Vernacular creativity, cultural participation and new media literacy: photography and the Flickr network." IR7.0: Internet Convergences, Brisbane, Australia.

Burgess, Jean, Helen Klaebe, and Moth Foth (2006) "Everyday Creativity as Civic Engagement: A Cultural Citizenship View of New Media." Communications Policy and Research Forum, University of Technology Sydney.

Burk, Nanci M. (2000) "Empowering at-risk students: Storytelling as a pedagogical tool." Paper presented at the annual meeting of the National Communication Association, Seattle, WA.

Cameron, Keith, ed. (1999) *National Identity*. Exeter: Intellect.

Carpenter, Gaylene (2004) "Collaborating to address cultural tourists' interests for experience." *e-Review of Tourism Research*, ertr.tamu.edu/pdfs/a-52.pdf (accessed March 11, 2005).

Carpentier, Nico (2007) "Participation and interactivity: Changing perspectives. The construction of an integrated model on access, interaction and participation." In Virginia Nightingale and Tim Dwyer (eds.), *New Media Worlds*, Oxford: Oxford University Press.

Carr, Nicholas (2006) "The new narcissism." *Rough Type*, February 17, www. roughtype.com/archives/2006/02/the_new_narciss.php (downloaded July 15, 2007).

Center for Digital Storytelling (2004) "Center for Digital Storytelling." www.story center.org/ (accessed October 1, 2004).

Center for Digital Storytelling (n.d.) "What is digital storytelling?" www.story center.org/whatis.html (accessed August 1, 2007).

Chambers, Robert (1995) "Poverty and livelihoods: Whose reality counts?" IDS discussion Paper 347. University of Sussex.

Chatzichristodoulou, Maria (2007) "From Entropy8Zuper! to Tale of Tales: Games and *The Endless Forest*." www.furtherfield.org/displayreview.php?review_id=283

Cheung, Charles (2000) "A home on the Web: Presentations of self on personal homepages." In David Gauntlett (ed.), *Web Studies: Rewiring Media Studies for the Digital Age*. London: Arnold, pp. 43–51.

*China Business Weekly*. 2005. "Reshuffle affecting telecoms industry." January 21, service.china.org.cn/link/wcm/Show_Text?info_id=118488&p_qry=sp (accessed June 3, 2005).

Cohen-Cruz, Jan (2006) *Local Acts: Community-Based Performance in the United States*. New Brunswick, NJ: Rutgers University Press.

conversegallery.com. 2005. "Converse Gallery." www.conversegallery.com/ (accessed June 2, 2005; since taken down, but examples can be found by searching the term on YouTube).

Coles, Robert (1997) *Doing Documentary Work*. New York: Oxford University Press.

College of Arms (n.d.) "The history of the Royal Heralds and the College of Arms." www.college-of-arms.gov.uk/About/01.htm

Collier, Paul and Anke Hoeffler (2002) "The political economy of secession." users. ox.ac.uk/~ball0144/self-det.pdf World Bank. Oxford, England and Oslo, Norway: Centre for the Study of African Economies, University of Oxford, and International Peace Research Institute.

Copestake, James, Monica Guillen Royo, Wan-Jung Chou, Tim Hinks, and Jackeline Velazco (2007) "An analysis of the multiple links between economic and sub- jective wellbeing indicators using data from Peru." WeD Working Paper 35. ESRC Research Group on Wellbeing in Developing Countries.

Corner, John (1994) "Mediating the ordinary: The 'access' idea and television form." In Meryl Aldridge and Nicholas Hewitt (eds.), *Controlling Broadcasting: Access Policy and Practice in North America and Europe*. Manchester: Manchester University Press.

Couldry, Nick (2000a) *Inside Culture: Re-imagining the Method of Cultural Studies*. London: Sage.

Couldry, Nick (2000b) *The Place of Media Power: Pilgrims and Witnesses of the Media Age*. London: Routledge.

Couldry, Nick (2006) *Listening Beyond The Echoes: Media, Ethics and Agency in an Uncertain World*. Boulder, CO: Paradigm Publishers.

Couldry, Nick (2008) "Mediatization or mediation? Alternative understandings of the emergent space of digital storytelling." *New Media & Society*, 10(3), 373–91.

Couldry, Nick and Anna McCarthy (2004) "Introduction: Orientations: mapping MediaSpace." In Nick Couldry and Anna McCarthy (eds.), *MediaSpace. Place, Scale and Culture in a Media Age*. London: Routledge.

Crossley, Michele L. (2003) (2nd ed.) *Introducing Narrative Psychology: Self, Trauma and the Construction of Meaning*. Buckingham and Philadelphia, PA: Open University Press.

Crowder, George (1991) *Classical Anarchism: The Political Thought of Godwin, Proudhon, Bakunin, and Kropotkin*. Oxford: Clarendon Press.

Cruz, Barbara (1996) *Frida Kahlo: Portrait of a Mexican Painter*. Berkeley Heights: Enslow.

CUHK (2004) "CUHK School of Hotel and Tourism Management co-organizes an exhibition on cultural tourism in China with Asia Tourism Exchange Center Limited to promote national tourism." *CUHK*. January 5. www.cuhk.edu.hk/ipro/pressrelease/040105e.htm (accessed June 8, 2005).

Davies, Diane (1999) "Towards devolution: Poetry and Anglo-Welsh identity." In Keith Cameron (ed.), *National Identity*. Exeter: Intellect.

Davis, Alan (2004) "Co-authoring identity: Digital storytelling in an urban middle school." *THEN: the journal about technology, humanities, education and narrative*, 1 (Summer). thenjournal.org/feature/61/

Davis, Marc and Michael Travers (1999) "A brief overview of the narrative intelligence reading group." *AAAI 1999 Fall Symposium on Narrative Intelligence*, North Falmouth, MA. www-2.cs.cmu.edu/afs/cs/user/michaelm/www/nidocs/DavisTravers.pdf (accessed November 22, 2004)

Dell'Aglio, Debora, Wendy Cunningham, Silvia Koller, Vicente Cassepp Borges, and Joana Severo Leon (2007) "Youth well-being in Brazil: An index for cross-regional comparisons". World Bank: Policy Research Working Paper, Report 4189, go.worldbank.org/N9OEBC2K60 (accessed September 5, 2007).

Deuze, Mark (2007) *Media Work*. Cambridge: Polity Press.

Dobson, Stephen (2005) "Narrative competence and enhancement of literacy. Some theoretical reflections." *seminar.net*.

Don, Abbe (1989–95) "We make memories." www.abbedon.com/project/wemake.html (accessed December 15, 2006).

Dovey, Jon (2000) *Freakshow: First Person Media and Factual Television*. London: Pluto Press.

Downing, John with Tamara Villarreal Ford, Genève Gil, and Laura Stein (2001) *Radical Media: Rebellious Communication and Social Movements*. London: Sage.

Dreyfus, Hubert L. and Paul Rabinow (1983) *Michel Foucault: Beyond Structuralism and Hermeneutics*. Chicago: University of Chicago Press.

Dwelly, Tim (2001) *Creative Regeneration: Lessons from 10 Community Arts Projects.* York: Joseph Rowntree Foundation.

Dyson, Anne Haas (1997) *Writing Superheroes: Contemporary Childhood, Popular Culture, and Classroom Literacy.* New York: Teachers College Press.

eastday.com. 2003. "Youth joins DIY bandwagon." eastday.com, October 9. service. china.org.cn/link/wcm/Show_Text?info_id=76866&p_qry=DIY (accessed May 26, 2005).

Erstad, Ola and James V. Wertsch (2008) "Tales of mediation: Narrative and digital media as cultural tools." In Knut Lundby (ed.), *Digital Storytelling, Mediatized Stories: Self-representations in New Media.* New York, Peter Lang, pp. 21–39.

Fisher, Matthew and Beth Twiss-Garrity (2007) "Remixing exhibits: Constructing participatory narratives with on-line tools to augment museum experiences." In Jennifer Trant and David Bearman (eds.), *Museums and the Web 2007: Proceedings.* Toronto: Archives and Museum Informatics, n.p.

Fiske, John and John Hartley (2003 [1978]) (rev. ed.) *Reading Television.* London: Routledge.

Florida, Richard (2004) *The Rise of the Creative Class.* New York: Basic Books.

Ford, Patrick K. (1992) *Ystoria Taliesin.* Cardiff: University of Wales Press.

Foucault, Michel (1978) *History of Sexuality, Part 1: An Introduction.* New York: Pantheon.

Franklin, Bob, ed. (2001) *British Television Policy: A Reader.* London and New York: Routledge.

Freeman, Jo (1971–3) "The tyranny of structurelessness" (online version based on three previous versions). www.jofreeman.com/joreen/tyranny.htm (accessed August 1, 2007).

Freire, Paulo (1972) *The Pedagogy of the Oppressed.* Harmondsworth: Penguin.

Frisch, Michael (1990) *A Shared Authority: Essays on the Craft and Meaning of Oral and Public History.* Albany, NY: SUNY Press.

Frisch, M. H. (1997) "What public history offers, and why it matters." *Public Historian*, 19, 41–3.

Ghanem, Elie (1998) "Social movements in Brazil and their educational work." *International Review of Education*, 44(2–3): 177–89.

Giddens, Anthony (1979) *Central Problems in Social Theory: Action, Structure and Contradiction in Social Analysis.* London: Macmillan.

Giddens, Anthony (1984) *The Constitution of Society: Outline of the Theory of Structuration.* Cambridge: Polity Press.

Gillard, Patricia (2002) "Museum visitors as audiences: Innovative research for online museums." In Tom O'Regan, Mark Balnaves, and Jason Sternberg (eds.), *Mobilising the Audience.* St Lucia, Queensland: University of Queensland Press, pp. 168–87.

Gillmor, Dan (2006) *We the Media: Grassroots Journalism by the People, for the People.* Sebastopol, CA: O'Reilly Media.

Gitlin, Todd (2001) *Media Unlimited. How the Torrent of Images and Sounds Overwhelms our Lives*. New York: Henry Holt.

Giunta, Edvige (2004) "Remembering ourselves, writing our histories: Memoir, oral history, and global communities." Paper presented at the XIII International Oral History Conference on Memory and Globalization, Rome.

Glassberg, David (1987) "History and the public: Legacies of the progressive era." *Journal of American History* 73, 957–80.

Goldbard, Arlene (2006) *New Creative Community*. Oakland, CA: New Village Press.

Graeber, David (2004) *Fragments of an Anarchist Anthropology*. Chicago: Prickly Paradigm Press.

Gramsci, Antonio (1999 [1932]) "Intellectuals." In Antonio Gramsci and David Forgacs (eds.), *The Antonio Gramsci Reader: Selected Writings 1916–1935*. London: Lawrence & Wishart.

Gray-Felder, Denise and James Deane (1999) "Communication for social change: A position paper and conference report, January, www.communicationforso cialchange.org/pdf/positionpaper.pdf

Griffith, Wyn (1950) *The Welsh*. Harmondsworth: Pelican.

Grollmann, Philipp and Felix Rauner (eds.) (2007) *International Perspectives on Teachers and Lecturers in Technical and Vocational Education*. New York: Springer.

Groundwater-Smith, Susan (2006) "Millennials in museums: Consulting Australian adolescents when designing for learning." *Forum of Museum Directors*, National Museum of History, Taipei.

Grubb, Benjamin and Jo Tacchi (2008) "Reaching out to communities: Creatively engaging the excluded." In Jerry Watkins and Jo Tacchi (eds.), *Participatory Content Creation for Development: Principles and Practices*. New Delhi. UNESCO.

Guest, Charlotte Lady (1849) *The Mabinogion*. Translated by Lady Charlotte Guest. www.gutenberg.org/dirs/etext04/mbng10h.htm. See also ebooks.adelaide.edu. au/m/mabinogion/guest/chapter12.html

Halvorsen, Thomas, Johan Hauknes, Ian Miles, and Rannveig Røste (2005) *Innovation in the Public Sector: On the Differences between Public and Private Sector Innovation*. Public Report No. D9. Oslo, Norway: NIFU STEP. www. step.no/publin/reports/d9differences.pdf

Hamelink, Cees J. (1995) *World Communication: Disempowerment and Self-empowerment*. Atlantic Highlands, NJ and London: Zed Books.

Harbage, Alfred (1947) *As They Liked It: An Essay on Shakespeare and Morality*. New York: Macmillan.

Harris, R. Carl, Stefinee Pinnegar, and Annela Teemant (2005) "The case for hyper-media video ethnographies: Designing a new class of case studies that challenge teaching practice." *Journal of Technology and Teacher Education*, 13(1), 141–61.

Hartley, John (1996) *Popular Reality: Journalism, Modernity, Popular Culture*. London: Arnold.

Hartley, John (1999) *Uses of Television*. London: Routledge.

Hartley, John (2008a) "Uses of YouTube: Digital literacy and the growth of knowledge." In Jean Burgess and Joshua Green, *YouTube: Online Video and the Politics of Participatory Culture*. Cambridge: Polity Press.

Hartley, John (2008b) "Problems of expertise and scalability in self-made media." In Knut Lundby (ed.), *Digital Storytelling, Mediatized Stories: Self-representations in New Media*. New York: Peter Lang.

Hartley, John, Gregory Hearn, Jo Tacchi, and Marcus Foth (2003) "The Youth Internet Radio Network: A research project to connect youth across Queensland through music, creativity and ICT." In S. Marshall and W. Taylor (eds.), *Proceedings of the 5th International Information Technology in Regional Areas (ITiRA) Conference 2003*. Rockhampton: Central Queensland University Press, pp. 335–42.

Hartley, John, Kelly McWilliam, Jean Burgess, and John Banks (2008) "The uses of multimedia: Three digital literacy case studies." *Media International Australia*, 128: 59–72.

Hawkes, Terence (1977) *Structuralism and Semiotics*. London: Methuen.

He, G (2001) "About CNTA: Chairman's words." www.cnta.com/lyen/2cnta/chairman.htm (accessed June 8, 2005).

Helff, Sissy (2008) "Scapes of refuge in Britain: Representing refugees in digital docudrama and mockumentary." In *Multiethnik Britain 2000+, Internationale Forschungen zur allgemeinen und vergleichenden Literaturwissenschaft*. Amsterdam: Rodopi, pp. 146–60.

Helff, Sissy (2007) "Signs taken for truth: Orchestrating transcultural aesthetics through narrative unreliability." In *Proceedings of the Conference of the German Association of University Teachers of English*, Vol. XXIX. Trier: Wissenschaftlicher Verlag, pp. 200–10.

Hermes, Joke (2006) "Citizenship in the age of the internet." *European Journal of Communication*, 21(3), 295–309.

Hesmondhalgh, David (2007) *The Cultural Industries*, London: Sage.

Highmore, Ben (2002) *Everyday Life and Cultural Theory*. London: Routledge.

Hill, Amy (2000) "Fearful and safe: Audience response to British reality programming." *Television and New Media*, 1(2): 193–213.

Hill, Amy (2006) "'Silence Speaks': Digital storytelling in South Africa: The men as partners experience." *The storyteller and the listener online*. storyteller-and-listener.blog-city.com/amy_hill.htm (accessed January 30, 2008).

Hockley, Luke (1996) "Inter-between: actus-done." *Convergence*, 2(2) (Autumn): 10–12.

Hofer, Mark and Kathleen Owings Swan (2006) "Digital storytelling: Moving from promise to practice." In Caroline Crawford et al. (eds.), *Proceedings of Society for Information Technology and Teacher Education International Conference 2006*. Chesapeake, VA: AACE, pp. 679–84.

Holland, Patrick and Graham Huggan (2000) *Tourists with Typewriters: Critical Reflection on Contemporary Travelwriting*. Ann Arbor: University of Michigan Press.

Holland, Patrick and Graham Huggan (2004) "Varieties of nostalgia in contemporary travel writing." In Tim Youngs (ed.), *Perspectives on Travel Writing*. Aldershot: Ashgate, pp. 139–51.

Hollway, Wendy (1984) "Gender difference and the production of subjectivity." In Julia Henriques, Wendy Hollway, Cathy Urwin, Couze Venn, and Valerie Walkerdine (eds.), *Changing the Subject: Psychology, Social Regulation and Subjectivity*. London and New York: Methuen.

Hooper-Greenhill, Eilean (1997) "Introduction: Towards plural perspectives." In Eilean Hooper-Greenhill (ed.), *Cultural Diversity: Developing Museum Audiences in Britain*. London: Leicester University Press.

Howell, Dusti and Deanne Howell (2003) "What's your digital story?" *Library Media Connection*, 40–1.

Howley, Kevin (2005) *Community Media: People, Places, and Communication Technologies*. Cambridge: Cambridge University Press.

HP (2005) "StoryCast: Simple, digital storytelling with photos and narration." HP labs. www.hpl.hp.com/research/storycast (accessed June 7, 2005).

Huggan, Graham (1994) *Territorial Disputes: Maps and Mapping Strategies in Contemporary Canadian and Australian Fiction*. Toronto: University of Toronto Press.

Huggan, Graham (2008) "Decolonizing the map: Postcolonialism, poststructuralism and the cartographic connection." In Graham Huggan, *Interdisciplinary Measures: Literature and the Future of Postcolonial Studies*. Liverpool: Liverpool University Press, pp. 21–33.

Hull, Glynda (2003) "Youth culture and digital media: New literacies for new times." *Research in the Teaching of English*, 38(2), 229–33.

Hull, Glynda and Michael Angelo James (2007) "Geographies of hope: A study of urban landscapes, digital media, and children's representation of place." In Peggy O'Neill (ed.), *Blurring Boundaries: Developing Writers, Researchers, and Teachers*. Creskill, NJ, Hampton Press.

Hull, Glynda A. and Mira-Lisa Katz (2006) "Crafting an agentive self: Case studies of digital storytelling." *Research in the Teaching of English*, 41(1), 43–81.

Hull, Glynda and Mark Nelson (2005) "Locating the semiotic power of multimodality." *Written Communication*, 22, 224–61.

Hunt, Alan and Gary Wickham (1994) *Foucault and Law: Towards a Sociology of Law as Governance*. London: Pluto.

Illich, Ivan (1973) *Deschooling Society*. Harmondsworth: Penguin.

Introna, Lucas and Helen Nissenbaum (2000) "Shaping the web: Why the politics of search engines matter." *The information society*, 16.

James, Jeffrey (2004) *Information Technology and Development: A New Paradigm for Delivering the Internet to Rural Areas in Developing Countries*. Oxford. Routledge.

Jenkins, Henry (2006) *Convergence Culture: Where Old and New Media Collide*. New York: New York University Press.

Jennings, Jeremy (1999) "Anarchism." In Roger Eatwell and Anthony Wright (eds.), *Contemporary Political Ideologies*. London and New York: Pinter, pp. 131–51.

Kajder, Sara (2004) "Enter here: Personal narrative and digital storytelling." *English Journal*, 93(3), 64–8.

Kajder, Sara, Glen Bull, and Susan Albaugh (2005) "Constructing digital stories." *Learning & Leading with Technology*, 32(5), 40–2.

Kamler, Barbara (2001) *Relocating the Personal: A Critical Writing Pedagogy*. Albany, NY: State University of New York Press.

Kay, Alan and Adele Goldberg (1977) "Personal dynamic media." *Computer*, 10(3), 31–41.

Keen, Andrew (2007) *The Cult of the Amateur: How the Democratization of the Digital World is Assaulting Our Economy, Our Culture, and Our Values*. New York: Doubleday Currency.

Kendall, Gavin and Gary Wickham (1999) *Using Foucault's Methods*. London: Sage.

Kidd, Jenny (2005) "Capture Wales: Digital storytelling at the BBC." *Cyfrwng: Wales Media Journal*, 2, 66–85.

Kingdon, Geeta and John Knight (2006) "Subjective well-being poverty vs. income poverty and capabilities poverty?" *Journal of Development Studies*, 42(7), 1199–224.

Kiran, M. S. (2008) "Challenging an asymmetric power relation: Media development for social change in Seelampur, India." In Jerry Watkins and Jo Tacchi (eds.), *Participatory Content Creation for Development: Principles and Practices*. New Delhi. UNESCO.

Klaebe, Helen (2006a) "The problems and possibilities of storytelling in public history projects." In *Proceedings of the International Oral History Conference: Dancing with Memory*, Sydney, eprints.qut.edu.au

Klaebe, Helen (2006b) *Sharing Stories: A Social History of the Kelvin Grove Urban Village*. Sydney: Focus.

Klaebe, Helen and Marcus Foth (2006) "Capturing community memory with oral history and new media: The Sharing Stories Project." Paper presented at the third International Community Informatics Research Network (CIRN) Conference.

Kovach, Bill and Tom Rosenstiel (2001) *The Elements of Journalism: What Newspeople Should Know and the Public Should Expect*. Crown, New York.

Kress, Gunter (2003) *Literacy in the New Media Age*. London: Routledge.

Kristof, Nicholas (2005) "Freeing sex slaves." *New York Times,* January 19. www.nytimes.com/packages/khtml/2005/01/19/opinion/20040119_CAMBODIA_FEATURE.html (accessed June 7, 2005).

Kropotkin, Peter (1892/1972) *The Conquest of Bread*, ed. Paul Avrich. New York: New York University Press.

Kropotkin, Peter (1902) *Mutual Aid: A Factor in Evolution*. London: Heinemann. www.pitzer.edu/~dward/Anarchist_Archives/kropotkin/mutaidcontents.html

Lambert, Joe (2000) "Has digital storytelling succeeded as a movement? Some thoughts." *dStoryNews* 2, September 20. www.dstroy.com/disfo/newsletter_02.html

Lambert, Joe (n.d.) "Facing the crisis: Interview with Joe Lambert." www.storycenter.org/diner/pages/joediner1.html (accessed October 2002).

Lambert, Joe (2002) *Digital Storytelling: Capturing Lives, Creating Community.* Berkeley, CA: Digital Diner Press.

Lambert, Joe (2003) *Digital Storytelling. Cookbook and Traveling Companion,* Version 4.0. Berkeley, CA: Digital Diner Press.

Lambert, Joe (2004) Interview with Jenny Kidd. Polverigi, Italy, February 7.

Lambert, Joe (2006) (2nd ed.) *Digital Storytelling: Capturing Lives, Creating Community.* Berkeley, CA: Digital Diner Press.

Lanham, Richard A. (2006) *The Economics of Attention: Style and Substance in the Age of Information.* Chicago: Chicago University Press.

Lankshear, Colin and Michelle Knobel (2007) "Sampling 'the new' in new literacies." In Michelle Knobel and Colin Lankshear (eds.), *A New Literacies Sampler.* New York: Peter Lang.

Lash, Scott and Celia Lury (2007) *Global Cultural Industry: The Mediation of Things.* Cambridge: Polity.

Lathem, Sandra, Cynthia Reyes, and Jing Qi (2006) "Literacy autobiography: Digital storytelling to capture student voice and reflection." In Caroline Crawford et al. (eds.), *Proceedings of Society for Information Technology and Teacher Education International Conference 2006.*Chesapeake, VA: AACE, pp. 700–4.

Laurel, Brenda (1986) "Towards the Design of a Computer-based Interactive Fantasy System." PhD thesis, Ohio State University.

Levine, Robert M. (1997) *Brazilian Legacies.* New York: M. E. Sharpe.

Levine, Robert M. and Crocitti, John J. (1999) *The Brazil Reader.* London: Latin America Bureau.

Lewis, Peter (2006) "Community media: Giving a 'voice to the voiceless.'" In Peter M. Lewis and Susan Jones (eds.), *From the Margins to the Cutting Edge: Community Media and Empowerment.* Cresskill, NJ: Hampton Press, pp. 13–40.

Liddington, Jill and Simon Ditchfield (2005) "Public history: A critical bibliography." *Oral History: The Journal of the Oral History Society,* 33, 40–5.

Ling, Tom (2002) *Innovation: Lessons from the Private Sector.* A "think piece" in support of the Invest to Save Study, *National Audit Office.* www.nao.org.uk/publications/nao_reports/02–03/innovation.pdf

Lister, Ruth (2004) *Poverty.* Cambridge: Polity.

Livingstone, Sonia (2007) "Engaging with media – a matter of literacy?" In *Transforming Audiences: identity/creativity/everyday life proceedings,* University of Westminster, London, September 6–7. eprints.lse.ac.uk/2763/

Livingstone, Sonia and Peter Lunt (1994) *Talk on Television: Audience Participation and Public Debate.* London: Routledge.

Lowenthal, Patrick and J. Dunlap (2007) "Digital Stories." In Patti Shank (ed.), *The Online Learning Idea Book: 95 Proven Ways to Enhance Technology-based and Blended Learning.* San Francisco: Pfeiffer, pp. 110–11.

Luna, Francisco Vidal and Herbert S. Klein (2006) *Brazil since 1980.* Cambridge: Cambridge University Press.

Lundby, Knut, ed. (2008) *Digital Storytelling, Mediatized Stories: Self-representations in New Media*. New York: Peter Lang.

Maddux, Cleborne and Rhoda Cummings (2003) "Information technology in education: Fads and the role of theory and research." In Caroline Crawford et al. (eds.), *Proceedings of Society for Information Technology and Teacher Education International Conference 2003*. Chesapeake, VA: AACE, pp. 2761–4.

Manovich, Lev (2001) *The Language of New Media*. Cambridge, MA and London: MIT Press.

Martin, Kirsty (2008) "Social change through local content creation: Case studies from Nepal." In Jerry Watkins and Jo Tacchi (eds.), *Participatory Content Creation for Development: Principles and Practices*. New Delhi. UNESCO.

Martin, Kirsty, Deepak Koirala, Rupa Pandey, Sita Adhikari, Govinda Prasad Acharya, and Kiran MS (2007) "Finding the local community in community media: Some stories from Nepal." *Asia Rights*, 8.

Martín-Barbero, Jesús (1993) *Communication, Culture and Hegemony: From the Media to the Mediations*. London: Sage.

Mateas, Michael and Phoebe Sengers (1999) "Narrative intelligence: Introduction to the AAAI 1999 Fall Symposium on narrative intelligence." North Falmouth, MA. www-.cs.cmu.edu/afs/cs/user/michaelm/www/nidocs/MateasSengers.pdf

Matthews, John (2002) *Taliesin: The Last Celtic Shaman*. Rochester, VT: Inner Traditions/Bear & Co.

May, Todd (1994) *The Political Philosophy of Poststructuralist Anarchism*. University Park, PA: Pennsylvania State University Press. caosmosis.acracia.net/wp-content/uploads/2007/07/todd-may-the-political-philosophy-of-poststructuralist-anarchism.doc

McAdams, Dan (1993) *The Stories We Live By: Personal Myths and the Making of the Self*. New York and London: The Guildford Press.

McClean, Shilo (2007) *Digital Storytelling. The Narrative Power of Visual Effects in Film*. Cambridge, MA: MIT Press.

McDury, Janice and Maxine Alterio (2002) *Learning through Storytelling: Using Reflection and Experience to Improve Learning*. London: Routledge Falmer.

McWilliam, Erica (2007) "Unlearning How to Teach." Paper presented at *Creativity or Conformity? Building Cultures of Creativity in Higher Education*, Cardiff: University of Wales Institute in collaboration with the Higher Education Academy, January 8–10. www.creativityconference.org/presented_papers/McWilliam_Unlearning.doc

McWilliam, Kelly (2008) "Digital storytelling as a 'discursively-ordered domain.'" In Knut Lundby (ed.), *Digital Storytelling, Mediatized Stories: Self-representations in New Media*. New York: Peter Lang.

Meadows, Daniel (2003) "Digital Storytelling: Research-based practice in new media." *Visual Communication*, 2(2), 189–93.

Mehra, Bharat, Cecelia Merkel, and Ann Bishop (2004) "The internet for empower-
    ment of minority and marginalized users." *New Media and Society*, 6, 781–802.

Mellon, Constance A. (1999) "Digital storytelling: Effective learning through the
    internet." *Educational Technology*, 39(2), 46–50.

Message, Kylie and Chris Healy (2004) "A symptomatic museum: the new, the NMA
    and the culture wars." *Borderlands e-journal*, 3(3), 1–11.

Michener, Victoria (1998) "The participatory approach: Contradiction and co-
    optation in Burkina Faso." *World Development*, 26(12), pp. 2105–18.

Midgley, James with Anthony Hall, Margaret Hardiman, and Dhanpaul Narine
    (1986) *Community Participation, Social Development and the State*. London
    and New York: Methuen.

Miller, Carolyn Handler (2004) *Digital Storytelling: A Creator's Guide to Interactive
    Entertainment*. Oxford: Focal Press/Elsevier.

Miller, Carolyn R. (1984) "Genre as social action." *Quarterly Journal of Speech*, 70(2),
    pp. 151–67.

Miller, Paul (2005) "Web 2.0: Building the new library." Ariadne, 45. www.ariadne.
    ac.uk/issue45/miller/

Mirza, Heidi Safia, ed. (1997) *Black British Feminism: A Reader*. London: Routledge.

Morris, Edward D. (1889) "The language and literature of Wales." *Proceedings of the
    Modern Language Association* 4(1), 4–18. inks.jstor.org/sici?sici=0030–
    8129%281889%294%3A1%3C4%3ATLALOW%3E2.0.CO%3B2–E

Murray, Janet (1997) *Hamlet on the Holodeck: The Future of Narrative in Cyberspace*.
    New York: The Free Press.

Murray, Janet (1999) (2nd ed.) *Hamlet on the Holodeck: The Future of Narrative in
    Cyberspace*. Cambridge, MA: MIT Press.

Murray, Janet (2004) "From game-story to cyberdrama." In N. Wardrip-Fruin and
    P. Harrigan (eds.), *First Person: New Media as Story, Performance and Game*.
    Cambridge, MA and London: MIT Press.

Nakakoji, Kumiyo (2005) "Seven issues for creativity support tool researchers."
    Workshop on Creativity Support Tools, Washington, DC, p. 69.

Nakakoji, Kumiyo, Atau Tanaka, and Daniel Fallman (2006) "'Sketching' nurturing
    creativity: Commonalities in art, design, engineering and research." Montreal:
    ACM Press, p. 1717.

Narayan, Deepa, with Raj Patel, Kai Schafft, Anne Rademacher, and Sarah Koch-
    Schulte (eds.) (2000) *Can Anyone Hear Us?* Oxford: Oxford University Press
    and the World Bank.

Narayan, Deepa, Robert Chambers, Meera Shah, and Patti Petesch (eds.) (2000)
    *Crying Out for Change*. Oxford: Oxford University Press and the World Bank.

Narayan, Deepa and Patti Petesch (eds.) (2002) *From Many Lands*. Oxford: Oxford
    University Press and the World Bank.

Nash, D.W. [David William] (1858) *Taliesin; or, the Bards and Druids of Britain. A
    Translation of the Remains of the Earliest Welsh Bards and an Examination of*

*the Bardic Mysteries*. London: John Russell Smith. books.google.com/books?id=SX4NAAAAQAAJ

Neilsen, Philip (2005) "Digital storytelling as life-writing: Self-construction, therapeutic effect, textual analysis leading to an enabling 'aesthetic' for the community voice." *Proceedings from the Speculation and Innovation (SPIN) Conference*, pp. 1–7. www.speculation2005.qut.edu.au/papers/Neilsen.pdf

Nichols, Bill (1991) *Representing Reality: Issues and Concepts of Documentary*. Bloomington and Indianapolis: Indiana University Press.

Nissley, Nick (2007) "Storytelling as a web-based workplace learning pedagogy." In Badrul Khan (ed.), *Flexible Learning in an Information Society*. Hershey, PA: Idea Group, pp. 86–95.

Nixon, Helen (2003) "Textual diversity: Who needs it?" In UoSA (ed.), *Proceedings of the International Federation for the Teaching of English Conference*. Melbourne: School of Education.

Notley, Tanya and Jo Tacchi (2004) "Online youth networks: Researching the experience of 'peripheral' young people in using new media tools for creative participation and representation." *3CMedia: Journal of Community, Citizens and Third Sector media*, 1, 73–81.

NYU Public History Program (2007) Public History. history.fas.nyu.edu/object/history.gradprog.publichistory.html

Ohler, Jason (2005) "The world of digital storytelling." *Educational Leadership*, 63(4), 44–7.

Ohler, Jason (2007) *Digital Storytelling in the Classroom: New Media Pathways to Literacy, Learning, and Creativity*. Thousand Oaks, CA: Corwin Press.

Oppenheimer, Todd (1997) "The computer delusion." *Atlantic Monthly* (July), 45–62.

Osmond, John (1995) *Welsh Europeans*. Bridgend: Seren.

Page, Nanette and Czuba, Cheryl E. (1999) "Empowerment: What is it?" *Journal of Extension*, 37(5). www.joe.org/joe/1999october/comm1.htm

Paré, Anthony (2002) "Genre and identity: Individuals, institutions, and ideology." in Richard Coe, Lorelei Lingard, and Tatiana Teslenko (eds.), *The Rhetoric and Ideology of Genre: Strategies for Stability and Change*. Creskill, NJ: Hampton, pp. 57–71.

Pariser, Eva (2000) "Artists' websites: Declarations of identity and presentations of self." In David Gauntlett (ed.), *Web Studies: Rewiring Media Studies for the Digital Age*. London: Arnold, pp. 62–7.

Parks, Will 2005. *Who Measures Change? An Introduction to Participatory Monitoring and Evaluation of Communication for Social Change*. South Orange, NJ: Communication for Social Change Consortium.

Pateman, Carole (1970) *Participation and Democratic Theory*. Cambridge: Cambridge University Press.

Paul, Nora and Christina Fiebich (2005) "The elements of digital storytelling." University of Minnesota School of Journalism and Mass Communication's Institute for New Media Studies. www.inms.umn.edu/elements

Pearce, Celia (2004) "Towards a game theory of game." In Noah Wardrip-Fruin and Pat Harrigan (eds.), *First Person: New Media as Story, Performance and Game.* Cambridge, MA and London: MIT Press.

Perkel, Dan (2006) "Copy and paste literacy: Literacy practices in the production of a MySpace profile." www.indexof.no/dperkel.pdf

Pickering, Mimi (2007) "Storytelling: Letter from Mimi Pickering," W. W. Kellogg Foundation. www.wkkf.org/Default.aspx?tabid=90&CID=385&ItemID=5000094&NID=5010094&LanguageID=0

Pink, Daniel (1999) "Publish or perish! The jeers and cheers of digital storytelling bootcamp," *Fast Company*, 21, January. www.fastcompany.com/magazine/21/perish.html

Pink, Daniel (2005) *A Whole New Mind: Moving from the Information Age to the Conceptual Age.* New York: Riverhead Books.

Porter, Bernajean (2006) "Beyond words: The craftsmanship of digital products." *Learning & Leading with Technology*, May: 28–31.

Potts, Jason, Stuart Cunningham, John Hartley, and Paul Ormerod (2008) "Social network markets: A new definition of the creative industries." *Journal of Cultural Economics*, April.

Powazek, Derek (1996–2005) *Fray.* www.fray.com/is (accessed March 2, 2006).

Proudhon, Pierre-Joseph (1851/1989) *General Idea of the Revolution in the Nineteenth Century.* Trans. John B. Robinson. London: Pluto Press.

Rennie, Ellie (2004) "The story so far: Digital storytelling, narrative and the new literacy." In P. Anastasiou and K. Trist (eds.), *Image, Text and Sound 2004: The Yet Unseen: Rendering Stories.* Melbourne: RMIT Informit Library.

Rex, Lesley A., Timothy Murnen, Jack Hobbs, and David McEachen (2002) "Teachers' pedagogical stories and the shaping of classroom participation: 'The Dancer' and 'Graveyard Shift at the 7–11.'" *American Educational Research Journal*, 39(3), 765–96.

Richards, Menna (2003) Presentation to the International Digital Storytelling Conference, November, BBC Wales, Cardiff.

Ritter, Alan (1980) *Anarchism: A Theoretical Analysis.* Cambridge: Cambridge University Press.

Ritter, Jonathan (2007) "Terror in an Andean key: Peasant cosmopolitans interpret 9/11." In Jonathan Ritter and Martin Daughtry (eds.) *Music in the Post 9/11 World*, New York: Routledge, pp. 177–208.

Robin, Bernard (2006) "The educational uses of digital storytelling." In Caroline Crawford et al. (eds.), *Proceedings of Society for Information Technology and Teacher Education International Conference 2006.* Chesapeake, VA: AACE, pp. 709–16.

Robin, Bernard R. and Melissa E. Pierson (2005, March). "A multilevel approach to using digital storytelling in the classroom." Paper presented at the annual meeting of the Society for Information Technology and Teacher Education, Phoenix, AZ.

Rocha, Jan (2000) *Brazil in Focus*. New York: Intellect Books.

Rodriguez, Clemencia (2001) *Fissures in the Mediascape: An International Study of Citizens' Media*. Cresskill, NJ: Hampton Press.

Roland, Craig (2006) "Digital storytelling in the classroom." *School Arts*, 105(7), 26.

Rothbard, Murray (1989 [1973]) *For a New Liberty: The Libertarian Manifesto*. New York: Fox & Wilkes.

Rudnicki, Anne, Alysa Cozart, Annapurna Ganesh, Carrie Markello, Sabrina Marsh, Sara McNeil, Heidi Mullins, Donna Odle Smith, and Bernard Robin (2006) "The buzz continues ... the diffusion of digital storytelling across disciplines and colleges at the University of Houston." In Caroline Crawford et al. (eds.), *Proceedings of Society for Information Technology and Teacher Education International Conference 2006*. Chesapeake, VA: AACE, pp. 717–23.

Russo, Angelina and Jerry Watkins (2007) "Digital cultural communication: Audience and remediation." In Fiona Cameron and Sarah Kenderdine (eds.), *Theorizing Digital Cultural Heritage*. Cambridge, MA: MIT Press, pp. 149–64.

Russo, Angelina, Jerry Watkins, Lynda Kelly, and Sebastian Chan (2006) "How will social media affect museum communication?" In *Proceedings Nordic Digital Excellence in Museums (NODEM)*, Oslo, Norway. eprints.qut.edu.au

Ryan, Marie-Laure (2004a) "Digital Media." in Marie-Laure Ryan (ed.), *Narrative Across Media: The Languages of Storytelling*. Lincoln: University of Nebraska Press, pp. 329–36.

Ryan, Marie-Laure (2004b) "Will new media produce new narratives?" In Marie-Laure Ryan (ed.), *Narrative Across Media: The Languages of Storytelling*. Lincoln: University of Nebraska Press, pp. 337–59.

Sahlins, Marshall (1972) *Stone Age Economics*. Chicago: Aldine-Atherton.

Salpeter, Judy (2005) "Telling tales with technology." *Technology & Learning*, 25(7), February. www.techlearning.com/shared/printableArticle.php?articleID=60300276 (accessed July 1, 2006).

Sayer, Christine and Deb Stumm (2008) "Queensland stories: Community, collections and digital technology at the State Library of Queensland." VALA 2008: Libraries/changing spaces, virtual places, Melbourne Exhibition and Convention Centre.

Schank, Roger (1990) *Tell Me a Story: Narrative and Intelligence*. Evanston, IL: Northwestern University Press.

Schank, Roger and Robert P. Abelson (1995) "Knowledge and memory: The real story." In Robert Wyer (ed.), *Knowledge and Memory: The Real Story*. Hillsdale, NJ: Lawrence Erlbaum, pp. 1–85.

Schank, Roger and Christopher Riesbeck (1981) *Inside Computer Understanding: Five Programs plus Miniatures*. Hillsdale, NJ: Lawrence Erlbaum.

Schlesinger, Philip (2003) "Introduction." In Jesús Martín-Barbero (ed.), *Communication, Culture and Hegemony: From the Media to Mediations*. London: Sage.

Schmidt, Nancy (1981) "The nature of ethnographic fiction: A further inquiry." *Anthropology and Human Quarterly*, 6, 8–18.

Schmidt-Belz, Barbara and Stefan Poslad (2003) "User validation of a mobile tourism Service." September 8. www.comp.lancs.ac.uk/computing/users/kc/mguides03/SchbelzPoslad-final.pdf (accessed March 11, 2005).

Schuler, Douglas (1994) "Community networks: Building a new participatory medium." *Communications of the ACM*, 1(37), 38–51.

Seiter, Ellen (2004) "Children reporting on-line: The cultural politics of the computer lab." *Television & New Media*, 5(2), 87–107.

Selber, Stuart A. (2004) *Multiliteracies for a Digital Age*. Carbondale: Southern Illinois University Press.

Servon, Lisa (2002) *Bridging the Digital Divide: Technology, Community, and Public Policy*. Oxford: Blackwell.

Shedroff, Nathan (1999) "Information interaction design: A unified field theory of design." In Robert E. Jacobson (ed.), *Information Design*. Cambridge: MIT Press, p. 137.

Shedroff, Nathan (2001) *Experience Design: A Manifesto for the Creation of Experiences*. Indianapolis, IN: New Riders.

Shneiderman, Ben (2002) *Leonardo's Laptop: Human Needs and the New Computing Technologies*. Cambridge, MA: MIT Press, pp. 12–13.

Silverstone, Roger (1999) *Why Study the Media?* London: Sage.

Silverstone, Roger (2007) *Media and Morality: On the Rise of the Mediapolis*. Cambridge: Polity.

Singer, Jefferson and Pavel Blagor (2004) "The integrative function of narrative processing: Autobiographical memory, self-defining memories and the life story of identity." In Denise Beike, James Lampinen, and Douglas Behrend, *The Self and Memory*. New York: Psychology Press, pp. 117–38.

Skeggs, Beverley (2004) *Class, Self, Culture*. London: Routledge.

Snyder, Ilana and Prinsloo, Martin (2007) "Young people's engagement with digital literacies in marginal contexts in a globalised world." *Language and Education*, 21(3), 171–9.

Sonesson, Göran (1997) "The limits of nature and culture in cultural semiotics." In Richard Hirsch (ed.), *Papers from the fourth bi-annual meeting of the Swedish Society for Semiotic Studies*, Linköping University, December. www.arthist.lu.se/kultsem/sonesson/CultSem1.html

Sonesson, Göran (2002) "The culture of Modernism: From transgressions of art to arts of transgression." In M. Carani and G. Sonesson (eds.), *Visio*, 3(3): *Modernism*, pp. 9–26. www.arthist.lu.se/kultsem/sonesson/Culture%20of%20Mod3.html

Spierling, Ulrike, Dieter Grasbon, Norbert Braun, and Ido Iurgel (2002) "Setting the scene: Playing digital director in interactive storytelling and creation." *Computers and Graphics*, 26(1), 31–44.

Sposito, Marília Pontes, and Carrano, Paulo César Rodrigues (2003) "Juventude e Políticas Públicas no Brasil." *Revista Brasileira de Educação*, 024 (September–December), 16–39. www.juventude.fortaleza.ce.gov.br/images/stories/juventude_e_polticas_pblicas_no_brasil.pdf

Springer, Julie, Sara Kajder, and Julia Borst Brazas (2004) "Digital storytelling at the National Gallery of Art." In David Bearman and Jennifer Trant (eds.), *Museums and the Web 2004*. Toronto: Archives and Museum Informatics.

Standley, Mark (2003) "Digital storytelling: Using new technology and the power of stories to help our students learn – and teach." *Cable in the Classroom*, 16–18.

Standley, Mark and Meg Ormiston (2003) *Digital Storytelling with PowerPoint: Teaching Powerful Storytelling*. Eugene, OR: Visions Technology in Education.

Stellin, Susan (2005) Fitting the world's biggest travel guide in a pocket. *New York Times*, March 8. www.nytimes.com/2005/03/08/technology/08handhelds.html (accessed March 9, 2005).

Stevens and Associates (2003) *The National Eisteddfod of Wales: The Way Forward*. Cardiff: Eisteddfod Genedlaethol Cymru, www.bwrdd-yr-iaith.org.uk/download.php/pID=44756

Straubhaar, Joseph, D. (1996) "The electronic media in Brazil." In Richard R. Cole (ed.), *Communication in Latin America: Journalism, Mass Media and Society*. Wilmington, DE: Scholarly Resources Press.

Stumm, Deb and Christina Sayer (2007) "Queensland stories: Content creation through personal histories and digital storytelling at the State Library of Queensland. Old stories, new ways." Paper presented at the National Oral History Conference, Brisbane, Australia.

Sweeder, John (2007) "Digital video in the classroom: Integrating theory and practice." *Contemporary Issues in Technology and Teacher Education*, 7(2), 107–28.

Tacchi, Jo (2007) "Ethnographic (per)versions and creative engagement through locally created content," paper presented at CMS Symbols – Symposia on Communication for Social Development, University of Hyderabad, India, 1–3 November.

Tacchi, Jo (2008) "Voice and poverty." *Media Development*, 1.

Tacchi, Jo and Benjamin Grubb (2007) "The case of the e-tuktuk." *Media International Australia incorporating Culture and Policy*, 125, 71–82.

*Tale of Tales* (2005a) "About Tale of Tales." tale-of tales.com/information.html (accessed August 2006; not currently available).

*Tale of Tales* (2005b) "The Endless Forest." www.tale-of-tales.com/TheEndlessForest/ (accessed October 2007).

*Tale of Tales* (2007) "About Tale of Tales." tale-of-tales.com/blog/?page_id=19 (accessed October 2007).

Tharp, Kevin W. and Liz Hills (2004) "Digital storytelling: Culture, media and community." In Stewart Marshall, Wal Taylor, and Xinghuo Yu (eds.), *Using Community Informatics to Transform Regions*. Hershey, PA: Idea Group, pp. 37–51.

Thomassie, J., J. Gruber, C. Dukehart, D. Gainer, G. Zoroya, and D. Teeuwen (2004) "Tale of two holidays." *USA Today*. www.usatoday.com/news/graphics/snsflyo ver/flash.htm (accessed June 7, 2005).

Thompson, Rachel (2007) "A biographical perspective." In Mary Jane Kehily (ed.), *Understanding Youth: Perspectives, Identities and Practices*. London: Sage.

Thumim, Nancy (2006) "Mediated self-representations: 'Ordinary people' in 'communities.'" In Stefan Herbrechter and Michael Higgins (eds.), *Returning (to) Communities. Theory, Culture and Political Practice of the Communal*. Amsterdam: Rodopi.

Thumim, Nancy (2007) "Mediating Self-representations: Tensions Surrounding 'Ordinary' Participation in Public Sector Projects." PhD thesis, Department of Media and Communications, London School of Economics and Political Science.

Thumim, Nancy. (2008) "'It's good for them to know my story': Cultural mediation as tensions." In Knut Lundby (ed.), *Digital Storytelling, Mediatized Stories: Self-representations in New Media*, pp 85–104. Peter Lang, New York.

Toffler, Alvin (1981) *The Third Wave*. London: Pan/Collins.

Torfing, Jacob (1999) *New Theories of Discourse: Laclau, Mouffe, Zizek*. Blackwell, Oxford.

Trendwatching.com (2005a) "Customer-made special." Trendwatching.com, May. www.trendwatching.com/newsletter/newsletter.html (accessed June 5, 2005).

Trendwatching.com (2005b) "Generation C." January. www.trendwatching.com/ trends/generation_C.htm (accessed May 21, 2005).

Tucker, Genevieve (2006) "First person singular: The power of digital storytelling." *Screen Education*, 42, 54–9.

Turner, Graeme (2005) *Ending the Affair: The Decline of Current Affairs in Australia*, Sydney: University of New South Wales Press.

University of Houston (n.d.) "Educational uses of digital storytelling." www.coe. uh.edu/digital-storytelling/ (accessed May 1, 2006).

Vergo, Peter (1993) "The reticent object." In P. Vergo (ed.), *The New Museology*, London: Reaktion Books, pp. 41–59.

Villarreal, Mary Ann (2004) "Finding our place: Reconstructing community through oral history." Paper presented at the IXIII International Oral History Conference on Memory and Globalization, Rome.

Viswanathan, Sujatha and Ravi Srivastava (2007) *Learning from the Poor: Findings from Participatory Poverty Assesments in India*. Manila: Asian Development Bank.

Vygotsky, L. S. (1978) *Mind in Society: The Development of Higher Psychological Processes*. Cambridge, MA and London: Harvard University Press.

Ward, Colin (1973) *Anarchy in Action*. London: Allen & Unwin.

Warschauer, Mark (2003) *Technology and Social Inclusion: Rethinking the Digital Divide*, Cambridge, MA: MIT Press.

Watkins, Jerry and Angelina Russo (2005a) "Developing communities and collections with new media and information literacy." In Edward A. Fox, Erich

Neuhold, Pimrumpai Premsmit, and Vilas Wuwongse (eds.), *Digital Libraries: Implementing Strategies and Sharing Experiences*. Bangkok: Springer, pp. 390–4.

Watkins, Jerry and Angelina Russo (2005b) "Digital cultural communication: Designing co-creative new media environments." In Linda Candy (ed.), *Creativity & Cognition: Proceedings 2005*. London: ACM Press, pp. 144–9.

Watkins, Jerry and Angelina Russo (2005c) "New media design for cultural institutions." In *Proceedings 2nd Conference on Designing for User eXperience*. San Francisco. eprints.qut.edu.au/

Watkins, Jerry and Angelina Russo (2007) "Participatory design and co-creativity in cultural institutions." In Patricia Sabine (ed.), *Museums in a Changing Climate*. Canberra: Museums Australia.

Watkins, Jerry and Jo Tacchi, eds. (2008) *Participatory Content Creation for Development: Principles and Practices*. New Delhi: UNESCO.

Watson, Richard, Sigmund Akselsen, Emmanuel Monod, and Leyland Pitt (2004) "The open tourism consortium: Laying the foundations for the future of tourism." www.opentourism.org/otc.pdf (accessed March 28, 2005).

Weber, Max (1978) *Economy and Society: An Outline of Interpretive Sociology*. Berkeley. Los Angeles, and London: University of California Press.

Weir, David (1997) *Anarchy and Culture: The Aesthetic Politics of Modernism*. Amherst: University of Massachusetts Press.

Wertsch, James V. (1985) *Vygotsky and the Social Formation of Mind*. Cambridge, MA and London: Harvard University Press.

Wertsch, James V. (1998) *Mind as Action*. Oxford: Oxford University Press.

Wertsch, James V. (2007) "Mediation." In Harry Daniels, Michael Cole, and James V. Wertsch (eds.), *The Cambridge Companion to Vygotsky*. Cambridge: Cambridge University Press.

Wertsch, James V., Pablo del Río, and Amelia Alvarez (1995) "Sociocultural studies: History, action, and mediation." In James V. Wertsch, Pablo del Río, and Amelia Alvarez (eds.), *Sociocultural Studies of Mind*. Cambridge: Cambridge University Press.

White, Sarah (1996) "Depoliticising development: The uses and abuses of participation." *Development in Practice* 6 (1), pp. 6–15.

Whitman, Walt (1995 [1883]) *Specimen Days and Collect*. New York: Dover.

Wikibooks (2005) "Digital storytelling," April 28. en.wikibooks.org/wiki/Digital_Storytelling (accessed June 6, 2005).

Wikipedia (2005) "Netizen," March 26. en.wikipedia.org/wiki/Netizen (accessed May 22, 2005).

Williams, Raymond (1974) *Television: Technology and Cultural Form*. London: Fontana.

Winsor, Dorothy A. (2003) *Writing Power: Communication in an Engineering Center*. Albany: State University of New York Press.

Woletz, Julie (forthcoming) "Digital storytelling from artificial intelligence to YouTube." In S Kelsey (ed.), *Handbook of Research on Computer Mediated Communication*. Hershey, PA: Idea Group Reference.

Worcman, Karen (2002) "Digital division is cultural exclusion: But is digital inclusion cultural inclusion?" *D-Lib magazine*, 8(3). www.delib.org/dlib/march02/worcman/03worcman.html

Worcman, Karen (2006) "Introdução." In Karen Worcman and José Vasquez Pereira, *História falada: Memória, rede e mudança social*. São Paulo: SESC SP, Museu da Pessoa, and Imprensa Oficial do Estado de São Paulo.

Woudhysen, Alice (2007) "Brazil: bridge-building needed for digital divide." *Global Technology Forum*, June 28. globaltechforum.eiu.com/index

Wu, Qiongli (2006) "Commercialization of digital storytelling: An integrated approach for cultural tourism, the Beijing Olympics and wireless VAS." *International Journal of Cultural Studies*, 9(3): 383–94.

Xinghan (2005) "ZSurvey.com business model analysis," March 10. www.starwww.com/expert/more.asp?name=article&id=397 (accessed March 29, 2005).

Xinhua (2005) "TV mobile phones facing barriers in China," February. news.xinhuanet.com/english/2005–02/18/content_2591900.htm (accessed June 10, 2005).

Xiudian, Dai (2007) "The digital revolution and development: The impact of Chinese policy and strategies." *Development*, 50(3): 24–9.

Yow, Valerie Raleigh (1994) *Recording Oral History: A Practical Guide for Social Scientists*. Thousand Oaks, CA: Sage.

Zimmerman, Eric (2003) "Play as research." In Brenda Laurel (ed.), *Design Research: Methods and Perspectives*. Cambridge, MA: MIT Press, pp. 176–84.

Zull, James E. (2002) *The Art of Changing the Brain: Enriching the Practice of Teaching by Exploring the Biology of Learning*. Sterling, VA: Stylus Publishing.

# Index